# Leibniz and Confucianism
# The Search for Accord

DAVID E. MUNGELLO

*The University Press of Hawaii* ⼤
Honolulu

**Library of Congress Cataloging in Publication Data**

Mungello, David E   1943–
  Leibniz and Confucianism, the search for accord

  Bibliography: p.
  Includes index.
  1.   Leibniz, Gottfried Wilhelm, Freiherr von, 1646–
1716.   2.   China—Civilization.   3.   Philosophy, Chinese.
4.   Confucianism.   I.   Title.
B2599.C5M86        193        77–4053
ISBN 0–8248–0545–3

*To Christine*
a childhood traveler on the *QE 1*

# Contents

# *Preface*

Symbols can have a power over our thoughts, especially if we experience them in person. I saw such a symbol on arriving in Hong Kong in the fall of 1973. There, in the harbor, was the wreck of the former luxury liner, the *Queen Elizabeth 1*. Half-submerged and lying on its side was a pride of twentieth-century Western technology, a carrier of fulfilled class dreams belonging to classes who viewed the struggling China of the 1950s with suspicion and misunderstanding.

The *Queen* had flourished and fallen as a technological victim to the society that created her. After being shunted from owner to owner, she was eventually bought by a Chinese shipping magnate and brought to Hong Kong, there to be outfitted as a floating university. Just a few days before her rechristening in January 1972, fire struck and left a burned and sunken hull. A court of inquiry cited labor unrest and sabotage, though one still hears dark rumors about insurance money. Left for two years to rust, the *Queen* became an object of fascination to visitors. She was a castoff of Western technology, yet many Westerners wondered how the Chinese could have so mishandled this prize. Viewed as a symbol, that ravaged hulk was the fruit of years of mutual misunderstanding between the West and China.

Eventually scrapping operations began, and, by the summer of 1974, the hull was barely discernible on the horizon. After the hull disappears, I believe the metaphor will linger. It will linger on the general level because of the continued misunderstandings between China and the West. It will linger on the personal level because of the depth of the struggle within individual minds over the Peoples Republic of China and the revolutionary, mystifying, and sometimes xenophoic things that are happening there. Good and moral things, by the most religious of definitions, have happened, and yet I sometimes find myself resisting accepting them as such. Is this the result of prejudice and resistance to change? Could there be any validity to this resistance? I believe it is something of both.

In the following study of Leibniz and Confucianism, I have attempted to investigate the particular form of misunderstanding and failure between China and the West that destroyed G. W. Leibniz' hopes of establishing an accord. Leibniz was deeply committed to an ecumenism that included not only the reunion of Catholic and Protestant Christendom but an ecumenism with which the religious and intellectual beliefs and practices of non-Westerners, such as the Chinese, could be reconciled. This is an investigation into how that commitment was pursued and some of the reasons why it failed.

The failure of Leibniz' search for accord is behind us. Will it remain the exclusive concern of historians, can it be used to foster harmony among different religious and ideological beliefs of the modern world? I believe it can. Consequently, my approach has been both historical and contemporary. I hope that this study will be read from the point of view of this dual spirit. And I hope that it will contribute not only to our thoughts but also to our search for an accord no less important to our day than it was to the age of Leibniz.

In my opinion, the section of the book that attempts to explain the reasons for Leibniz' ecumenical failure is the weakest portion of the work. A less competent man should always be aware of his inadequacies when criticizing one of greater ability. The fact remains, however, that Leibniz failed in his attempt, and I believe that the reasons for his failure extend beyond philosophic expertise. Leibniz did not limit himself to his areas of expertise, and I believe that this refusal of limitation is a sign of his intellectual integrity. I chose to pursue the reasons for Leibniz' failure because these seemed to be the logical conclusion of this study. If this book opens up a road to further consideration of Leibniz' work, then perhaps it will honor him in a way that transcends my more obvious criticism.

I would advise the reader against taking my judgments as utterly final. At times the geographical, chronological, and metaphysical distances that separated the material with which I was dealing were so great that I often felt only one step from falling into a chasm of confusion. No doubt scholarly progress will enable those who follow me to place that chasm further behind them, and this book must ultimately be judged by them as well as by the present readers. I only hope that this book sustains the trust and confidence in me that so many have shown in the path of its creation. To them, I would like to take this opportunity to express my gratitude.

This book began as a doctoral dissertation at the University of California at Berkeley, and I am indebted to the committee members: Professors Tu Wei-ming (chairman), Benson Mates, and Frederic Wakeman, Jr. Professor Walter H. O'Briant read a draft of the dissertation. Dr. Joseph Smith and the Division of Overseas Ministries of the Christian Church (Disciples of Christ) assisted in my stay in Hong Kong and, indirectly, helped make possible the research visit to Rome and Hanover. Members of the Society of Jesus and, in particular, Fr. Edmond Lamalle, archivist, and Fr. Josef Fejér, assistant archivist, of the Roman archives of the Society of Jesus, facilitated research in Rome. Dr. Albert Heinekamp, Frau Sigrid Pilawa, and the staff of the Niedersächsische Landesbibliothek were both efficient and cordial in assisting my research at the Leibniz archives in Hanover and in subsequent correspondence. The Orientalia Division of the Library of Congress promptly responded to my queries. Expressions of indebtedness for specific forms of assistance are noted at appropriate points in the text.

It was my good fortune to have had the stimulation of other Leibniz projects during the final stages of composing this work. Professors Henry Rosemont, Jr., and Daniel J. Cook shared their work in translating Leibniz' *Discourse on the Natural Theology of the Chinese,* and Thatcher Deane shared the current results of the Leibniz-Bouvet correspondence project.

I am deeply indebted to Henry Rosemont, who gave a great deal of assistance in the final revisions of the manuscript. I have no doubt that without his assistance this work would be less than it is. Alfred Jensen's paintings and conversation on the *Book of Changes* befuddled me valuably, and I am indebted to my friend Carol Karasik for introducing me to them. My teacher, Professor Carl H. Pfuntner, gave support and "philosophy" throughout the several years' process. My friend Jay C. Bishop, Jr., contributed several painstaking drawings. For sustaining me in the trying moments, I thank my family and, in particular, my wife, to whom this book is dedicated.

# 1
## *Leibniz' Contact with China*

Gottfried Wilhelm Freiherr von Leibniz (Lai-pu-ni-tz'u) was born at Leipzig in Saxony on 23 June 1646. His family was of the minor nobility, but of modest means, and remained so after his father, a professor of moral philosophy at the local university and an apparently pious man, died six years later in 1652.[1] Leibniz' mother, who died during his eighteenth year, was herself orphaned at an early age and raised in an academic environment supplied by a professor of theology and by a professor of law who also served as her guardian. During his early education, Leibniz' precociousness led him to the text of the Roman historian Livy and other extracurricular reading; a minor crisis was created by the objections of his pedantic instructor, but the situation was resolved in Leibniz' favor. After this, he was given free access to his father's considerable library and succeeded in mastering Latin by his twelfth birthday.

At fifteen, he matriculated at the University of Leipzig, where he continued his independent approaches to knowledge. There he made his acquaintance with the writings of Descartes and felt himself provoked into a difficult choice between the substantial forms of the scholastics and the mechanistic philosophy of the moderns. (i.e. Cartesians). His increasing tendency toward the latter led him to the study of mathematics, but Leibniz never lost his interest in scholastic concerns, even though his approach to these problems may have been quite modern. This interest is shown by his concern with the great medieval issue of realism versus nominalism: he favored the latter in his bachelor's dissertation, *Disputatio metaphysica de principio individui* (A metaphysical disputation on the principle of individuation) (1663), a work guided by the distinguished Aristotelian Jacob Thomasius.[2]

Following his studies at Leipzig, Leibniz was attracted for six months to Jena where he studied with the mathematician and moral philosopher Erhard Weigel. Though an opponent of the more rigid scholastics, Weigel sought a reconciliation of modern philosophy with that of Aristotle. Concentrating upon the study of jurisprudence, Leibniz readily obtained the degree of master of philosophy but received a significant setback when he was rejected as a candidate for the doctoral degree in law at Leipzig. A restriction in the number of candidates seems to have combined with the precedence of several senior candidates to eliminate Leibniz. Soon afterward, he left Leipzig and thereafter rarely returned. Instead he went to Nuremberg and later, matriculating at the University of Altdorf, obtained the doctorate in law with distinction by writing the philological and juridical thesis *De causibus perplexis in jure* (On difficult problems in law).

In 1667, after rejecting the offer of an academic position at Altdorf, and after a brief experience as secretary to a Rosicrucian society, Leibniz met Johann Christian Boineburg. The tolerance evident in Boineburg's Gallican Catholicism—Boineburg was a convert from Lutheranism—may have attracted Leibniz, whose ecumenical Lutheranism and youthful brilliance clearly impressed Boineburg. For a young man of Leibniz' ambitions, Boineburg's contacts provided an important stepping-stone to recognition, and Leibniz' dedication of his *Hypothesis physica nova* (New physical hypothesis) (1671) to Oldenburg, the secretary of the Royal Society in London, was probably done at the suggestion of Boineburg, a friend of Oldenburg's.[3] When Boineburg introduced the young man to the elector and archbishop of Mainz, Johann Phillip, the result was the beginning of a long and intricate political career. As a politician, Leibniz was brilliantly naive in his ideas. The notion of the young Leibniz traveling to Paris in 1672 with a plan for Louis XIV's armies to invade the Turkish infidels in Egypt instead of the Protestants in Germany[4] seems almost absurd in modern times; yet one can see in this plan an early sign of the vision that was so much a part of Leibniz' later work in international law, science, and religion.

At that time, Paris was the intellectual as well as the political capital of the Western world, and for some time Leibniz had been eager to go there. The visit must have been highly stimulating because we see Leibniz engaging in a wide range of invention and investigation. In the area of mechanical arts, he improved Pascal's calculating machine by adding the functions of multiplication and division to its repertoire of addition and subtraction. He made inventions in the fields of navigation, hydrostatics, pneumatics, optics, and watchmaking. This was an age unlike our own in several ways. Breadth of knowledge rather than intense specialization was part of the fashion, and not only was Leibniz sensitive to fashion, but his abilities also matched the times. He was eminently qualified for the baroque ideal of "savant," a notion that gave a learned man authority to speak in a wide range of fields.

While in Paris, Leibniz made the acquaintance of the eminent theologian Antoine Arnauld and the mathematician Christian Huygens. Leibniz' visit to London in 1673 was for the direct purpose of helping to present to Charles II a proposal from the elector of Mainz. But when Charles proved no more interested than did Louis XIV, Leibniz turned an abortive political mission to intellectual advantage by meeting some of the great scientific minds of the seventeenth century then residing in London, among them Oldenburg and the chemist Robert Boyle. When news reached London early in 1673 that the elector of Mainz had died, Leibniz returned to Paris. The death of the elector, combined with Boineburg's death just a few months before, left Leibniz completely without a patron and with declining means of support. He remained temporarily in Paris and even considered permanent residence there. It was during these years that he developed his infinitesimal calculus.

Finally, Leibniz accepted a third offer from the duke of Hanover and took up duties as librarian and councilor at the court. His choice of service appears to have been a wise one, especially for a man of his interests. Even before his arrival, the court had been a unique ecumenical center in which a Catholic monarch, Duke John Frederick, ruled over predominantly Protestant subjects. Certain elements in both France and Rome were looking toward Hanover as the key to reunion with the Northern German Protestants. And nearly coinciding with Leibniz' arrival at Hanover in 1677, the Spanish Franciscan Christophede Spinola arrived to conduct irenic negotiations with the consent of both the pope and the emperor of the Holy Roman Empire.[5]

The continuity of Hanoverian ecumenism was assured when Ernest Augustus succeeded his brother in 1679. Leibniz' new patron, a tolerant Lutheran, continued the irenic discussions and gave Spinola one of the warmest welcomes received from a Protestant court when the latter returned to Hanover in 1683. Leibniz took an increasingly prominent role in these negotiations until he finally became chief Lutheran negotiator in later discussions with Ernst, landgrave of Hessen-Rheinfels; Monsignor Paul Pelison court historian to Louis XIV; and Bossuet, bishop of Meaux.

Aside from its ascendency as an ecumenical center, Hanover was also rising to political prominence. Leibniz' participation in this growing power was directly dependent on the favor of those ruling in Hanover. Consequently, his influence was particularly strong in the late seventeenth century, when he was held in great favor by Sophia, the electress of Hanover, and her daughter, Sophia Charlotte. When the latter married Frederick of Brandenburg (later Frederick I, the first king of Prussia), Leibniz' influence spread to Berlin, where it was instrumental in establishing the Prussian Academy of Sciences, whose presidency he was honored with in 1700.

With the death of Sophia Charlotte in 1705, and that of Sophia in 1714, Leibniz' influence waned accordingly. Furthermore, when through the English Act of Settlement, Georg Ludwig, duke and elector of Hanover, became George I of England in 1714, Leibniz did not participate in this extension of influence. His past disputes with English thinkers, particularly with Isaac Newton over the priority of the invention of the infinitesimal calculus,[6] contributed to the court's decision to have Leibniz remain in the obscurity of Hanover. There, though increasingly out of favor, he proceeded with his final achievements. These included a popularized summary of his philosophy in the *Monadology* (1714); correspondence with the English theologian and Newtonian, Samuel Clarke (1715–1716);

and his major statement of views on Chinese philosophy, the *Discourse on the Natural Theology of the Chinese,* completed just a few months before his death on 14 November 1716.[7]

On his deathbed, Leibniz is said to have refused the sacrament. Because of his infrequent church attendance and rare communion, the general consensus was, ironically, that he was an unbeliever and consequently no clergyman would preside at the funeral. Only his secretary, Eckhart, attended him at the grave.[8]

## The China Mission

The connection between ecumenism and missionary activity was very strong in Leibniz' mind and, as with so many other elements in Leibnizian philosophy, the theme can be traced to his youth. Although Lutherans had shown little missionary zeal, a small but significant group of faculty at Wittenburg, starting in 1651, began to favor some form of missionary activity. Among these was the preacher Dilher of Nuremberg, who befriended and patronized Leibniz during his stay in the city in 1666–1667.[9] Among the authors of works on China with whom Leibniz was familiar and communicated were G. Spizel, author of *De re literaria Sinensium* (Leiden, 1660), and Athanasius Kircher, S. J., author of *China monumentis qua sacris qua profundis illustrata* (1667).[10] It was through Kircher's work that Leibniz acquired at least part of his knowledge of the important Jesuit missionary Matteo Ricci, although Ricci's journals were also widely available in several translations in seventeenth-century Europe. As a Jesuit, Kircher belonged to a group that would assume great importance in Leibniz' ecumenical thinking.

Perhaps Leibniz' earliest contact with members of this order came through Boineburg's private secretary, the Jesuit Johann Gamans of Aschaffenburg. He introduced Leibniz to several intellectually prominent Jesuits, including Kircher, who shared Leibniz' interest in developing a universal language, and Adam Kochanski, court mathematician to King John Sobieski of Poland.[11] From 1670 to 1698, Leibniz corresponded with Kochanski, and they shared a common interest in China. Kochanski was, moreover, a correspondent of Ferdinand Verbiest, a leading Jesuit in the China

mission, and he aided in the unsuccessful Jesuit effort to have Peter
the Great open up the overland route to China.[12]

Andreas Müller, provost of Nicolaikirche in Berlin, had been appointed by Frederick William, the Great Elector, in the capacity of
adviser on Chinese affairs and the possible establishment of a Far
Eastern trading company. Most of Müller's work was sent to Leibniz via Johann Elsholz, physician to the Great Elector, and in 1679
Leibniz addressed a list of fourteen questions regarding Müller's
unpublished *Clavis Sinica* (Key to Chinese) to Müller via Elsholz.
Judging from the questions, Leibniz appears to have imbibed Müller's intriguing but linguistically debatable theory that the Chinese
language is pictographic rather than semantic or phonetic.[13] It was
this pictographic thesis that later brought accusations of heresy and
caused Müller's dismissal by the pious Frederick William. Specifically, the attack was directed toward Müller's defense of the
Chinese language, which must, so the accusation went, be the product of the devil since a pictographic representation of God in the
word for God would be equivalent to making a graven image and
would violate the Second Commandment.

In Paris and under the editorship of the Chinese missionary
Philippe Couplet, S. J., the Jesuits published *Confucius Sinarum
Philosophus* (1687), an attempt to translate several Chinese
classics, including the Confucian *Analects,* the *Great Learning,* and
the *Doctrine of the Mean.* Franz Merkel claims that Leibniz, in a
letter to Ernst, landgrave of Hessen-Rheinfels, dated 9/10 December 1687, demonstrated that he had made a close reading of the
book in the year of its publication.[14] However, in view of Leibniz'
infrequent references to the work in later writings, it is questionable
just how much he assimilated from *Confucius Sinarum Philosophus.* Nevertheless, at least one sinologist has felt that this Jesuit
compilation directly influenced Leibniz' philosophy.[15]

A copy of *Confucius Sinarum Philosophus* can be found today
in Leibniz' library preserved in Hanover, and though it contains little marginal notation in Leibniz' hand, we can probably assume
that he was familiar with its contents. Influence is quite another
question. One doubts whether his familiarity with the book or the
mental stimulation he received from it could compare with his reactions to the treatises on Chinese religion and culture by the mission-

aries Longobardi and Sainte-Marie, received at a much later date. Both the marginal notation in these two treatises and the consequent production of his own treatise on Chinese philosophy indicate they had a much greater influence on Leibniz than the *Confucius Sinarum Philosophus*.

If one divides Leibniz' development of understanding of China into early, middle, and late phases, his reading of *Confucius Sinarum Philosophus* belongs to an early phase. Although the work is a substantial piece, perhaps Leibniz was simply unprepared, given his knowledge of China in 1687, to be very influenced. At any rate, *Confucius Sinarum Philosophus,* along with more than fifty titles on China and Asia, is present in Leibniz' library. Given the extent of Leibniz' intellectual contacts, he was probably aware of every significant work on China produced in Europe in the seventeenth century.

In a letter written in 1716 to Peter the Great of Russia, Leibniz concedes his debt to Frs. Kircher and Couplet.[16] In this letter, Leibniz explains how he believes that God has decided to have the sciences of learning extended throughout the world and that Peter is in an ideal position for being an instrument to that end by drawing knowledge from both Europe and China. As an aid in propagating this extension of knowledge, Leibniz claims to have discovered the secret of deciphering the "characters" (i.e., diagrams) of the ancient sage Fu Hsi and to have discovered correspondences between his binary mode of arithmetic and that of Fu Hsi's diagrams. In addition to crediting Fr. Bouvet with having assisted his discovery by sending a Chinese copy of Fu Hsi's diagrams, Leibniz credits Fr. Kircher for *China illustrata* and Fr. Couplet presumably for the *Confucius Sinarum Philosphus*, which supplied him with the information on which he based his discovery.

Reading works by Kircher and Couplet, and communicating with them and with other scholars such as Andreas Müller, was a mere preliminary to a much deeper involvement with the China mission. This involvement began with Leibniz' visit to Rome in 1689 and his meeting with Claudio Filippo Grimaldi, S. J.[17] A member of the China mission, Grimaldi was in Rome for a visit before returning to China, where he would succeed Ferdinand Verbiest, S. J., as head of the Chinese Bureau of Mathematics. This was the beginning of a direct source of information not only from Grimaldi but also, by the latter's introduction, from other members of the mission. It is perhaps difficult for someone today to see the significance of this contact, but in the seventeenth-century setting, where formal news media were nearly nonexistent, where the secondary literature of scholars was unreliable, and where direct access to China was practically impossible for a man of Leibniz' commitments, the importance of this contact was crucial to Leibniz' interests in China.

Exclusive reliance upon Jesuit sources left no way to check some of the Jesuits' more partial interpretations of Chinese culture. Fortunately, Leibniz did have a few non-Jesuit contacts with China. In approximately 1707, for instance, Leibniz spoke with a Fr. Cima, a missionary recently returned from China. Father Cima was an Italian of the Augustinian order, an order that had traditionally opposed the Jesuit position in the China mission. Though agreeing that the K'ang-hsi emperor was enlightened, Fr. Cima was far less optimistic than Bouvet and other Jesuits on the chances for the monarch's conversion.[18]

The Jesuits themselves provided a limited corrective to one another's interpretations. For example, when Grimaldi told Leibniz that using mathematical instruments and books, the K'ang-hsi emperor studied for three or four hours daily with Verbiest, there were few offsetting views to counteract Leibniz' overoptimism regarding the use of his combinatory art in China and his belief that knowledge of the sciences could be attained only through geometry. Later, another Jesuit tutor to the K'ang-hsi emperor, Joachim Bouvet, would point out in a letter to Leibniz that there had been great exaggeration of the emperor's interest in European knowledge, but Leibniz had to wait several years for this rectifying opinion. Leibniz shared with the Jesuits the view that European science was the key to Christianity's reception in China, and he shared the belief held by many Jesuits that knowledge of these sciences could foster religious piety.[19]

It was this belief that helped found, as well as eventually frustrate, the ecumenical efforts of Leibniz and certain Jesuits in China. Leibniz had failed to comprehend the limitations of these universal sciences, both for the Chinese and for the West. Furthermore, in his concern that the West should profit as much as China in an exchange of ideas, culture, and artifacts, and in his belief that the revealed religion of the West would be an equal trade for the natural theology and ethics of China, Leibniz was negotiating both sides of the ecumenical discussion. He thought that Bouvet and the other Jesuits were accurate interpreters of the Chinese position, when actually they seem to have been projecting a good deal of their own needs onto the Chinese. In fact, China was not interested in having religion revealed on the terms that Leibniz and Bouvet set. They might have been open to elements of what Leibniz and Bouvet proposed—if these elements had been couched in something more akin to the Confucian-Christian synthesis suggested by Matteo Ricci.[20]

## The Rites Controversy

Since Leibniz' ecumenical plans for China were so closely tied to the Society of Jesus, any difficulties for the latter would inevitably affect Leibniz. With a group as talented, disciplined, and spiritually ambitious as the Jesuits, conflict with outsiders was inevitable. The order had been founded in the sixteenth century by the Basque Ignatius of Loyola (1491–1556). Instead of stressing contemplative mysticism and the notion of an elect, Ignatius emphasized the ability of all to reach God through will and purpose. To this end, he devised his *Spiritual Exercises* as a manual to cultivate the disciplined experience of both heaven and hell. An intense experience of the senses in the secluded atmosphere of an organized spiritual retreat was stressed; one was prepared by the exercises of this manual to make his choice for God's will.[21] Christ was transformed from an object of quiet reverence into a militant figure leading his disciplined order into battle against the devil. This militancy and the "corpselike obedience" of the Jesuits were fundamental because, in their view, obedience possessed a saving power.

The Protestant suspicion toward the methods of *Spiritual Exercises* was intensified by Ignatius' view that obedience must be unlimited, even to the point of violating one's convictions. Critics called it an "obedience unto sin," but obedience was not a new element in Christianity. The difference was that whereas previous religious orders had directed their obedience toward a cloistered setting, the Jesuits aimed at carrying their obedience into the secular world. The Jesuit prescription was *contemplativus in actione*—contemplation in action.

There were several theological bases for the disputes of the Jesuits with other Roman Catholics and Protestants. The Jesuit stress upon free will conflicted with the emphasis upon grace by the Lutherans, Calvinists, and Jansenists. The latter were the leading opponents of the Jesuit order in France and included some of the most brilliant intellectuals of the day. The *Provincial Letters* (1665–1666) of the mathematician and philosopher Blaise Pascal set forth the essential Jansenist position in the debate, while Antoine Arnauld, a later correspondent of Leibniz', was the leading Jansenist polemicist.[22]

As an extension of their emphasis on free will, the Jesuits tended toward absolution and the judging of sin in terms of the intention of the will. Following Aristotle's *Nichomachean Ethics,* which stressed the conscious basis of moral judgment, the Jesuits applied moral evaluation to an act only if the will and reason were present and not hindered, for example, by fear. In his *Provincial Letters,* Pascal accused the Jesuits of sanctioning (1) the notion of the ends justifying the means and (2) the swearing of false oaths and the practice of deception. Yet the Jesuit casuists recognized only two permissible forms of deception: amphiboly, that is, the use of ambiguity to confuse the listener; and *reservatio mentalis* (mental reservation), that is, mentally formulating the complete truth but suppressing certain parts in its oral expression.

Another basis of dispute, particularly between the Jesuits and the Dominicans, was the issue of "Probabilism" versus "Probabiliorism." Though Probabilism can also be traced to Aristotle's *Nichomachean Ethics,* it was first formally presented in a complete theological and philosophical structure in 1577 by the Dominican monk Bartholomeus de Medina. Initial adherents of the position were drawn from several religious orders, but by the end of the sixteenth century the Jesuit casuist Vasquez adapted the position for the Jesuits, who became progressively more identified with it while the Dominicans moved toward the less lenient position of Probabiliorism.

The frequent discrepancy between the actual situation with the penitent and the cases in the Jesuit confessional manuals served to point up the problem. According to Probabilism, if two contradictory positions regarding the law can be merely entertained, the law need not be applied by the confessor. According to Probabiliorism, the nonobservance of the law is justified only if the probabilities against it are greater than those in favor of it. By the late sixteenth and early seventeenth centuries, moral laxity in the administration of confession by the clergy was evident. Stimulated by an article against "Laxism" by Pascal in the *Provincial Letters,* Pope Alexander VII condemned certain of the more extreme principles of Probabilism. Popes Innocent XI and Alexander VIII further limited Probabilism, while the Dominicans in Rome exerted pressure for a victory of Probabiliorism over the Jesuits' Probabilism.

Jesuit laxity in the confessional may have been a source of contention in Europe, but the members of the order in the field were realizing that a less rigid view of doctrine and rites provided room for maneuvering that could be converted into a highly useful proselytizing tool among foreign peoples. The conflict in the famous Rites Controversy centered precisely on the validity of this looser approach. Was it heresy, or was it expediency in the positive sense? Was it the fruit of Jesuit aggression, or the serving of God's will? Whose method was that of the true Christ?

As applied to the Chinese Rites Controversy, the essential positions began to solidify around 1610. There were those, primarily Jesuits, who held that the Chinese ancestral rites and the ceremonies in honor of Confucius were not essentially religious but social and civil in character; they also felt that ancient Chinese terms such as *shang-ti* (King-on-high) and *t'ien* (Heaven) were suitable equivalents of the Christian God. The opponents of this view, who tended more and more to be associated with the Dominicans, Franciscans, Augustinians, and the French Society of Foreign Missions (Société des Missions étrangères), held that the Chinese rites were religious in character and that only a new Chinese term, such as *t'ien-chu* (Lord of Heaven), could be used with validity to render the term "God."

In Europe, a tremendous propaganda battle began to emerge that in the late seventeenth and early eighteenth centuries centered at Paris. In 1697, Joachim Bouvet, one of the first French Jesuits

sent to China, returned to Paris to secure funds and recruits for the
mission and to publish his *Portrait historique de l'Empereur de la
Chine* (Historical portrait of the emperor of China), a flattering ap-
praisal guaranteed to show the Chinese K'ang-hsi emperor in his
most enlightened aspects and calculatingly dedicated to Louis XIV.
In 1697, Louis le Comte, a fellow member with Bouvet of the first
group of French Jesuits in China, also returned to Paris to publish
his *Nouveaux Mémoires sur l'État present de la Chine* (A report on
the present condition of China). The work is a lengthy two-volume
book, filled with descriptions and illustrations on a wide variety of
topics ranging from the manner in which the emperor received the
missionaries on their arrival in Peking to the character of the
Chinese spirit.

In 1698, Charles le Gobien, S. J., published *Histoire de l'Edit de
l'Empereur de la Chine en faveur de la Religion Chrestienne* (The
history of the edict of the emperor of China in favor of the Christian religion). Although Le Gobien had not traveled to China, he
had access to field reports through his Paris office, which acted as a
clearinghouse for the European dissemination of these reports. The
Chinese edict referred to in Le Gobien's work was one of religious
toleration for Christians, issued by the K'ang-hsi emperor in 1692.
The extended, complicated negotiations and court lobbying that led
up to the edict are described in detail and certainly not in a manner
unsympathetic to the Jesuit fathers, who a good deal of the time
seem to have been in a state of considerable uncertainty about their
status and even their lives. The Edict of Toleration, which is translated and quoted in full by Le Gobien,[23] was a great triumph for the
Jesuits, and the contrast with Louis XIV's revocation of the Edict
of Nantes in 1685 must have been striking to many, at least Protestant, eyes. Yet the Jesuits were not trying to criticize their patron so
much as encourage him in his support of the China mission and Jesuit techniques.

But the French were not of one opinion on this matter. In China,
in 1693, the year following the K'ang-hsi emperor's Edict of
Toleration, Charles Maigrot, the vicar apostolic of Fukien and an
associate of the Society of Foreign Missions, issued a decree that
forbade Chinese Christian neophytes in his region to participate in
Confucian or ancestral ceremonies and condemned the use of *t'ien*

and *shang-ti* as equivalents for God. In France, Antoine Arnauld was writing his seven-volume critique of Jesuit methods, *Morale pratique des Jésuites* (The moral practice of the Jesuits). The Jesuit confessor of Louis XIV, Michel le Tellier, wrote his highly controversial *Défense des nouveaux chrétiens* (Defense of the new Christians), to which the Dominicans responded with *Apologie des dominicains* (Apology of the Dominicans). The entire debate was degenerating into heated and superficial polemics when in 1700 the Society of Foreign Missions, after having referred the matter to Rome for a decision, nevertheless convened a commission itself to examine the recently published works of Le Comte and Le Gobien.[24]

Among the main issues investigated was the extent to which China had possessed the knowledge of the true faith. The climate, however, was too politicized and controversial for genuine discussion to occur, and the commission ended with each side holding to more rigid views on the matter than before the investigation had begun. Leibniz watched these events with dismay. His inclusion of Jesuit writings in his *Novissima Sinica* (Latest news from China) (first edition, 1697; second and enlarged edition, 1699) and his correspondence clearly show him to be a Jesuit sympathizer, but he feared that the growing feelings against Jesuits' methods would lead Rome to rulings that could destroy the China mission.[25]

### The Question of Influence

The emergence of correspondences between the philosophy of Leibniz and that of China brings up the question of whether Leibniz was influenced by China. There seems little reason to suggest that Leibniz himself influenced China, although the attainment of such an influence through Jesuit missionaries and an ecumenical form of Christianity was a goal that he and other Europeans attempted unsuccessfully to realize. The late E. R. Hughes suggested that key Leibnizian notions of a "simple substance" and "pre-established harmony" were influenced by his reading of *Confucius Sinarum Philosophus*.[26] Hughes is correct in linking the period of Leibniz' initial exposure to that collection of translations of Chinese classics in 1687 with the particularly fertile years of 1686–1690 during which Leibniz corresponded with Arnauld. The year 1686 was crucial in the transition from Leibniz' youthful atomism to the development of his mature philosophy of the spiritual atom, or what was eventually to be called the "monad."

Nevertheless, an examination of the Leibniz-Arnauld correspondence, which seems to have served as a catalyst for developing these notions, shows that the more substantial half of that correspondence, along with the composition of the *Discourse on Metaphysics,* had been written by the end of 1686. Since 1686 was one year prior to the publication of *Confucius Sinarum Philosophus,* the influence of the latter upon these notions could not have been formative.[27] Moreover, we have already noted the infrequent explicit references to *Confucius Sinarum Philosophus* in Leibniz' writings. There is, however, a difference of opinion among Leibniz scholars as to the importance to be assigned to the *Discourse on Metaphysics.* Although Bertrand Russell thought it Leibniz' best account of his philosophy, Leroy Loemker regards it as an incomplete and inadequate account preceding Leibniz' full development of the notions of *vis viva* (force), the gradations of individual substances and their perceptions and appetites, and the nature of corporeal beings.[28] The difference in interpretation seems to follow a difference in emphasis between Russell and others, who stress the logical ingredients of Leibnizian philosophy, and Loemker who emphasizes the *Discourse on Metaphysics* as part of Leibniz' larger theological plan.

Another reason for minimizing the possibility of Chinese influence by way of *Confucius Sinarum Philosophus* is that Leibniz' knowledge of China in 1686 was very undeveloped. His intensive contact with the China mission did not begin until his visit to Rome and acquaintance there with the Jesuit Grimaldi in 1689. Additionally, his most complete formulation of views on Chinese philosophy, the *Discourse on The Natural Theology of the Chinese,* was not composed until 1716, the year of his death and long after his philosophy had come to maturity.

In *Science and Civilisation in China,*[29] Joseph Needham has suggested that the modern European philosophies of organism, by which the perennial conflict between theological idealism and mechanical materialism could be overcome, are traceable to Leibniz, where they stop. Needham believes that Leibniz may have borrowed his synthesis from the organic world view of the Chinese, and particularly from Sung Neo-Confucianism. Later chapters in this study will consider the nature of the transmission of ideas from China to Leibniz, but for the moment I would suggest that the Chinese influence on Leibniz was more corroborative than germinal. It is my belief that an examination of Leibniz' contact with China will show that the significance of the relationship resided as much in the ecumenical potential that was never realized as in the history of that contact. That potential is not a speculative reconstruction on my part but is evident from Leibniz' philosophical and religious premises and plans, even though the reasons for its failure may require some explanation.

But what of the correspondences that existed between Leibniz and China—correspondences between Leibniz' organicism and Neo-Confucian organicism, between Leibniz' concept of the monad and the Neo-Confucian concept of *li* (principle), between Leibniz' binary arithmetic and the hexagrams of the *Book of Changes,* between Leibniz' tendency to reduce physics and ethics to the more common denominator of the monad and the Chinese tendency to merge the natural world with the moral world, between Leibniz' notion of force *(vis viva)* and the Chinese notion of *ch'i* (material force)? If these are not to be explained by the cultural diffusion of ideas from China to Leibniz, and if mere coincidence seems overburdened by such a degree of similarity, then could spontaneous generation explain these correspondences?

The spontaneous generation of similar ideas in cultures removed in time and distance from one another is a view that has often attracted adherents by default—that is, by the absence of documented evidence showing actual diffusion of elements from one culture to another. Since there is an inherent demand in cultural diffusion for documentation that can never be fully satisfied, the absence of confirmed diffusion may indicate a lack of knowledge rather than a lack of diffusion. Yet the point comes where the absence of cultural diffusion seems to be a justifiable hypothesis and specific notions of spontaneous generation arise. There is the similarity of external conditions or of interior human structure, resulting in similarity in thought perhaps akin to Jungian archetypes and the universal unconscious. Another explanation of spon-

16

taneous generation is that there is a similar complex of human needs that arises in far-removed races and tends to require a similar type of gratification.

Leibniz' view of spontaneous generation in China is consistent with his mathematical and logical preferences. In his *Discourse on the Natural Theology of the Chinese* 31,[30] Leibniz describes Chinese views and worship of God as fully in accord with natural law, which is "engraved in our hearts." This implication of spontaneous generation is supported when Leibniz, in the same section, refers to the Chinese heavenly commandment and law as equivalent to the Western "light of reason." Yet Leibniz recognizes the possibility that cultural diffusion played some role in developing ancient Chinese culture. In the *Discourse* 24 and 32,[31] he refers to the possibility of certain knowledge having been diffused to China from the "Patriarchs." This reference, however, is not necessarily to the Hebraic Abraham and his immediate descendants. It is quite possible that Leibniz has in mind the Figurist view of Joachim Bouvet and other Jesuits who held that some knowledge was transmitted to China by certain patriarchal figures who were neither Western nor Chinese but universal figures who transmitted knowledge to the West and China in common. (See chapter 3.) Finally, Leibniz' suggestions of cultural diffusion would account for only part of the Chinese learning that Leibniz perceives as bearing great similarity to European knowledge.

Leibniz explains the concurrence of correspondences between his own and Chinese philosophy as the result of his view of truth being universal in its validity. It is in Leibniz' tendency to see these correspondences as corroborations of truth that one sees a diminishment of the possibility that China had an appreciable influence on him. It was this overemphasis on interpreting correspondences in terms of universal truth, rather than any similarity of needs or common interior human structure, that led to an imbalance in Leibniz' ecumenism and perhaps condemned it to its ultimate failure even as it began its mission.

But why should one devote a book to a failure? It occurs to me that Leibniz scholars might be inclined to ask this question, particularly since Leibniz was so successful in other areas. It has generally been recognized that Leibniz' efforts as a political pamphleteer and jurist fell considerably short of his achievements in logic, mathematics, and metaphysics. What makes a study of Leibniz' search for accord and its failure worthy of attention is the monumental scope of the project and the fact that it was severely hindered by the neglect of certain very basic insights into the nature of religious experience. The failure of genius always makes an interesting tale, and I believe that this one has much to teach us. Perhaps no less because we too are prone to a similar neglect.

# 2
## Leibniz' China Interpreters

The key interpreters of China on whom Leibniz relied were all missionaries, primarily of the Jesuit order. They included Frs. Matteo Ricci, Nichola Longobardi, Antoine de Sainte-Marie, Claudio Filippo Grimaldi, and Joachim Bouvet, of whom only the last two were contemporary to Leibniz. Much of the sixteenth century was marked by the failures of the Portuguese from their position at Macao and the Spaniards from the Philippines to establish a missionary and trade base on the Chinese mainland. When the first penetrations were made, the effort was dominated by Italian Jesuits who entered by way of the Jesuit bases in India and Macao. Matteo Ricci's entry onto the mainland in 1683 was not first chronologically, but he easily qualifies as the father of the China mission. Ricci came trained in the most current European science of his day and is said to have been an outstanding pupil at the Roman College. There he was trained by the leader of Jesuit astronomy and author of the Gregorian calendar, the German Christopher Clavius, the same Clavius who later, just before his death in 1611, was to prove cautiously receptive to the views of Galileo.[1]

### Matteo Ricci, S. J.

Matteo Ricci (Li Ma-t'ou, 1552–1610) was born in Macerata and entered his novitiate at Rome. He reached Macao in 1582 and one year later at Canton entered the Chinese mainland. There he spent the remaining twenty-eight years of his life acquiring a knowledge of Chinese language and culture that few Westerners have known. Of the five interpreters discussed in this chapter, Ricci attained the greatest respect among the Chinese literati, particularly as the author of works written in Chinese.

Ricci represented a new approach in missionary methods. Disagreeing with the rigid Spanish and Portuguese treatment of foreign people as pagans whose traditional culture conflicted with Christianity, Ricci and others in the Society of Jesus sought more of a reconciliation of the native culture with Christianity. These differences in approach would eventually give rise to the protracted debate known as the Rites Controversy, which did great damage to the Christian mission in China. The differences between the accommodation and the Europocentric attitudes came to settle on specific questions involving terminology: Should a traditional Chinese term such as *shang-ti* be used for God or should the nontraditional but native *t'ien-chu* be used or should there be a Chinese transliteration of the Latin *Deus?* Another specific issue on which the debate focused was whether the rites to Confucius and to one's ancestors constituted idolatry: Were such practices religious—and therefore a violation of the First Commandment—or merely civil and social? The accommodation viewpoint tended to accept *shang-ti* and *t'ien-chu* as suitable equivalents for God (Ricci had originated this usage) and to regard the Confucian and ancestral rites as primarily civil and social in character.

Ricci's authority and influence were such that his position on the Chinese rites was accepted with only quiet objection, and the long debate on the rites question did not really begin until after his death in 1610. His views on China were presented to Europe in 1615 in a Latin edition of his journals entitled *De propagatione Christiana apud Sinas* (On the propagation of Christianity among the Chinese), which had been extensively edited and amended in translation from the original Italian by Ricci's co-worker, the Belgian Nichola Trigault, S. J. (Chin Ssu-piao, 1577-1628).

Ricci's journals were widely read in seventeenth-century Europe and appeared in a number of Latin, French, German, Spanish, and Italian editions. From Leibniz' general familiarity with seventeenth-century works on China and from his specific familiarity with Ricci's views, we might assume that he had read the journals.

Yet while frequent citations of the works of Sainte-Marie and Longobardi appear in Leibniz' *Discourse on the Natural Theology of the Chinese* of 1716, he makes little reference to Ricci's journals. The most specific reference appears in a two-page discussion of the journals found among Leibniz' papers at Hanover.[2]

On one side of the Rites Controversy of 1610–1742 were those Christians who stressed some common ground for reconciling Western and Chinese beliefs. These were the advocates of adapting Christianity to the native culture. They were opposed by those who refused to separate Christianity from European culture. The latter held that there was little or no basis for reconciliation and that Chinese religious practices violated the essence of the "true faith." The view sympathetic to the Chinese rites, which became increasingly associated with the Jesuit order, tended to reject modern Confucianism as a distortion of the original canon. By doing so, the missionaries avoided facing the modern Chinese skepticism on the subject of spirits and souls and also the lack of a clearly defined divinity. In rejecting the moderns and going back to the classics, the fathers followed a very old Chinese practice of returning to the original canon to seek the "true" meaning of the ancients. Far from being a sign of disintegration of classical authority, such a practice had traditionally been a recurring sign of the great vitality in the Confucian tradition.

We may ask to what extent the Christian fathers observed more than the *forms* of this traditional Confucian practice and to what extent there was a basis to their interpretation of the "true" meaning of the ancients. Though there was a real familiarity with the classics on the fathers' part, their position cannot be reviewed solely in terms of doctrine but must include reference to a key Jesuit concern—namely, conversion through a blending of Christianity with the native culture. Such conversion through cultural assimilation, rather than through less subtle methods of propagation in which the missionary maintains his foreign status, remained an essential distinction for the China mission.

Matteo Ricci was aware of the strong strain of xenophobia that seems to ebb and flow as a perennial stream in China.[3] The more he observed the Chinese, the more he tended to conclude that Confucian culture was too embedded to be displaced by Christianity. The

:ianists would be outdistanced by Joseph Henry-
nare, S. J. (Ma Jo-se, 1666–1736), who represents
gh-water mark in Jesuit attempts to reconcile Sung
iism, the orthodox philosophy of seventeenth- and
:ury China, with Christianity. Although Ricci re-
:ient Chinese *shang-ti* as equivalent to the Christian
ed short of including the more modern Neo-Confu-
n as *wu-chi* (Ultimate of Nonbeing) and *t'ai- chi* (Su-
e) in that equation. Prémare was to identify the Neo-
-*chi* with the Christian God and to regard *t'ai-chi* as

plain Ricci's sympathy for contemporary Chinese on
missionary expedience raises the issue of
i.e., crafty and duplicitous tactics. But it is difficult
d the fundamental Jesuit notion of *contemplativus in*
mplation in action) without the conviction in Christ.[5]
at Ricci's *Journals,* we find a strong devotion to duty
itolerant pronouncements whenever he came across
lered to be ignorance or superstition. This was parti-
regard to the "sect of idols" or "school of Satan,"[6]
is for the faith of the Buddhist priests, who he even-
were often low on the social ladder. When the Jesuit
itered the Chinese mainland, they adopted the cloth-
ddhist priests. Perhaps projecting from their experi-
, they believed that this was the most expedient ap-
tural assimilation. They soon recognized the humble
: priests and so adopted the more revered robes of the

extent, Ricci also criticizes Taoism, but for a six-
y European, he displays remarkably little Christian
Vhere chauvinism does emerge, the object is usually
and, this writer feels, closely linked with Ricci's desire
the faith. In noting the friendships that Ricci slowly
h certain literati, one wonders to what extent the long
tion of these Confucianists was responding to the
tivated ways of this priest. It is unlikely that his com-
Christian moral maxims would have attained its at-
ilarity among the literati had not some depth of ac-

brilliance of Ricci's insi
may have been out of th
to tolerate complement:
tianity admission into t
this admission would be
place what was a traditic
Buddhism. This insight
himself with contempoi
coloring and to avoid tl
schools of the time that
rate Confucian, Buddhis
to emphasize the social
mentary religious aspec
attacking Buddhism, wh:
tian path.

Frequently, both sides
ably on certain elements
ence between the sides wa
Chinese rites condemned
the legendary sages of the
the classical canon aroun
later. Among those sym
sometimes a tendency to
cius together, but there v
interpretation for viewing
single, continuous traditic
people as Bouvet and the
origin linking Europe with
cients that Leibniz saw a I
in the diagrams of the *Boo*

Ricci was an outstand
commodating Christian in
pretation heavily favored t
ci was far less critical of cc
held the accommodation
Chinese was a distinguishii
to understanding the high
held. In the next century,

porary Conf
Marie de Pré
perhaps the h
Neo-Confucia
eighteenth-ce:
garded the ar
God, he stop,
cian terms su
preme Ultima
Confucian w:
secondary.[4]

Trying to e
grounds of
"Jesuitism"-
to comprehen
*actione* (cont
When we loo:
spiked with :
what he cons
cularly true i:
his designatic
tually realize:
fathers first e
ing of the Bt
ence in Japa
proach to cu
status of the:
literati.

To a lesse
teenth-centu:
chauvinism.
quite specific
to propagate
developed w
moral cultiv
spiritually c:
mentary on
tributed po;

cord existed between the two.[7] Many of the Chinese were experienced practitioners of moral discipline and were unlikely to be deceived by mere craft.

It is possible to view Ricci's empathy with the Confucian literati as a reaction to their fewer superstitions, at least as Ricci viewed them in relation to the Buddhist and Taoist adherents. But Ricci's fundamental objection to Buddhism may have stemmed from the realization that religious temperaments responding to Christianity would very often be the same temperaments that were attracted to Buddhism. This notion is evident when one examines the former commitment of many of Ricci's literati converts. For instance, the Buddhist commitment applied to both the family and the person of Hsü Kuang-ch'i (1562–1633), also known by his baptismal name of Paul Hsü. It applied also to (Michael) Yang T'ing-yün (1557–1627) and to the converted viceroy of the province of Shantung, Feng Mu-kang.[8] Moreover, Ricci was anxious about the recent resurgence of Buddhism along with its tendency to be increasingly syncretized with Confucianism and Taoism. Consequently, his program for conversion through assimilation included caustic attacks upon Buddhism combined with treatises written to appeal specifically to the literati.

The most influential of these treatises was the *T'ien-chu shih-i* (The true meaning of God), which, characteristically of the accommodation method, emphasizes logical persuasion rather than spiritual or scriptural authority.[9] The arguments are presented in the form of a dialogue between a Chinese literatus and a Western scholar. Ricci's aim was captured in the phrase attributed by Ricci to Hsü Kuang-ch'i: *"Pu Ju i Fo"* (Complete Confucianism and displace Buddhism).[10] Consequently, the *T'ien-chu shih-i* attempts to refute the Chinese religious sects of Buddhism and Taoism by lumping them together into the single category of *"Fo-Lao"* (literally, "Buddha–Lao-tzu" or "Buddhism–Taoism").[11] This reductionism may not be entirely due to Ricci's bias but may also reflect the religious syncretism prominent in the Ming period (1368–1644). Though Ricci accepts the syncretism when it merges Buddhism with Taoism, he is critical of the syncretic tendency when it includes Confucianism. Consequently, he strongly rejects the blending of Confucianism, Buddhism, and Taoism that was variously known as *san-chiao i-ho* (the harmonization of the three teachings) or *san-han chiao* (the three teachings united). Ricci is far more favorable toward Confucianism, which he tries to reconcile with Christianity by emphasizing the common basis of both in natural reason.

The *T'ien-chu shih-i* emphasizes philosophy and religion in China since the composition of the Confucian classics, from which Ricci quotes. It is now generally believed that, apart from the *Analects,* Confucius' role in the composition of the classics was minimal. There was, however, a traditional view, which Ricci may have shared, that Confucius' role in the formation of the classics was closer to authorship. Ricci's emphasis on Confucius contrasts with the position of later Europeans sympathetic to the Chinese rites, including Leibniz, who stressed the period leading up to and sometimes including Confucius, as opposed to the post-Confucius era.

Writing from an anti-Buddhist perspective similar to that of the *T'ien-chu shih-i,* Ricci in his *Journals* attacks the Pythagorean doctrine of the transmigration of souls and indirectly attempts to refute the Buddhist notion of the transmigration of the soul. Here again, one must fault Ricci on his treatment of Buddhism. Greater familiarity with Buddhist doctrine would have indicated that only in the grossest Buddhist view is the *soul* said to transmigrate. On the contrary, one finds repeated references in Buddhist literature to the denial of the existence of a soul, along with the acceptance of transmigration. (True to the Christian tradition, Leibniz also rejected transmigration of the soul when it appeared in the context of Pythagoreanism, though he accepted many other Pythagorean notions.)[12]

Ricci was exposed to a Buddhism that had degenerated from an earlier apogee in Chinese history and had since become blended with a number of Taoist and popular religious customs. On the other hand Buddhism was undergoing a limited revival during the Ming period and Ricci's balance of favor toward the Confucianists and his criticism of the Buddhists are simply unjustified by any impartial standard. Ricci might have been offended by certain practices in the local Buddhist temples, but he was also exposed to articulate proponents of Buddhism and surely they would have confirmed that Buddhism in essence was not an idol-worshipping religion and contained little theism. But Ricci was not prepared to listen to these Buddhist spokesmen. His description of debates with them represents an embarrassing lapse in a generally fair and perceptive mind.[13]

The fact is that there were bases of Buddhism from which similarities between it and Christianity could have been established as effectively as between Confucianism and Christianity, had Ricci been sufficiently objective and willing or had circumstances been ripe for such an effort.[14] Our own era is participating in attempts at accord between Christianity and Buddhism by a number of people, including the Jesuit William Johnston, who is discussed in the concluding chapter.

When we deal with Ricci's treatment of Chinese thinkers who stand outside the orthodox Confucian path, the customary praise for Ricci must abate. For example, Ricci had some contact with the learned Chinese iconoclast Li Chih, who was attempting a new synthesis of various schools including Buddhism and Confucianism. But Li Chih had placed himself beyond the pale of current Confucianist orthodoxy, and this fundamental fact seems to have diminished him in Ricci's eyes. Otto Franke, in his article on the contact between Ricci and Li Chih, suggests that not only could Li Chih have corrected Ricci's erroneous view that ancient China was Confucianlike, but Li and his heretical followers might also have provided a more lasting alliance with the Christian mission than did the orthodox literati Ricci chose to cultivate.[15]

Franke's suggestions are intriguing, but they contradict the fundamental approach of Ricci and the Jesuits that relies on cultivating the powers that be. To the extent that Li Chih dissociated himself from those powers, he could not have been accepted without a basic shift in method. One deficiency of this approach was that it tended to place the Jesuits outside the most creative cultural currents of the day. In Ricci's time, such a current was shared by Li Chih. Later, in Bouvet's time, the most creative current was shared by Ming loyalists and others, whose research and new conclusions on the *Book of Changes* appear to have eluded Jesuits working on the same classic. Since the Jesuits tended to align themselves with the status quo, any shift in power would require a rapid shift in allegiance. Sometimes, as in the transition from the Ming to Ch'ing dynasties in the mid-seventeenth century, they were capable of such a fast transition. Where the transitions were more subtle, as in changing cultural conceptions among the literati, the Jesuits were less successful.

### Nichola Longobardi, S. J.

Nichola Longobardi (Lung Hua-min, 1565–1655) was born into a patrician family at Caltagirone, Sicily and entered the novitiate at Messina in 1582. After arriving in China in 1597, he worked with Ricci as one of the pioneer missionaries, though their techniques differed. Longobardi combined pious zeal and technical skill with tireless energy, but he was far less refined than Ricci in his knowledge of philosophy and theology.[16] While Ricci inclined toward the cultivation of literate Chinese, Longobardi excelled in programs such as the campaign of street preaching aimed at the people in the suburbs of Shao-chou which, according to Ricci's evaluation, was successful.[17] Yet Longobardi was not without literary ability. Sometime around 1600, he expressed his critical attitude toward the Chinese rites in an unpublished Latin manuscript, *De Confucio ejusque doctrina tractatus* (A treatise on Confucius and his doctrine), which was condemned by the vice-provincial, François Furtado, S. J. Consequently, the work was temporarily suppressed; later it was translated into Spanish and published by Fr. Domingo Navarette in his *Tratados* (Madrid, 1676–1679).[18] It was later translated into French by Monsignor de Cicé and published by the Society of Foreign Missions as *Traité sur quelques points de la religion des chinois* (A treatise on several matters of the Chinese religion), hereafter referred to as *Religion Treatise* (Paris, 1703). It was this French version that had a great influence upon Leibniz when its completed form came into his hands late in 1715. While this work reflected an outlook which differed from that of Ricci, Longobardi was not outspoken in his differences while Ricci lived. Yet on many matters involving the mission, Ricci and Longobardi appear to have been in basic agreement, and Ricci appointed him as his successor just before dying.[19]

After Ricci's death Longobardi openly sided with the emerging position critical of the Chinese rites and rejected the cautious course pursued by Ricci and favored by such prominent Chinese converts as the "Three pillars of the early Catholic Church" *(K'ai-chiao san-ta chu-shih)*—(Paul) Hsü Kuang-ch'i, (Michael) Yang T'ing-yün, and (Leo) Li Chih-tsao (1570–1630). At the Nanking mission, Alfonso Vagnoni, S. J. (Wang Yi-yüan, 1566–1640) had become overintoxicated by initial success and became less cautious in his methods. With Vagnoni, Longobardi favored a more open approach and—against the advice of the Chinese Christian literati—suggested petitioning the emperor for formal recognition of freedom to practice Christianity. (On the other hand, Vagnoni did not share Longobardi's objections to using traditional Chinese terms to refer to God.) The less cautious tactics of the Jesuits exposed them to attack from their Chinese enemies, and in 1617 there began a brief suppression of Christianity. In 1622, Longobardi was succeeded as head of the mission by João de Rocha, S. J. (Lo Huai-chung, 1561–1633), though he remained active in the China mission until his death in 1655 at the venerable age of ninety.

The tendency to interpret Chinese beliefs in terms of Christian equivalences in objects of worship rather than seeing the functions of that worship is common to nearly all Europeans of this period. But what distinguishes Longobardi's interpretations from those of Ricci, Bouvet, and Leibniz is a certain coarseness of view. This is apparent in his tendencies to presume a correspondence between Chinese and gentile (i.e., non-Christian) philosophies as a whole *(Religion Treatise* 3:1) or between Chinese and European idolatry *(Religion Treatise* 13:1). To be fair, one should note the existence of forced tendencies on the part of both those sympathetic to, and those critical of, the Chinese rites; but in sum, it seems that Longobardi's views are less discriminating than those of Ricci and Bouvet.

Longobardi relied far more upon the views of contemporary Chinese in formulating his interpretation of the Chinese than did Ricci and those sympathetic to the Chinese rites. The use of his conversations with Chinese literati as source material gives the reader an unusually direct access to Chinese views, particularly when he includes long quotations from these men. As with any oral device, however, there are qualifying factors of which Longobardi shows little awareness. For instance, he cites the spoken views of "Dr.

Paul" (Hsü Kuang-ch'i) that the Chinese *shang-ti* (King-on-high) could not be equivalent to the Christian God, that neither the ancient nor modern Chinese would have had any recognition of this God, and that the fathers proposed these Chinese equivalents to avoid alienating certain Chinese scholars (*Religion Treatise* 17:34). We do not know when Hsü may have said this, but it is probable that it was after his conversion of 1603, particularly since he had not attained the *chin-shih* (doctoral) degree before that date and would not have borne the title of "Dr." until a year later. Consequently, Hsü's views cannot be assumed to be completely unbiased or representative of Confucianism. Furthermore, in any conversation with Longobardi, Hsü would have been quite aware that he was talking with a priest, especially if he himself professed the faith.

Another pertinent conversation between Longobardi and a literati convert—this time with "Dr. Michael" (Yang T'ing-yün)—is reported at length in the *Religion Treatise* 17:19–32. In the course of this conversation, Yang criticizes Confucianism for neglecting the other life and praises Buddhism for proposing an eternity and paradise (*Religion Treatise* 17:24). Yang's reference to a Buddhist paradise probably means the Western Paradise of Amitabha, which became an object of great attention to many devotees of this popular form of Buddhism. Actually, this paradise was not a permanent abode like that of the Christian heaven, but only a rewarding way station for those on their way to Nirvana, technically not a place so much as a state of consciousness in which desire is extinguished.

In his praise of Buddhism and throughout the entire conversation, Yang gives evidence of syncretic tendencies. In the *Religion Treatise* 17:32, discussing the notion that all things are one, he responds to an objection of Longobardi's by saying that if the three sects of Confucianism, Taoism, and Buddhism followed their respective doctrines in their purity, they would remove practices contrary to Christianity. One can almost feel the discomfort such syncretic attitudes created in Longobardi. For Ricci, it was just such a searching openness that would encourage accord. To the extent that a syncretic attitude is much more willing to allow—indeed, seek—substitutions than is a dogmatic attitude, Ricci could use this syncretic attitude to create a role for Christianity by the displacement of Buddhism. The substitution would be possible because Buddhism and Christianity share similar approaches and concerns. Yang reflects this shared concern in his praise for Buddhism's attention to the afterlife, also a fundamental Christian concern.

Although the syncretic attitudes of Yang and other Chinese literati accepted this displacement of Buddhism by Christianity, Li Chih and his followers would probably have rejected it. The Li Chih group would perhaps have been more inclined to displace Confucianism, but Ricci had set the Jesuits of the China mission on a path toward a Confucian-Christian synthesis in which Buddhism was the inevitable choice for elimination. For reasons of doctrinal belief and temperament, Longobardi could not work with such syncretic approaches. In his eyes, they amounted to building the Church in China on sand.

Longobardi states that in their emphasis on objects of worship rather than substance of worship, Chinese religious notions are not equivalent to those of Christianity because they are only superficially spiritual and lack any true conception of a divinity who dispenses recompense and retribution (*Religion Treatise* 16:4). The concept *li* (principle) was used by those sympathetic to the Chinese rites, and by Leibniz in particular as a basis for finding a Chinese equivalent for the Christian God. This concept is defined by Longobardi as "prime matter" (*Religion Treatise* 14:18) and elsewhere as "universal substance" (*Religion Treatise* 17:28). He defines the complementary of *li* (that is *ch'i*) as "primeval air" (*l'air primogéne*) (*Religion Treatise* 14:19).

Leibniz later criticizes this interpretation of *li*, as is discussed in chapter 4, and he does so on valid grounds. The Chinese did not view *li* as material substance. Given his definition of *li*, Longobardi is able to interpret the Chinese view as materialistic and lacking the spirituality found in Christianity. Yet though his definition of *li* is inaccurate, Longobardi's treatise deserves attention, for when Leibniz composed his *Discourse on the Natural Theology of the Chinese* he relied primarily not on Ricci's journals but on the treatises of Longobardi and Sainte-Marie.

### Antoine de Sainte-Marie, O. F. M.

Antoine de Sainte-Marie, alias Antonio Caballero a Santa Maria (Li An-tang, 1602–1669), was born at Baltanás, Spain, on 20 April

1602.[20] He entered the Order of Friar Minors (Franciscans) in 1618 and traveled to the Philippines in 1628.[21] In 1633, Sainte-Marie sailed for China from Manila in the company of the Dominican Juan Bautista de Morales and fellow Franciscan Francisco Bermúdez. His initial contacts with Jesuits in China were very unfavorable. This was due to more than interorder and nationalistic rivalries, for the situation of Christianity and the Jesuits at that time in China had become very delicate because of the persecution led by the scholar-official Shen Ch'üeh. As a new arrival in China, Sainte-Marie was insensitive to the situation and, in a scene with comic overtones, the Jesuits had him kidnapped by Chinese Christian laymen and removed from the tense Nanking area. In a tribute to Sainte-Marie, a recent Jesuit historian describes him as holding no grudges in the aftermath of the kidnapping.[22]

Sainte-Marie, along with Morales, Bermúdez and Francisco Díez, began to question Jesuits and Chinese Christians and to compile for their superiors a report critical of Jesuit methods. In February 1636, Sainte-Marie sailed for Manila with the completed reports and, though imprisoned by the Dutch en route, reached Manila in June 1637. These reports have become primary sources for the study of the Rites Controversy, though in terms of Sainte-Marie's contribution they reflect less than three years' experience in China whereas his later *Mission Treatise* reflects over thirty years of experience. In 1643, he received the decrees appointing him prefect apostolic in China. By 1649, he was locating in Shantung Province where, with some financial assistance from Adam Schall at Peking, he established a long-lasting mission. In the persecution of 1665, he was banished with other missionaries to Canton. He acquired a knowledge of Chinese sufficient to collaborate in the writing of several books in Chinese on religious themes, including *T'ien Ju yin* (Christianity and Confucianism compared) (1664).[23] Throughout, he remained a persistent critic of the Jesuit position that was sympathetic toward the Chinese rites. He died at Canton on 13 May 1669.

Longobardi, Vagnoni, and, to a lesser extent, Visdelou[24] were rare Jesuits who deviated from the predominantly sympathetic position toward the Chinese rites. As the controversy intensified, the Jesuit order became more exclusively identified with the sympathetic position and, for the most part, criticism of this accommodating view in missionary methods came from non-Jesuit orders such as the Dominicans, Franciscans, Augustinians, and the Society of Foreign Missions. The Spaniard Morales, head of the Dominican order in China, and Sainte-Marie led the formal opposition to the Jesuits' methods in the mid-seventeenth century. The Franciscans and Dominicans were closely associated with the fortunes of Spain and Portugal. Consequently, the eclipse of these powers in the seventeenth and eighteenth centuries left these orders in a weakened position and led to resentment of the rise of the Society of Jesus in China. Yet the existence of Portuguese Jesuits blurs any clear-cut alignment in the matter. Additionally, the sixteenth and early seventeenth-century prominence of Italian Jesuits gave way to the late seventeenth- and eighteenth-century dominance of German and, particularly, French members, signifying a northerly shift in European political power. The methods of the Franciscans and Dominicans were far harsher and less subtle than those of the Jesuits who seemed more conscious of the need to correct some of the uncompromising elements that led to the missionary disaster in Japan during the first half of the seventeenth century.

The smoldering Rites Controversy flamed up in 1648 when Morales protested that the adaptiveness of the Jesuit methods defiled Christian doctrine by admitting various native Chinese superstitions into the practice of Christianity. Father Morales' intemperate behavior led to his expulsion by the Chinese, who were probably goaded on by the Jesuits, and Morales traveled to Rome to tell his story. In response, the Jesuits sent Fr. Martin Martini (Wei K'uang-kuo, 1614–1661) to Rome, and he presented the Jesuit side of the question so effectively that by 1656 he had secured perhaps the only markedly pro-Jesuit decree in the controversy. Sainte-Marie was quite aware of this background of events and in his *Mission Treatise* (pp. 10–11 and 47–49) specifically attempts to refute several of the views that Martini presented at Rome. In the same passage, Sainte-Marie states that he met with Martini in 1659, just after the latter's return from Rome, and personally disagreed with him.

Sainte-Marie completed his *Mission Treatise* in December 1668. Its full title is *Traité sur quelques points importants de la mission de la Chine* (Treatise on a few important points of the mission of China).[25] This title represents the French translation made from the original Spanish edition and published at Paris in 1701. It was in this form that the treatise came into the hands of Leibniz, who made considerable use of its contents. Leibniz was aware of the treatises by Longobardi and Sainte-Marie as early as 1709, though he did not see copies of them until late in 1715.[26] Then, in January 1716,[27] Leibniz wrote of his plan to use the Chinese sources of Longobardi and Sainte-Marie in composing a discourse in French on the high quality of ancient Chinese philosophy. This essay materialized as the *Discourse on the Natural Theology of the Chinese.*

### Claudio Filippo Grimaldi, S. J.

Claudio Filippo Grimaldi (Min Ming-wo, 1638–1712) was born in the Piedmont, in northwestern Italy, on 27 September 1638 and entered the Society of Jesus just over nineteen years later. After a long voyage of two years' duration, he arrived in Canton in 1669. He was soon residing in Peking, where in 1671 he constructed a model of a steam-turbine road carriage.[28] He and Verbiest were of great assistance to the K'ang-hsi emperor (r. 1662–1722) in dealing with the Russian embassy of Nikolai Gavrilovitch Spathary in 1676, since Spathary's knowledge of Latin provided the Jesuits with a medium of communication not possessed by the Chinese.[29] In the years of 1683 and 1685, Grimaldi accompanied the K'ang-hsi emperor on excursions to Tartary. He departed from Canton in 1686 for a return voyage to Europe where, at Rome in 1689, Leibniz made his acquaintance.

Leibniz' papers indicate that this acquaintance occurred at an early stage of his developing knowledge of China. In the Leibniz-Grimaldi file at Hanover, one can find notes made by Leibniz from a conversation with Fr. Grimaldi, presumably in Rome in 1689. In these notes, a mathematical basis for the relationship is definitely established. Leibniz was aware that Grimaldi was an associate of and designated successor to Ferdinand Verbiest, S. J. (Nan Huai-jen, 1623–1688), who had achieved a position of great influence in the Chinese court. Leibniz connects Verbiest with the Chinese "Tribunal in Mathematics," of which he was director.[30] The formal name of this agency was the Bureau of Astronomy *(Ch'in t'ien chien)*, and it dealt with astronomy as well as mathematics. Essentially the bureau was responsible for composing the official calendar—a task of supreme importance in China—but it was also involved with developing hydraulic and mechanical instruments. Verbiest had tutored the youthful K'ang-hsi emperor in geometry, philosophy, music, and, whenever possible, religion. In consequent years, astronomy, mechanics, and hydraulics provided the basis for the K'ang-hsi emperor's interest in foreign missionaries on the bureau. As Verbiest's associate, Grimaldi would have been part of these activities and would have shared this access to the Chinese throne. His knowledge of China would be considered as remarkable today as it was in the seventeenth century. Given Leibniz' orientation toward court politics, his expertise in mathematics, and his encyclopedic interests, it is not surprising that the stimulus provided by Grimaldi should have been an important factor in Leibniz' subsequent interest in China.

While in Rome, Leibniz wrote a letter, dated 19 July 1689, containing a list of thirty questions for Grimaldi to answer at his leisure.[31] The questions reflect little knowledge of China. Typically Leibnizian in scope, they cover a broad range of topics—plants, and agriculture, the production of paper, silk, porcelain, and leather, medicine, geometry, astronomy, chemistry, metallurgy, machines, and instruments with military and nautical uses. In his short introductory letter to this list, Leibniz mentions his awareness of the great antiquity of Chinese culture and anticipates the notion of an exchange of learning—an idea that is to become prominent in his later writings. He states that in exchange for the great mathematical sciences of the Europeans, the Chinese could teach Europeans the natural arcana they have observed through their long history. Furthermore, the ancient imperial traditions are present in China in a way now lost to Europe because of migration of populations, and Leibniz believes we could learn much from the records of this tradition preserved in China. Possibly, Leibniz implies, we could also learn much about Europe by studying these records. In this letter and list we see Leibniz' encyclopedic mind responding to a stimulus supplied by conversations with Grimaldi. Leibniz' notions of Chinese antiquity are general and unrefined, in the manner of a bright mind quickly catching on to a new subject. But we are observers at the still-early stages of a process that is to end twenty-six years later with a knowledge of China rare among Europeans of his day.

Sometime before leaving Rome, Leibniz met with Grimaldi and received answers to most of his thirty questions.[32] In response to Leibniz' query concerning Chinese astronomy, Grimaldi makes the interesting reply that Chinese celestial observations are not very trustworthy. He characterizes Chinese astronomers as mercenary men whose astronomy is determined more by their search for material rewards than for truth. The reference here is possibly to Mohammedan astronomers who had imported Arabic astronomical knowledge and techniques into China. These Mohammedans seem to have been essentially observers of celestial movements whose rigidity in outlook increased in proportion to their decline in knowledge of applied and theoretical mathematics.

By the time the Jesuits arrived, the Mohammedans appear to have degenerated into mere meticulous recorders of what they observed. In tests played out before the court, the Jesuits were able to demonstrate a superior ability in calculating precise times for eclipses and in suggesting reforms for the calendar. Since members of the Jesuit society such as Johann Adam Schall von Bell (T'ang Jo-wang, 1592–1666) and Ferdinand Verbiest had been involved in direct and bitter confrontations with the Mohammedans over these points, Grimaldi could hardly be expressing a detached opinion on their merits. At any rate, Grimaldi's first-hand accounts probably laid the foundation for Leibniz' later low opinion of the knowledge of mathematical sciences in modern China. His low regard for modern Chinese knowledge led Leibniz to support the view held by Ricci—a view later emphasized by Bouvet and the Figurists—that only the ancient Chinese possessed an understanding of the sciences consonant with a knowledge of the True Religion.

Joseph Needham's extensive investigation of Chinese science has given us reason to doubt this seventeenth-century evaluation of Chinese mathematical astronomy. Needham believes that the overly low assessment was caused by two main factors. First, there was a deterioration of a sophisticated Chinese astronomical tradition late in the Ming dynasty (1368–1644). This would help explain why Grimaldi, among others, viewed the Chinese astronomers of the late Ming as mere observers and recorders of celestial phenomena.

Second, and perhaps more significant, Needham maintains that the Jesuit astronomers did not devote sufficient effort to studying Chinese astronomical records because they carried a firm and unshakable conviction in the superiority of European science.[33] Finally, apart from Needham's argument, it should be noted that the Jesuits' scientific integrity in their work in astronomy in China, and specifically in their presentation of Copernican heliocentric theory, was not always as unimpeachable as their writings might indicate.[34]

Leibniz' letters to Grimaldi emphasize astronomy and mathematics, no doubt reflecting Grimaldi's expertise in these fields in China. Leibniz' letter of 21 (?) March 1692 is of additional interest in that it refers to an exchange between Terrentius (Johann Terrenz Schreck; Teng Yü-han, 1576–1630), a Jesuit astronomer in China and the famous European astronomer Johannes Kepler (1571–1630).[35] According to Leibniz, Terrentius wrote to Kepler in 1623 concerning astronomical matters and Kepler replied in 1627.[36] In his letter, Kepler made some comments on the origin of Chinese civilization that bear a remarkable similarity to the Noachide theory later to become prominent among the Jesuits.

According to the Noachide theory, the three sons of Noah— Sham, Ham, and Japheth—spread throughout the world, the descendants of Japheth, the oldest, travelling to northeast Asia. They took with them God's Law, which over the years became corrupted, though elements of it can still be detected in such doctrines as the virgin birth of the Prince of Millet (Hou Chi), said to be the first ancestor of the Chou dynastic line. The Society of Foreign Missions opposed this theory on the grounds that it diminished the authority of the Jews as the chosen people. If God's Law were carried to other peoples of the world, the line of descent from Noah to Abraham, Moses, and the prophets would no longer have such singular authority to speak for God. It was also said to diminish the importance of Christ's redemption of man.

I am unable to ascertain whether Kepler's notions have any direct link with the Noachide theory, but Leibniz does say that Kepler identified King Yao with Japheth's son, Javan. Legendarily speaking, Yao has several predecessors, including Fu Hsi and the Yellow Emperor (Huang Ti), but Kepler is apparently referring to the earliest Chinese ancestor. Besides Javan, Japheth's six sons include Ma-

gog, Madai, Tubal, Meshach, and Tiras.[37] Kepler also claimed that
Tubal was the ancestral father of the Tartars, although Leibniz believed that the Chinese and Tartars were more dissimilar in origin
than this.

In spite of Leibniz' disagreement on the origin of the Tartars, he
was later to be generally sympathetic to the view, held by so many
Jesuits, that ancient China did possess the True Law and that this
was the basis on which cultural accord between China and the West
could best be established. This view is implicit in Leibniz' letter of
20 December 1696 to Grimaldi, in which he presents his binary
system of mathematics.[38] This appears to be the last letter of
significance between Leibniz and Grimaldi preserved in the Hanover files. Soon afterward, the more important correspondence
with Bouvet begins.

### Joachim Bouvet, S. J.

Joachim Bouvet (Po Chin, 1656–1730) was among the first group
of French Jesuits to enter China. Five of them arrived in Peking in
1688. Two of the group, Bouvet and Jean-Francois Gerbillon
(Chang Ch'eng, 1654–1707), were ordered by the court to remain at
Peking and use their mathematical and technical training in support of astronomical and other activities for which the Jesuits were
now responsible.[39] This was not the first French mission sent to
China, for the Society of Foreign Missions had emerged from a
Parisian seminary founded in 1633 to train missionaries in methods
of foreign proselytizing. Unlike the other orders engaged in China,
however, the missionaries of this society were secular clergy and
unaffiliated with any religious order. Their efforts were spread
throughout Siam and Indochina, as well as parts of China itself,
and were not concentrated upon Peking as were those of the
Jesuits.[40]

The rivalry between the Portuguese and Spanish missionaries
and interests present from earlier times now intensified with the entry of the first French Jesuits, who unlike the German Jesuits in
China were closely allied with their home state. The king of Portugal was highly protective of his official status as patron of the
religious missions in China, and to minimize conflict the French
stressed the scientific rather than the religious nature of their first

officially patronized mission.[41] It was not long before the French achieved formal recognition of their separation from the Portuguese mission. In Bouvet's participation in the ensuing rivalries and intrigues, he appears to have expressed devotion to France, but even more to the Jesuit cause in which his commitment to Christ was profoundly embedded.

Unlike the missionary careers of Ricci and Longobardi, Bouvet's stay in China was from the start spent almost entirely at the center of imperial power. Even his trip to Europe in 1697–1699 was made partly in the capacity of an official gift-bearer of the K'ang-hsi emperor and partly to seek reinforcements from France for the Jesuit cause.[42] His association with the K'ang-hsi emperor seems to have been among the closest of all the Jesuits. His activities included tutoring the royal family,[43] helping at the emperor's command, to survey the area around Tientsin as a basis for a flood control project,[44] and, like Ricci, composing treatises in Chinese on Christian themes that would appeal to the literati.[45] Bouvet assumed a leading role on the side sympathetic to the Chinese rites and became associated with the Figurists, who emphasized the common origin of Chinese and Western cultures. His participation in the Rites Controversy included letters written from Peking to a number of European correspondents, one of whom was Leibniz.

Writing from Paris on 10 November 1701, the Jesuit Fr. Le Gobien forwarded a letter from Bouvet, along with a covering note, to Leibniz.[46] Le Gobien's note states that since Bouvet's letter of 8 November 1700 an additional letter of 2 December 1700 had arrived, reporting that the Jesuits had consulted the K'ang-hsi emperor on the question of Chinese rites. Their written petition gives some indication as to how much the Jesuits had mastered the delicate art of memorializing the emperor. Rather than merely asking the emperor for clarification, their petition in fact went on to offer a set of tentative explanations of the rites by which the Chinese honored Confucius and their ancestors. Their explanations emphasized the "good reasons"[47] on which these ceremonies were founded. The prescribed manner in which a Chinese emperor responded to a memorial was generally either to return it unsigned, indicating disapproval, or to accept it, sometimes with short comments appended in vermilion. Le Gobien tells us that the emperor accepted

the Jesuit explanation without alteration and that the decision acquired the force of law on 30 November 1700.

Here we have one of the less admirable instances of Jesuit pro-
cedure. Several years of proximity to the throne had given the
Jesuits access to the seat of power. They were quite right in recognizing the supremacy of the Chinese emperor as head of both
administrative and religious affairs in China. By writing an interpretation of Chinese rites that carefully appealed to the K'ang-hsi
emperor's own views, while simultaneously expressing the dominant Jesuit view of sympathy toward the rites, the Jesuits had resolved the question in a manner acceptable to the Chinese. But the
rites question for Europeans and for missionaries in China was not
resolved merely by the emperor's concurrence that the nature of the
Chinese rites was completely civil and social. A question of Christian doctrine could not be settled by political authority, and certainly not by Chinese political authority alone. The eventual rulings
of Rome—*Ex illa die* (1715) and *Ex quo singulari* (1742)—went
against the Jesuits, though political pressures were applied from
both sides. The Jesuit position was not, however, simply a matter
of political intrigue. There was a definite doctrinal view justifying a
sympathetic interpretation of Chinese rites that had been developed
by the society through years of experience, discussion, and reflection. Yet one would also probably have to concede that there was
something in the methods and outlook of the Jesuits which helped
to predispose this sympathetic interpretation even before the interpretation was begun. Bouvet's letters indicate a substantial concern
for the reasoning that went into the Jesuit interpretation. They also
indicate his own political motives. His letters were quite influential
in shaping Leibniz' views on China.

# 3
# *Leibniz and Bouvet*

Leibniz' China interpreters divide into two groups. In the first, we find missionaries such as Ricci, Longobardi, and Sainte-Marie, all of whom lived before Leibniz' time and with whom he made contact only through their written works. In the second group, we find missionaries who were contemporary to Leibniz and with whom his contact was direct, both through correspondence and, occasionally, personal meetings. Principal among these was Bouvet.

Projection of European concepts and needs upon Chinese culture was a characteristic of both groups, but with Bouvet the projection differed in its specific form. Longobardi and Sainte-Marie laced their writings with extensive quotations from the Chinese classics. Bouvet pays frequent veneration to the classics, but his approach is more that of universalist and syncretizer than scholar. His hypotheses are far more daring than those of Longobardi and Sainte-Marie, whose interpretations tend to be so literal that they often mislead. Because Longobardi and Sainte-Marie are negative in their interpretations of Chinese culture while Bouvet is highly creative, it is not surprising that Leibniz cast his lot with the latter.

## The Relationship

The Leibniz-Bouvet correspondence is one of the most important sources for the study of cultural relations between Europe and China in the late seventeenth and early eighteenth centuries. The

correspondence has been frequently cited by scholars and interest
has extended to the Far East. Early in the twentieth century, the
Japanese scholar Gorai Kinzō traveled to Germany, where he
copied the Leibniz-Bouvet correspondence out of the Leibniz archives at Hanover. Upon returning to Japan, he included parts of
this correspondence in his study on the influence of Confucianism
on German political thought.[1] Gorai's rendering of this correspondence was later translated into Chinese by Liu Pai-min and published in 1941 as part of a study on the *Book of Changes*.[2]

The Leibniz-Bouvet correspondence consists of at least fifteen
letters dating from the year 1697 to 1707 or shortly thereafter.[3] The
exchange of letters was irregular, for a while Bouvet was clearly the
initiator and was active in the early correspondence, his last recorded letter to Leibniz is dated 8 November 1702. Leibniz then wrote
five more letters which, if the archives are complete, remained
unanswered.

Bouvet's sudden silence would probably be explained more by a
change in priorities or interests than by any lack of vigor, since he
continued to be active in the China field until his death in 1730. The
Rites Controversy was at its peak between 1700 and 1704, at which
time Pope Clement issued his decree disapproving the Jesuit position and dispatched his representative, Tournon, to China. The
Tournon mission of 1704–1710 marked the beginning of the end of
Jesuit success in China. Perhaps Bouvet felt himself so embroiled
in this struggle that he could no longer find the time to carry on a
correspondence with Leibniz. With the European tide apparently
turning against the Jesuits, Bouvet may have felt that the real fight
was now to be one of devoting all effort to cultivating the support
of the K'ang-hsi emperor and allied forces in China as a counter-
vailing force against anti-Jesuit hostility in Europe. Possibly Bouvet regarded the correspondence with Leibniz as expendable or, less
cynically, perhaps he really did intend to continue, but demands
were such that he could no longer find the time.

Though the lapse of the Bouvet correspondence greatly reduced
Leibniz' direct contact with the China missionary field, Leibniz
maintained indirect contact through his European correspondents.[4]
Furthermore, not all Jesuits lost interest in corresponding with
Leibniz. In January 1706, Bartholomew des Bosses, a prominent

Jesuit theologian and mathematician at the Jesuit seminary at Hildesheim, initiated an extensive correspondence with Leibniz that continued until the latter's death. Many of their letters refer to news and concerns of China, for Des Bosses was in touch with missionary currents at Rome and elsewhere. Leibniz expressed his disappointment over Bouvet's lack of response in several letters to Des Bosses.[5] Naturally, Leibniz would have been disappointed by the abrupt end of a correspondence so auspiciously begun and in which he had been such an active participant. It was no doubt with Leibniz' assistance that Bouvet's correspondence was extended to a larger European audience with the publication in the journal *Mémoires de Trévoux* in 1704, of Bouvet's long letter to Leibniz of 4 November 1701.[6]

Leibniz' initial interest in China can be traced to his reading of books on the subject from as early as the 1660s and his concern with Chinese as a universal language during the 1670s. This initial stage can be distinguished from a second stage in the development of Leibniz' knowledge of China, beginning with the meeting with Grimaldi at Rome in 1689 and Leibniz' subsequent intensification of interest in China. A third stage coincides with the Bouvet correspondence from 1697 to 1707. The culmination of Leibniz' understanding was not to come until the last year of his life. This is the period in which others were increasingly abandoning Leibniz to the isolation and declining influence of his situation at Hanover. It was during this final stage that Leibniz discovered the Longobardi and Sainte-Marie treatises and their translations of Chinese philosophical texts, and it was at this time that his mature assimilation of Chinese civilization was expressed in his treatise on Chinese natural theology in 1716.

The relationship between Liebniz and Bouvet was tactical from both sides. It was a symbiosis fed on the one hand by Leibniz' reputation and wisdom and on the other by Bouvet's knowledge of Chinese culture and contacts with the K'ang-hsi emperor. Bouvet needed support for his missionary projects. For example, he required four or five fellow missioners for the tasks of compiling a new commentary to the Chinese classics and editing a new Chinese dictionary for Europeans. His hope was that Leibniz' standing in Europe would influence Louis XIV's Jesuit confessor, François la

Chaise,[7] and his secretary, Antoine Verjus, S. J., to seek support from French sources. In turn, Leibniz needed the cooperation of the Jesuits for his ecumenist cause.

Initial contact between Bouvet and Leibniz was made through the intermediary Verjus. Leibniz was in correspondence with Verjus concerning the China mission and had sent him several copies of the first edition of the *Novissima Sinica* (1697).[8] When Bouvet returned to Europe in 1697 with the intention of gathering further support for the Jesuit cause, he presumably read one of these copies of the *Novissima Sinica*. Consequently, Bouvet sent Leibniz a copy of his recently published *Portrait historique de l'Empereur de la Chine* (Historical portrait of the Emperor of China) along with a letter dated 18 October 1697.[9] Leibniz answered on 2 December 1697 by forwarding through Verjus a letter which—in addition to requests for information on the Chinese language, history, and so forth—asked that he be permitted to reprint Bouvet's *Portrait historique* in the second edition of *Novissima Sinica*.[10] Bouvet was happy to oblige, and the *Portrait historique* was reprinted in the 1699 edition.

On 28 February 1698, just before departing from La Rochelle for China, Bouvet wrote to Leibniz. In this letter he refers to the *Book of Changes* and briefly describes what has come to be known as the Figurist view of Chinese history. Bouvet believed that the lines of the hexagrams composed by Fu Hsi were in fact the first characters, that is, the basic linguistic units, of the Chinese language and culture. In effect, one sees here the Pythagorean implications of a common denominator for both an arithmetical and linguistic system in which language can be analyzed with mathematical precision. This notion coincided with the belief, so prevalent among certain Europeans, including Leibniz, that a "key" to the Chinese language could be developed. Reflecting a more practical awareness of the Chinese language, Bouvet in a letter to Leibniz of 19 September 1699 shows a certain caution toward their chances for developing the sort of key conceived by Andreas Müller of Berlin, who spoke of the common origin of Chinese characters and Egyptian hieroglyphs. Yet Bouvet himself believed in the theory of common origin.

In his letter of 28 February 1698, Bouvet refers Leibniz to Fr.

Couplet's *Confucius Sinarum Philosophus* for a representation of
these ancient Chinese characters. In fact, Bouvet believes that the
diagrams of Fu Hsi concentrate not only arithmetical and linguistic
elements but also the natural principles of all sciences. This
metaphysically complete system was thought to have been lost by
the Chinese long before the time of Confucius (551?–479? B.C.),
though the diagrams themselves have remained known to the
Chinese through their classic, the *Book of Changes*.

Bouvet and Leibniz shared a common assumption of the
age—namely, that "reason" was absolute in commanding assent
and led to confirmation of the "true religion," Christianity. Bouvet
believed that the conversion of the Chinese to Christianity could be
accomplished by reteaching the Chinese what had previously been
part of their knowledge. Leibniz subscribed to this view, particularly since he himself was working on an arithmetical common
denominator for solving general problems of knowledge. One can
imagine his excitement when he later discovered the similarities in
progression between the hexagrams and his own binary arithmetic.

Bouvet was always pressed in trying to find time to respond to
Leibniz' many questions and suggestions for ambitious schemes.
Practical matters frequently interfered, both from the European
and from the Chinese ends. In his letter of 19 September 1699, written just after his return to Peking, Bouvet refers briefly to distractions connected with his return journey to China. Though Louis
XIV had subsidized the initial Jesuit mission of 1685, he was un-
willing to underwrite the sending of additional Jesuits to China.
Since Bouvet had returned to Europe in 1697 not only at the K'ang-
hsi emperor's request but also to expand the China mission, his
efforts were aimed at finding additional support. Thus the publication of *Portrait historique* (1697) was, in part, a propaganda
maneuver. The arrangement that Bouvet eventually made was with
a French glass producer in search of profit. This Jean Jourdan de
Groussay agreed to invest in a ship carrying a cargo of glasswares,
and he included passages for several Jesuits only after Bouvet convinced him of their potential usefulness as negotiators when the
cargo arrived in China. Consequently, the ship *Amphitrite* brought
ten additional Jesuits to the China mission.[11]

Bouvet probably had some share in selecting these Jesuits. Two in particular came to share Bouvet's interest in the *Book of Changes*. Father Joseph Prémare joined Bouvet in developing Figurist theories and later wrote a lengthy study on the manifestation of Christian dogma in the diagrams of the *Book of Changes*.[12] Another member of the group traveling to China on the *Amphitrite*, Fr. Jean-Baptiste Régis (Lei Hsiao-szu, 1664–1738) made a Latin translation of the *Book of Changes*, even though he was apparently not a Figurist.[13]

Before describing more of the Leibniz-Bouvet correspondence, it may be useful to refer to a piece written by Leibniz that represents one of several anticipations of similarity between his philosophy and that of China. The setting is a New Year's letter of 1697 addressed to his patron, Rudolphus Augustus, duke of Brunswick-Lüneburg-Wolfenbüttel.[14] The ostensible purpose of the letter is to propose the coining of a medallion that would contain Rudolphus Augustus' image on one side and the *Imagio Creationis* (Image of Creation), an exemplification of the dyadic or binary system, on the other. The letter provides a glimpse of how Leibniz' mathematical ideas intersect with his ecumenical interests in religion and politics, for Leibniz believes that his binary system presents an instance of how God created the world out of the units of 0 (Nothing) and 1 (God). It is this process that Leibniz refers to as the "secret of creation."

Though he had been told by Grimaldi in Rome that the K'ang-hsi emperor was being tutored in mathematics and geometry by Verbiest, Leibniz had received little information regarding China on which to base his notion of potential similarities between the hexagrams of the *Changes* and his binary progression. Yet in the discussion of the *Imagio Creationis,* Leibniz says that he has communicated his concept of number in the "secret of creation" to Grimaldi in the hope of appealing to the emperor's interest in number.[15] He feels that the Chinese response to European mathematics may enable the binary system to operate as a tool, if not to convert the emperor to Christianity, at least to bring him into some ecumenical accord with Christian principles by demonstrating the universal validity of these principles.

Bouvet's letter of 8 November 1700 from Peking was sent to the French Jesuit Charles le Gobien with the request that it be forwarded to Leibniz. Le Gobien, too, was intimately involved with the Jesuit mission in China and had authored the *Histoire de l'Edit de l'Empereur de la Chine en faveur de la Religione Chrestienne* (Paris, 1698). In a previous letter,[16] Bouvet had described Le Gobien's role as that of a clearing house for the release of Jesuit reports from China. It was Le Gobien who decided which of the reports were to be released to the public, and consequently it was to Le Gobien that Leibniz wrote for information on China. Le Gobien forwarded Bouvet's letter along with a covering letter dated at Paris, 10 November 1701. This covering letter mentions the receipt of a new letter from Bouvet, dated 2 December 1700, announcing that the K'ang-hsi emperor had accepted the Jesuits' memorial as a valid explanation of Chinese rites as of 30 November 1700. In effect, Le Gobien fully accepts this resolution of a doctrinal question by the political authority of the Chinese emperor. In supporting this official acceptance of the Jesuits' action, Le Gobien notes that the "senior missionaries," that is, the Jesuits, have spent the past thirty or forty years studying this matter at Peking and in consultation with Chinese savants. Consequently, they would have a better understanding of the situation than the "new missionaries," that is, the non-Jesuit orders, that have resided in China for a mere twelve to fifteen years and in locales far from the capital. (Actually, although Le Gobien assumes otherwise, court obligations were frequently a hindrance to comprehension of Chinese culture in that their official duties kept the Jesuits involved at the Manchu court and limited their contact with the Chinese literati.) Le Gobien concludes his letter with praise for Leibniz' *Novissima Sinica*.

As a stimulus and source of information on China, the Leibniz-Bouvet correspondence ended when Bouvet's last letter reached Leibniz, probably in 1703. Leibniz' interest in China was still intense and his assimilation of Chinese philosophy would not peak until his composition of the *Discourse* in 1716. For this reason, I place the Leibniz-Bouvet correspondence in an intermediate stage in the development of Leibniz' understanding of Confucianism. There are, however, exceptions to this placement. There are several notions about Chinese culture that reached their mature development in Leibniz' thought at the time of his exchanges with Bouvet. These include certain premises of natural theology in regard to the

Chinese that were shaped by Bouvet's Figurist views. They also include Leibniz' ideas on the arithmetical progression embodied in the diagrams of the *Book of Changes*. The three letters from Bouvet to Leibniz (8 November 1700, 4 November 1701, and 8 November 1702) considered in the following section represent the culmination of the correspondence in that they are the last letters that Bouvet wrote. More significantly, for the purposes of this study, these three letters contain most of the basic information that Bouvet transmitted to Leibniz on the key subjects of natural theology and the *Book of Changes*.

## The Letters

### Bouvet's Letter of 8 November 1700
### to Le Gobien and Leibniz

Bouvet's letter of 8 November 1700, forwarded to Leibniz by Le Gobien, cites the *Book of Changes* as the oldest work of China and perhaps of the world. In this position, Bouvet is in accord with several modern sinologists who defend the *Book of Changes* as the oldest extant Chinese work. Disagreeing with many critics of his own time, Bouvet praises the *Changes* as the source of all Chinese science and of a philosophy perhaps superior to that of contemporary Europe. While admiring the text of the *Changes,* Bouvet believes that many of the commentaries written on it are full of errors and, expressing a characteristic missionary's complaint, notes that a section in the *Changes* on divination is pure superstition.

Bouvet compares the corpus of the *Changes* to a precious residue left from antiquity. Time has since overlaid this corpus with errors that obscure what the original patriarchs taught to their descendants. Placing the origins of China back 3000 or 4000 years prior to A.D. 1700, Bouvet refers to Fu Hsi as the first legislator who composed this famous diagram of 64 figures and 384 lines. The reference here is to either the circular or the square arrangements in the Prior to Heaven order *(Hsien-t'ien tzu-hsü),* in which each of the 64 figures contains six lines. These figures when multiplied together, yield a total of 384 lines. Bouvet believes that this diagram summarizes in a Pythagorean fashion the perfected state of the sciences of arithmetic, music, astronomy or astrology, medicine, and physics possessed by the Chinese forefathers.

Bouvet detects a great accord between the knowledge of the Chinese ancients of 4000 years ago and that of Western sages of antiquity. He claims that the figures of Fu Hsi were invented as universal symbols for the same purpose as the figures of the Hermes Trismegistus of the West—that is, to represent these extremely abstract principles. The many commentaries on the work written by authors, including Confucius, in the intervening 3000 years, dating from the time when Fu Hsi's system was understood down to A.D. 1700, are seen by Bouvet to have merely obscured the original import of Fu Hsi's figures. Consequently, he has left aside all the Chinese commentaries in order to study these figures as an independent unit and believes he has arrived at a solution by means of numerical analysis and combination.

Bouvet agrees with other "disciples"—it is not certain whether the reference here is to Chinese disciples or European Figurists—that Fu Hsi was not a Chinese but a universal figure whose system comprehends all other sciences. Bouvet and those of his fellow missionaries known as Figurists had held the view that Fu Hsi was not a Chinese but the original lawgiver of all mankind. This lawgiver was said to be recognized in different societies with different names—Fu Hsi among the Chinese, Hermes Trismegistus among the Egyptians and Greeks,[17] Enoch among the Hebrews, Zoroaster among the Persians.

Bouvet regards the Prior to Heaven diagram as reflecting a general method of science that combines three sets of numerical progressions, geometrical figures and proportions, and laws of statics designed to order the sciences and make rational God's creations. In short, everything is reduced to number, weight, and measure. The science of this method derives from a system of numbers, a double set of numbers on a geometrical plane and solid, linked in such a way as to yield all the harmonies of music. Furthermore, Bouvet sees the 64 hexagrams and their 384 lines as representing the harmonies of celestial movement, with all the necessary principles that explain the nature of all things and the causes of generation and corruption. In his eyes, all this reinstates the lost music of China, lost some fifteen to twenty centuries ago, and also that of Greece, including the three musical systems of diatonic, chromatic, and harmonic scales. Detecting a correspondence between the numbers of Fu Hsi and those of Pythagoras and Plato, Bouvet is led to believe that they stem from the same system. He notes a further correspondence to the numerical mysteries of the Cabala and consequently comes to link the ancient Chinese philosophy with that of Plato and the ancient Hebrews, treating them all as the common revelation of the Creator.

Bouvet severely criticizes Maigrot of the Foreign Mission, who in 1693 as bishop of Conon and vicar apostolic in Fukien had mandated all priests of his vicarate to discontinue using the Chinese *t'ien* and *shang-ti* as equivalents for the Christian God. Bouvet urges that the missionaries, instead of completely rejecting the notion of equivalents, should study the ancient classics associated with Fu Hsi and Confucius to see how the later Chinese had distorted what was once a religion in consonance with Christianity. This would be preferable to dwelling on the corruption of these post-Confucius writings and insisting, as did Maigrot, that the Chinese abandon these customs as corrupt. Bouvet thinks that such severity will place an insuperable obstacle in the path of converting the Chinese and lose a hundred years of missionary effort. The abortive missionary experience in Japan might well have been in his thoughts.

Bouvet suggests a gradual and compromising path in spite of the fact that such a path may be less convenient to the Holy See, the congregation, and the vicars apostolic.[18] He proposes that all the missionaries join together to study the ancient Chinese classics and use the Chinese custom of veneration of antiquity to overcome modern corrupt interpretations of the classics and restore the true philosophy of Fu Hsi. In the process, "the light of right reason" would be employed. By rejecting current interpretations of the classics and proposing what he regards as their original meaning, Bouvet follows an approach that has traditionally been part of the Confucian tradition—namely, that of returning to the *true* meaning of the classics. This search and debate had been under way in China for over 2,000 years.

Noting the necessary connection between the "true philosophy," which the Chinese of antiquity had, and the "true religion," which is Christianity, Bouvet thinks that the task of showing the Chinese the erroneous and superstitious nature of their post-antiquity philosophy is very feasible. Besides involving the literati in the effort to establish Christianity in China, Bouvet also suggests directing a particular work at the K'ang-hsi emperor. He conceives of this work as the reestablishment of the sciences of ancient China in accordance with the system of Fu Hsi and thinks it would give the emperor such pleasure that it would be circulated throughout the realm bearing the force of law. Such an outcome would both elevate the status of Christianity and also confirm the common nature of Chinese antiquity with Christianity.

### Bouvet's Letter of 4 November 1701 to Leibniz

Bouvet could have learned of Leibniz' binary arithmetic through two sources. The first is Leibniz' letter to Grimaldi of 20 December 1696 containing a two-page explanation of Leibniz' binary system of numerical progression.[19] The second source is Leibniz' letter to Bouvet of 15 February 1701 written from Braunschweig.[20] From Bouvet's frequent references to Grimaldi and from his acquaintance with the Leibniz-Grimaldi exchanges, we might assume that Bouvet saw Leibniz' 1696 letter to Grimaldi. In any case, something seems to have triggered Bouvet's enthusiastic response of 4 November 1701. The 1701 and 1702 letters by Bouvet to Leibniz constitute the more substantial sections of Bouvet's part in the correspondence. A letter of 15 February 1701 would seem to have had just sufficient time to travel from Europe to Peking—delivery took at least seven months—and to have arrived in time to stimulate Bouvet in his response of 4 November 1701.

In the letter of 4 November 1701,[21] Bouvet sees Leibniz' numerical calculus as beneficial to the religious causes of both the missionaries and ecumenism. He notes the marvelous similarity between Western and Chinese principles and sees them as having a common basis in the science of numbers found in both Fu Hsi's diagram and Leibniz' calculus. He also believes that Fu Hsi's numerical system, now lost, explained all the Chinese sciences, including those of physical principles and causes of generation and corruption. Bouvet refers specifically to Leibniz' numerical table with its double geometrical progression that corresponds to the system of Fu Hsi. He then suggests that were Leibniz to continue his binary arithmetic from the fifth degree (that is, 00 000 or 32) to the sixth degree (that is, 000 000 or 64), substitute broken and unbroken lines for 0 and 1 respectively, and then curve the result into a circular form, the result would correspond to the circular arrangement found in Fu Hsi's Prior to Heaven diagram, of which Bouvet encloses an example.[22] A photographic reproduction of the diagram that Bouvet enclosed in his letter to Leibniz of 4 November 1701 appears in Diagram 1.

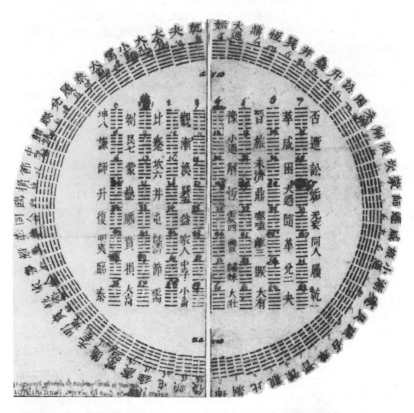

Diagram 1.    The Prior to Heaven hexagram order (*Hsien-t'ien tzu-hsü*). A reproduction of the diagram that was enclosed with Bouvet's letter to Leibniz of 4 November 1701 (*Leibnizbriefe* 105, pp. 27–28). Courtesy of the Leibniz Gesellschaft, Niedersächsische Landesbibliothek, Hanover, Germany.

Although Bouvet stresses a correspondence with the cirular arrangement of the diagram, he quite clearly intends a correspondence with the rectangular arrangement also, since the latter consists of the same 64 hexagrams but in a different geometrical order. Bouvet refers to the broken and unbroken lines 0 and 1 as "two universal and magical symbols" that contain the principles of all knowledge. Bouvet describes the second figure in the Prior to Heaven diagram as a magical square arranged within a circle. This too is attributed by Bouvet to the authorship of Fu Hsi.

Employing the Prior to Heaven diagram, Bouvet and Leibniz were able to draw correspondences between its order and the binary progression by letting a divided line in the hexagram represent 0 and an undivided line represent 1. A binary progression is thus derived. For example, *k'un* ☷ , the first hexagram in the upper left-hand corner of the square arrangement in the Prior to Heaven diagram, would in the denary system represent 0, which for purposes of clarification will be represented as 000 000. Following the sequence in the square arrangement, the second hexagram, *po* ☶ , would be 1 in the denary system and 000 001 in the binary system. The third hexagram, *pi* ☵ , would be 2 and 000 010; *kuan* ☴ would be 3 and 000 011; and so on up to *ch'ien* ☰ , the sixty-fourth hexagram, which would be 63 in the denary progression and 111 111 in the binary.

In regard to the square arrangement in the Prior to Heaven diagram, Bouvet and Leibniz diverged from the traditional transformation of the diagrams, which changes from the bottom upward; for example, using the traditional transformation, 000 001 would be rendered as *fu*[b] ☳ instead of *po*. However, this probably represents more a sign of the flexibility of the system than ignorance of the Chinese tradition. Bouvet must have been aware of the more traditional method, and Leibniz shows in his letter to Des Bosses of 12 August 1701 that he is capable of counting the lines from the bottom up.[23] It would certainly be consistent with Bouvet's belief that the hexagrams contained the key to all ancient Chinese sciences to treat the diagrams in as fluid a manner as possible.

Apparently out of the scientific stimulus he had received in his Paris and London visits (1672–1676), Leibniz developed his analysis of the dyadic or binary (i.e., base of 2) arithmetical progression

and in 1679 presented his findings in a paper, *De Progressione Dya-
dica.* In contrast to the binary base, Europeans had been employing
a denary (i.e., base of 10) progression. In his later *Explication,*
Leibniz holds that a denary base is neither of the highest antiquity
nor is it necessarily superior to other systems, though it has acquired a certain unique facility among us through habit.[24] According to Leibniz, the Greeks and Romans were aware of its advantages and yet did not utilize it. Leibniz traces its introduction to
Europe via the Spanish Moor influence of Gerbert (d. 1003), later
known as Pope Sylvester II. Apparently, along with it came the
"place value" characteristic that Europe had learned in the sixteenth century from the Arabs, who in turn trace it back to A.D.
sixth-century Hindus.[25] Leibniz based his analysis upon the recognition that certain properties of numerical systems are common to
all numbers and that, while 10 has acquired an easy familiarity
among Europeans, the selection of a base number is in fact rather
arbitrary and need not be 10: it could be 2 or 12 or any number.

Actually, the correspondences Bouvet perceived between Leibniz' binary system and the Prior to Heaven order of the hexagrams
emerge from the basic fluidity of that order, which permits several
possible readings. The square arrangement within the circular
might be read horizontally beginning with *k'un* from left to right
and from top to bottom, as Bouvet seems to have done; or it might
be read horizontally beginning with *ch'ien* from right to left and
from bottom to top, as the Neo-Confucian philosopher Shao Yung
(1011-1077) seems to have done. The circular arrangement presents
similar alternatives if one reads the lines of each hexagram from the
center outward. Reading in this way, a binary progression is made
possible by moving counterclockwise in a semicircle, from *k'un* at
the bottom up through *kou* ≡ , then leaving off and picking up
with *fu* at the bottom to trace another semicircle by moving
clockwise through *ch'ien.*

It is interesting to note that the research of Hu Wei (1633-1714)
and other contemporary Chinese scholars was leading them at this
same period to different conclusions. For example, they attributed
the Prior to Heaven diagram not to Chinese antiquity but to the
much later creation of Shao Yung of which more will be said
below. In contrast to this, Bouvet thinks the Chinese commen-

tators, including Confucius, are very mistaken in their analyses. Continuing with his letter of 8 November 1700, Bouvet relates how his discovery of the correspondence between the ancient Chinese system and Leibniz' numerical calculus raised both his esteem of Leibniz and his hopes that the ancient system of science might be recovered. There seems little doubt that it also raised Bouvet's hopes for converting the Chinese.

Bouvet refers favorably to Leibniz' plan for a Universal Characteristic that would represent thoughts in the same way that universal characters represent laws, calculations, and demonstrations of reason.[26] He thinks such a genre would correspond both to the ancient hieroglyphs of the Cabala and to the characters of Fu Hsi, which he identifies with the double geometrical system of Leibniz. One could use this system to order all phenomena in terms of genus and species in a natural metaphysic. Bouvet offers the organic metaphor of a genealogical tree proceeding from the trunk down to the smallest subdivision of a branch. The sign of the point ($\cdot$), the simplest sign, represents unity and is the characteristic sign of both the first principle and the transcendent being. The two genres that arise from the point, or first principles, are perfection and imperfection, represented by the binary number of two points ($\cdot\cdot$) and by the ternary number of three points ($\cdots$), respectively. Or they can be represented by two lines, one whole line (——) representing the perfect number and one broken line (— —) representing the imperfect number.

Bouvet applies the double geometrical progression to colors by reducing color to the two simplest components of light and darkness and degrees of variation therefrom.[27] Light at its most intense would be white; in a lesser state of intensity, yellow. Shadow at its most intense would be black; in a lesser state of intensity, blue. (Bouvet's emphasis on degrees of variation is very similar to an emphasis found in Leibniz.) Bouvet correlates these four primary colors with the eight trigrams by grouping two trigrams with each primary color. He then introduces these eight trigrams as the fundamental figures of Fu Hsi and the foundation of all sciences. In attributing the trigrams to Fu Hsi, Bouvet is in accord with Chinese researchers of both his own and more modern times. It is by means of similarities and analogies drawn from the progressions found in figures of the Prior to Heaven diagram that Bouvet feels confident he can explain principles of many types of science.

Bouvet explains the Chinese emphasis on the third (trigram) order and the sixth (hexagram) order in a very Pythagorean manner by squaring 8, the number of trigrams, to yield 64, the number of hexagrams or six-lined figures. Bouvet also relates these to the eight degrees of Aristotelian qualities. In applying the figures to colors, Bouvet sees sixty-four colors grouped into eight types, each of which breaks down into eight degrees. The result is that everything can be translated into a continuum in which one thing varies only a slight degree from the thing beside it. This is highly reminiscent of Leibniz' tendency to view things in terms of gradations. Bouvet holds that what explains colors can also explain all phenomena. By determining the two simplest elements, one can explain all species. For example, one might assign 4 to white, 8 to black, 2 to heat, 6 to cold, 5 to dryness, and 7 to dampness; then one might refer to the seventh grade or degree of dryness, since each element in turn breaks down into eight degrees of gradation. With such a tool, Bouvet believes it is possible to attain a precision akin to the exactness by which one refers to the 360th part of a circle or to a celestial sign as the twelfth part of the zodiac.

Bouvet calls Fu Hsi the prince of philosophers and thinks that if Aristotle and other great Western philosophers were viewed from the right perspective, the fundamental similarity of their ideas would be understood. Quickly moving to cut off any suspicion that he is elevating China over his "dear fatherland" Europe, Bouvet holds that European attainments are superior to modern Chinese achievements and again puts forth the proposition that Fu Hsi was not Chinese, but a universal figure. He identifies Fu Hsi with such characters of the Levant as Zoroaster, Enoch, and Hermes Trismegistus and draws support for this identity from an analysis of several Chinese hieroglyphs and even from the name Fu Hsi itself. Bouvet rightly points out that the character $fu^a$ is composed of the character for man $(jen^a)$ and for dog $(ch'\ddot{u}an)$. Bouvet thus interprets $fu$ as meaning man-god, or the wise dog who comes and searches out causes and principles, and claims that Hermes Trismegistus is also represented by the head of a dog on a human body.[28] He interprets the character for the name $Hsi^a$ as referring to sacrifice and to Fu Hsi's role as the director of sacrifices. This claim is supported by a closely related term, *hsi*[b], which refers to sacrificial victims. Bouvet also claims that Fu Hsi is referred to by the alternative name *"Taï-hao,"* a term he interprets as signifying "thrice great," the same meaning assigned to the name Trismegistus.

Bouvet notes that if we believe Chinese chronology, Fu Hsi lived 4600 years ago—once more a variation in Bouvet's chronological placement of Fu Hsi—and his work represents the oldest monument on earth. Bouvet associates such antiquity with an awareness of the Creation and sees this awareness reflected in the six degrees (i.e., lines) of generation, representing the six days of labor, and then the lapse into the mystery of the seventh, corresponding with the Sabbath. Bouvet further notes that according to Fu Hsi, Heaven and Earth are said to be the first degree of natural production, akin to the unbroken and broken lines in the diagrams. He quotes a passage from the *Record of Rites (Li Chi)*—*"T'ai-i fen erh kuei t'ien-ti"*—and translates it as "the great unity, or to say the same thing, the triple unity (for the two hieroglyphs *t'ai-i* contain these three meanings) is the principle of Heaven and Earth." A less trinitarian rendering might be: "The Supreme Unity divides and forms Heaven and Earth."[29]

To show that this *t'ai-i* (Supreme Unity) is equivalent to the supreme deity, *shang-ti*, Bouvet cites the *Shih chi* (Historical records) of Ssu-ma Ch'ien (145–90 B.C.). Here, Bouvet claims, it is said that in ancient times one sacrificed and offered victims of the first order to *t'ai-i*, which is the same as the Maximal One.[30] Bouvet then presents the radical claims that eventually became known as the Figurist view. He states that the ancient Chinese understanding included not only seeing God as Creator and Principle of all natural things, but also encompassed the mystery of the Holy Trinity. Bouvet claims that there are numerous passages in ancient Chinese books that confirm a knowledge of sin, the punishment of evil, angels, the first man (i.e., Adam), the corruption of human nature by sin, the Flood, the Incarnation of Christ to come, and Christ's redemption of man. In short, Bouvet states that at one time in the past, China had a very clear conception of the Divinity.[31]

Bouvet believes there is a technique present in the construction of Chinese characters that was developed not by the Chinese but by the ancient fathers of the world. To support his point, he postulates similarities in sound and meaning between the most ancient Chinese characters and the Egyptian language, and he believes these similarities are still apparent in spite of historical alterations in the language. Even the most tolerant reader would hesitate over the sweeping nature of such comparisons, but Bouvet promises that should he find the time, he will make some "surprising" remarks on these similarities. (Unfortunately, he never found the time.)

Bouvet explains that distractions have prevented the French Jesuits from carrying out their plan of sending yearly messages to Europe explaining the Chinese science and other matters, but he is hopeful that the situation will shortly improve. He expresses the wish that Leibniz will communicate his own discoveries and those of his academy so that the missionaries will have tools with which to destroy the demonic empire and establish Christ's realm in China. On the concept of using knowledge as a tool for religion, Bouvet and Leibniz agree. In this regard, they reflect the optimism toward potential fruits to be harvested from the application of knowledge, a view symptomatic of the emerging European Enlightenment.

Apparently in response to Leibniz' request for information on the Chinese language, Bouvet answers that Fr. Claude de Visdelou (Liu Ying, 1656–1737) is in the early stages of translating a Chinese dictionary into a European language. He adds that he himself would like to write an analysis of the language, but it would distract him from more important duties involving religion and science. Bouvet notes that as soon as the dictionary being translated from Chinese into Tartar (i.e. Manchu) is completed, missionaries will render it into Latin or French. One wonders whether Bouvet eventually participated in this project and whether the result is the dictionary that is said to rest among his manuscripts in the library collection at Le Mans, France.[32]

Speaking as a proselytizer, Bouvet stresses the need to wait for the right moment to introduce their discovery (i.e., the connection between numbers and creation) to the K'ang-hsi emperor. But the emperor is not as accessible to Bouvet now as he was earlier when he was indulging his fascination for European science with Jesuit tutors. Bouvet requests further information on Leibniz' theory so that he will have sufficient knowledge to make the full case the emperor will demand. He explains that since returning from his trip of 1697-1699 to Europe, his only direct service to the emperor has been working with three other Jesuits, among them Fr. Antoine Thomas (An Tuo, 1644-1709), constructing a map to include the imperial hunting grounds.

In response to overly optimistic claims by certain Europeans, and to the questions of a Mr. Scrokins and Fr. Kochanski—at Leibniz' suggestion, Kochanski submitted a list of questions to Bouvet in 1697[33]—Bouvet gives the sobering reply that the emperor cannot read any European language. Once, Bouvet relates, the emperor and the crown prince showed enough curiosity to have the letters of the alphabet written for them and to have the missionaries read from a European book, but never with the desire of learning the language. On the other hand, the emperor and some of his children have found European numerals simpler than the Chinese for calculation and so they use a table of sines and logarithms modeled by Bouvet on those used in France. Ever conscious of a universal logic of arts and sciences, Bouvet argues that if one could grasp the logical connection Bouvet and Leibniz presume to exist among the Chinese characters, the Chinese language could be used without the tiresome study the language now requires.

Bouvet concludes this letter with analyses of several Chinese characters that he claims have been in use by Oriental philosophers for 4500 years. These characters signify the Sovereign Being, the equivalent of the Christian God, which they recognized and worshipped in that time. Bouvet begins with his very Pythagorean premise that the arithmetical and geometrical basis of all Chinese science is reflected in the construction of the Chinese character for the deity. It should be noted, however, that "arithmetical" and "geometrical" are not necessarily synonymous; at least one interpreter of the *Book of Changes* disagrees with Bouvet and Leibniz and claims that the progression found in the *Changes* is arithmetical rather than geometrical (see the appendix).

Bouvet holds that the signs of the point (·) and unity (——) are the two simplest elements to be imagined. Bouvet's claim that in antiquity the character represented by the point and pronounced "*chu*[a]" expressed the idea of master or Sovereign Lord is supported by the identity of this character with the more modern *chu*[b],

which bears a similar meaning. Bouvet again invokes the quotation
from the *Record of Rites (Li Chi)*—*"T'ai-i fen erh kuei
t'ien-ti"*—to signify that *t'ai* represents the many and *i* the one and
that together they represent the number three or triple unity. To
support this notion, Bouvet quotes a phrase from an unspecified
Chinese dictionary, *"T'ai-i han-san"* (The Great Source contains a
unity), to make the point that the one and the many certainly involve a trinity. Furthermore, Bouvet holds that the character *t'ai* is
composed of *ta* (great) plus the point *chu* (master) and together signifies "one, three together (i.e., trinity) greatest." When *ta* (great)
is combined with the word for unity, *i,* the result is *t'ien* (Heaven),
in the archetypal or spiritual rather than material sense. His-
torically speaking, *t'ai-i* was originally a Taoist term. It is said to
have first appeared in Eastern Chou dynasty (770–221 B.C.) literature, where it had the same meaning as *tao*. It was later introduced
into the Han dynasty (206 B.C.–A.D. 221) state religion and
associated with the great sacrifice by the emperor on T'ai moun-
tain.[34]

Bouvet refers to the characters *ti* and *shang-ti* as being the most
commonly used in referring to the Sovereign Lord. Bouvet analyzes
*ti* to be composed of *li*[c], which he interprets as "first established,"
and *chin,* a standard or sign of authority. Bouvet interprets this as
referring to God's sovereign authority in the world. He next
analyzes the characters *chu*[b] and *tsai*. *Chu*[b] (master) is composed of
*Wang*[a] (king) and the point *chu*[a] (master). The hieroglyph *tsai* is
composed of *mien* (which signifies a cover in the form of a roof and
denotes Heaven) and *shih,* located at the bottom of the character.
This same figure, according to Bouvet, signifies the number 10 for
the Chinese, the Egyptians, and the Romans. Bouvet claims that
*shih* signifies the universality of all things, just as Pythagoras
represented all things by the four figures 1, 2, 3, 4, which together
total 10. The third element of the character is found in the middle
and, as above, is *li*[c] denoting building and elevation.

### Bouvet's Letter of 8 November 1702 and Leibniz' "Explication"

Bouvet's letter of 8 November 1702 is considerably briefer than
that of 4 November 1701, perhaps because he had not yet received

Leibniz' reply to his last letter.[35] In the opening lines, Bouvet relates that during the past year he has continued his study of the Chinese classics and has discovered in them a great similarity with religion. He says they use a path that can easily and naturally lead not only to comprehension of the Creator and natural religion but also to understanding of Jesus Christ and difficult Christian truths. He holds that a near-complete system of the true religion is to be found in the Confucian classics and that this system includes the mysteries of the incarnation of the Word, the life and death of the Savior and the principal functions of the latter's holy ministry contained in prophetic manner (prophetic because the classics were written before the birth of Christ).

For nearly 2000 years, Bouvet believes, the Chinese have been without any knowledge of the true God because they have lost both the hieroglyphic significance of these characters and also the wisdom of the classics. Ultimately, he contends, only a superficial part of the doctrine has been perpetuated. The essence of this lost knowledge is universal, predating the Chinese as a race. The Chinese have conserved this essence more faithfully than any other (gentile) tradition. Here Bouvet's call is to the *true* meaning of the classics, an appeal that has always commanded respect among Confucianists and has been a key concern in a continuing debate at the core of the Confucian tradition.

Bouvet discusses the way in which the Chinese, like the Greeks, have distorted their original history from Fu Hsi down to Confucius. He feels that they have couched this period in a historical allegory or historical poem in order to better explain the system of ancient religion. Within this context, he sees two paths. Some have abandoned the ancient traditions, corrupted their manners, and constructed a religion reflecting the disorder of their passions. (It is not certain to what extent this reference goes beyond the atheistic tendencies that developed within Confucian tradition to encompass the Taoist and Buddhist beliefs.) Others have tried to maintain the purity of the original doctrine and to this end have preserved many of the ancient practices of religion. This may be seen in a precise analysis of the hieroglyphs the ancients employed to embody the principles of arithmetic, geometry, astronomy, astrology, music, metaphysics, physics, and so forth. Bouvet concedes the still flimsy nature of some of his ideas but notes that he has had success with testing several of them, particularly those mentioned in his letter to Leibniz of the previous year, 1701.

Bouvet reemphasizes the importance of his common interests with Leibniz in understanding antiquity and analyzing the characters of language. In praising Leibniz' knowledge in this area, he asks that Leibniz recommend to Fr. Verjus books that might be helpful in this task.[36] He briefly cites a plan to compile a new set of commentaries to the Chinese classics and a new dictionary, all of which, he feels, would substantiate his theories on reestablishing the ancient and universal sciences of China, once synonymous with the natural law of religion. To this end, he will need the assistance of several fellow missionaries, and he asks that Leibniz use his influence with Frs. Verjus and La Chaise to help secure funds from the French court for this project.

The extent to which Leibniz was influenced by Bouvet's letters is documented in the short piece by Leibniz entitled *Explication de l'arithmétique binaire,* which appeared in a 1703 edition of *Mémoires de l'Académie des sciences.*[37] This essay begins with a brief presentation of his dyadic or binary mathematics, which he calls a "double geometrical progression." There follows a presentation of some similarities between his dyadic and the 4000-year-old lines of Fu Hsi. Leibniz' material is taken almost entirely from Bouvet's letters, particularly from that of 4 November 1701. (The "Explication" text mistakenly dates this letter 14 November.) Aside from his statement that the Chinese have been without the true significance of Fu Hsi's diagrams for over a thousand years— Bouvet places the loss as being close to 3000 years in duration— Leibniz presents Bouvet's ideas accurately.

Leibniz presents two bases for establishing similarities between certain Chinese and European notions and their universality. The first is in regard to numbers and the second concerns language. Besides sending Bouvet a description of his dyadic, Leibniz had also sent a description of his plan for a Universal Characteristic, and Bouvet's analysis of certain ancient Chinese characters indicates that he is in accord with Leibniz' ideas on the matter. In his paper, Leibniz seems more cautious than Bouvet in asserting that the Chinese language possesses such logical bases in its structure;

however, he hopes that Bouvet is right and that the Chinese characters will yield evidence of a logical system which operates in a manner akin to calculation. This hope was probably stimulated by the recognition that European knowledge of Leibniz' day was attributing to Hermes Trismegistus the invention of number and language just as Bouvet was attributing origins of number and language to Fu Hsi.

In his presentation of the Universal Characteristic in the manuscript *Scientia Generalis. Characteristica*[38], Leibniz uses demonstration rather than experiment although he considers both to be paths to certain knowledge. He seeks to construct an "alphabet of human thought" that will function as a type of calculus and likens this language to the arithmetic of Pythagorean numbers or a Cabala of mystic vocables. Leibniz distinguishes between *contingent truths,* which involve truths of fact and whose demonstration requires an infinite analysis capable only by God, and *necessary truths* or truths of reason, whose demonstration involves a finite analysis within the range of human ability. Leibniz implies that this Universal Characteristic will involve truths of a necessary nature, but that careful construction of a system of characters is necessary to make them amenable to calculation. By "signs" Leibniz means the symbols our thoughts use to signify things—for example, words and letters, chemical, astronomical, and Chinese figures; hieroglyphs; musical, cryptographic, arithmetical, and algebraic notions. By "characters" Leibniz means signs that are written, drawn, or carved.

Leibniz plans a system of characters capable of such precise calculation that mental error would be equivalent to an error of computation. In a rather incredible, if not, to modern minds, naïve view, Leibniz speaks of a result in which philosophical disputation would be replaced by a smooth exchange between two computers. In this context, discussing philosophy would be akin to sitting down with one's abacus and calling to a friend: "Let us calculate." Obviously such a situation would be ideally suited to an academy of scholars whose origins might transcend national lines. Referring in addition to his ecumenical plans, Leibniz believes it is hopeless to think of resolving controversies among the sects—religious and philosophical sects tend to converge in Leibnizian philosophy—

until complex reasonings can thus be reduced to simple calculations and vague words delineated by precise characters.[39]

## Bouvet, Leibniz, and the *Book of Changes*

The *Book of Changes* has a continuous tradition of commentaries that revolve around the twin themes of divination and philosophy. Sometimes one theme will dominate over the other, as in the case of the Sung Neo-Confucian philosopher Chu Hsi, who interpreted the *Changes* more as a divinatory than philosophical text.[40] The somewhat earlier Neo-Confucian philosopher, Shao Yung (1011–1077) emphasized the philosophical significance. Bouvet made little use of this particular commentarial tradition.

The significance of Bouvet's omission appears when one considers the tradition as it stood at Bouvet's time. Seventeenth-century Chinese scholarship was undergoing a revival of an intensive textual study devoting considerable effort to the *Changes*. In about 1661, Huang Tsung-hsi (1610–1695) wrote *I-hsüeh hsiang shu-lun* (A treatise on the symbols and numbers of *Changes*-learning). This work, in six chapters, attempted to sort out actual origins from the legendary ones attributed by Sung thinkers to certain diagrams of the *Changes*. Though several studies were written on the *Changes*, perhaps the most influential was that of Hu Wei (1633–1714) entitled *I-t'u ming-pien* (An elucidation of the diagrams of the *Changes*) in ten chapters (1706). This work is of particular interest because it was completed while Hu was residing in the same city, Peking, and apparently at the same time, around 1700, as Bouvet when he was writing the above-cited letter to Leibniz.[41] Furthermore, during his stay of 1699–1701, in Peking, Hu frequently discussed his ideas with prominent official literati such as Li Kung, Chin Te-ch'un, and Wan Ssu-t'ung, the latter of whom was writing a preface to Hu's *I-t'u ming-pien*. These discussions would indicate that the *Book of Changes* was a prominent topic of interest among Chinese literati contemporary to Bouvet, yet Bouvet gives little indication of having been in touch with such contemporary interest.

Another sign of Bouvet's isolation from life outside the court appears in his letter to Leibniz of 19 September 1699 where he states that Manchu is the dominant language in the Chinese empire. Actually, the Manchus represented a small and isolated warrior elite in a nation of over 100 million. Very few Chinese learned Manchu, but Manchus increasingly learned Chinese. This phenomena is a recurring one in Chinese history, where military and political conquerers of China are in the end "conquered" by Chinese culture. Unless Bouvet is speaking of anything but a purely "official" and court dominance of the Manchu language, his statement is misleading.

These signs indicate the extent to which the Jesuits at Peking were isolated from literate Chinese society. In contrast, Jesuits who worked in the Chinese provinces were frequently in close touch with a wide range of literati thinking. This was certainly the case with Joseph Prémare, S. J., Bouvet's fellow Figurist.[42] The isolation of Jesuits at the imperial court was furthered by Chinese loyalty to the Ming dynasty, a native Chinese dynasty displaced in 1644. Among Chinese scholars there was a strong resistance to participating in the intellectual life of the new rulers who represented an alien northern race. These Manchus, like all foreign peoples, including Europeans, were barbarians who had to prove their civilized status in order to be even partially accepted in Chinese eyes. Feeling a sense of insecurity and cultural inferiority in their new hegemony, the Manchus sought to establish their credentials by embracing traditional forms of Chinese culture, which consisted predominantly of Sung Neo-Confucianism. In this practice they continued the policies of the Ming rulers who had institutionalized Sung Neo-Confucian commentaries on the classics as the basis of the civil service examinations. But the vital and creative intellectual life of learned Chinese was reacting against Neo-Confucianism and the speculative textual studies of Sung Neo-Confucianism.

In the renewed search for the "true" meaning of the classics among Chinese literati, there arose an emphasis on careful and extensive textual research that was particularly apparent in reference to the *Book of Changes*. Isolated in the court life of the Manchus and a growing but still limited number of Chinese collaborators, Bouvet and the other Jesuits were apparently cut off from this new research on the *Book of Changes*. Consequently, it appears that Bouvet had limited contact with the critics of Neo-Confucianism and did not understand that the Prior to Heaven hexagram order, which he believed to be the work of the ancient Fu Hsi, was probably the unique rearrangement of the Neo-Confucianist Shao Yung.

Hu Wei must be seen as one of these critics of Neo-Confucianism. In contrast to the approach of Bouvet, who ignored previous Chinese commentaries on the *Changes* as misleading, Hu Wei takes his essential task to be that of sorting out the original corpus of the *Changes* from contributions by later commentators. To this end, his work—unlike that of Bouvet, or even of Longobardi or Sainte-Marie—is arranged with sections of extensive quotations from these commentaries, followed by sections containing Hu Wei's own comments and conclusions on the given issue. The work is divided into ten chapters, each of which takes up a specific diagram or set of diagrams such as the River diagram, the diagrams associated with the Five Forces and Nine Colors, the Dragon diagram, and so forth. The sixth and seventh chapters, however, pursue the Prior to Heaven diagrams of the *Changes,* and the eighth chapter considers the diagrams of the Posterior to Heaven learning. In the seventh chapter, is found the same Prior to Heaven diagram that Bouvet sent to Leibniz.[43]

Hu aligns the theories on change of King Wen, the duke of Chou, and Confucius with the original theories of Fu Hsi.[44] However, he thinks that beginning with the Han period, certain Taoist elements had become confused with the original body of the *Changes*. In particular, he believes that from the time of the Sung dynasty notions of change associated with these three—Lao-tzu (the supposed originator of Taoism), Lieh-tzu (a Taoist author who shares with his work of debatable origin and authenticity), and Ch'en T'uan (who lived circa 906–989 and was a famous practitioner of Taoist immortality techniques)—have been used to interpret Fu Hsi's work rather than the more rightful notions of King Wen, the duke of Chou, and Confucius.

In Hu's view, Confucius held that numbers and words make up the entire content of the *Changes* and that heavenly images and calendrical calculations, which assume such great importance in the views of Taoists, are not involved. Hu further describes Confucius as maintaining that the changes operate through processes whereby the even numbers 2, 4, and 8 are generated. A view of creation associated with the double geometrical progression of a numerical sequence involving 2, 4, 8, 16, 32, 64, and on into infinity is not a product of the ancient Chinese sages, such as Fu Hsi, but of the mathematical learning or numerology of Shao Yung.

Hu cites Chu Hsi to the effect that Shao Yung's mathematical learning stems from the Taoist Ch'en T'uan, who mistakenly identified the Taoist Great Origin learning with the learning of the ancient sages. Hu holds that Ch'eng I was the last scholar to emphasize the "Ten Wings" (ten appendices) of the *Changes* and therefore able to distinguish the Huang-Lao (Yellow Emperor—Lao-tzu) elements of Taoism, which had become mixed with the original *Changes,* from authentic elements derived from the ancient sages. As a result, Ch'eng I was able to see the Prior to Heaven diagram as a Taoist addition and to separate it from the original text of the *Changes.* Hu maintains that since the end of the Sung and early Yüan periods, no one else has made such a separation. He attempts to correct this lapse.

Since Hu's work denies both Fu Hsi's authorship in the Prior to Heaven diagram and a double geometrical progression in the original *Changes* diagrams, Bouvet could hardly agree with his position without altering some of his own theories. If one applies Hu's conclusions, then Bouvet's claim to having discovered the original meaning of the *Changes* diagrams must be translated into a discovery of a much later, and Taoist-influenced, corruption of these diagrams.

Even though Hu's work was based on careful textual research, it hardly represents the final word on the diagrams of the *Changes.* It does, however, represent a significant contribution to studies of the *Changes* and at least demands an answer. If Hu's work betrays a weakness of abstractive powers that typifies many works of Ch'ing philological scholarship, perhaps Bouvet's and particularly Leibniz', powers in this area could have provided valuable rebuttals to certain of Hu's points. Unfortunately, the evidence gives no grounds for assuming that Bouvet was even aware of Hu's theories, and consequently the problem was never presented to Leibniz. We are left with pieces that only imply their roles in a larger puzzle.

### Leibniz' Last Words on the *Book of Changes*

From 1706 to 1716, Leibniz carried on a an extensive correspondence in Latin with Bartholomew des Bosses, a Jesuit theologian who had a great interest in mathematics.[45] The correspondence is marked by frequent references to the China mission, and an enclosure within his letter to Des Bosses dated 12 August 1709 is particularly significant of Leibniz' attempt to synthesize what he had received from his Chinese interpreters. In the enclosure, which may have been written as early as 1701, Leibniz cites a collection of writings received and published by the directors of the Society of Foreign Missions seminary, a missionary group unsympathetic to the Chinese rites and to Jesuit methods in China. The writings include references to the debate among Jesuit missionaries in China shortly after Ricci's death in 1610 in which Longobardi, then head of the Jesuit mission, arranged to have both sides of the question presented. On the side unsympathetic to Chinese rites were Frs. Francesco Pasio (Pa Yung-lo, 1554–1612), Jean Ruiz (João Rodrigues; Lu Jo-han, 1561–1633), and Sabatino de Ursis (Hsiung San-pa, 1575–1620).[46] The side sympathetic to Chinese rites included Frs. Diego de Pantoja (P'ang Hsün-yang, 1571–1620) and Alfonso Vagnoni (Wang Yi-yüan, 1566–1640). Leibniz states that those who followed Longobardi's position held that the Chinese recognized no incorporeal things and consequently were unaware of gods, angels, and souls; moreover, they claimed the Chinese *shang-ti* was not equivalent to the Christian God.

In a preview of the argument later developed in far greater detail in his *Discourse on the Natural Theology of the Chinese,* Leibniz cites and then rejects the argument of those unsympathetic to the Chinese rites. He describes them as believing that the Chinese have known no spirituality and that things emerge from the principle *t'ai-chi,* which contains *li,* defined as the prime material and substance of a thing, and *ch'i* (primitive ether), defined as approximating matter. (The questionable validity of these definitions is discussed in the following chapters.)

After some discussion, Leibniz gives his reasons for rejecting these views. He believes it is insufficient to claim that the Chinese lack equivalences to Christianity because their texts lack references to incorporeal substances or rewards in another life. Even the Old Testament contains little reference to incorporeal substances or such rewards. Furthermore, he claims that the Chinese would not have cultivated either ancestors or good merit without having some understanding of the power of giving thanks to a supreme force. Leibniz maintains that the ancient Chinese did teach of divine things and spirits.

In a technique much duplicated in the later *Discourse,* Leibniz borrows part of Longobardi's interpretation, though not his conclusion, to see *t'ai-chi, li,* and *ch'i* as corresponding to a Christian or Platonic Trinity in which *t'ai-chi* represents the power or first principle, *li* the knowledge of ideas or essences, and *ch'i* the will or love that is called spirit. *Li* is taken as a source of emanations for which a fountain metaphor is proposed. In further discussion of the equivalences between the "philosophy," by which he means natural theology, of ancient China and Christianity, Leibniz presents a brief analysis of correspondences between Fu Hsi's recognition of the origin of things out of the binary units of one (——) and nothing (— —) and the Christian view of Creation which Leibniz sees represented in his binary progression of 1 and 0.

Through the detection of this correspondence, Leibniz implies that he and Bouvet have helped resolve the Rites Controversy, which was then under way in Europe and stood as a direct obstacle to Leibniz' ecumenical plans. However, writing in 1710 to Des Bosses,[47] Leibniz bemoans Bouvet's failure to continue their collaboration and to supply further information he has requested. Since Bouvet has sent no letter explaining the sixteen Chinese volumes he has received, Leibniz complains that he is unable to decipher the content of these works.[48] With this lapse in communication from Bouvet, Leibniz' sources of information on China were diminishing. It was only with the arrival in late 1715 of copies of the treatises by Longobardi and Sainte-Marie and their generous quotations from the Chinese classics that Leibniz was stimulated into his most philosophically substantial work on China—the *Discourse on the Natural Theology of the Chinese.*

Leibniz' last written words on the diagrams of the *Changes* appear in the concluding sections of the *Discourse.* There he adds little to what he had synthesized in his "Explication" of 1703, except for specifying several other scholars also engaged in the pursuit of understanding Chinese culture. These include the German Andreas Müller, who investigated the meaning of the Chinese characters, and the Arab Abdalla Beidavaeus, who wrote on Chinese mathematics.[49] In explaining the similarity between his binary mathematics and Fu Hsi's diagrams, Leibniz refers to his former teacher, the Pythagoreanist Erhard Weigel of Jena.[50] Leibniz also makes a criticism that resembles the criticisms of Hu Wei and could conceivably refer to several of the same Taoists whom Hu criticized: Leibniz states that those Chinese who lost the true significance of the *Changes* diagrams deviated from their real meaning by interpreting them in terms of strange symbols and hieroglyphs.[51]

# 4
# The Discourse on Chinese Philosophy: Part I

## The Work and Its Stimulus

The direct stimulus for Leibniz' writing of the *Discourse on the Natural Theology of the Chinese* came from Nicholas Remond, chief counsel to the duke of Orleans and a follower of Nicholas Malebranche (1638–1715). Inspired by a reading of Leibniz' *Theodicy,* Remond initiated a correspondence by writing a letter of praise to Leibniz in 1713.[1] In a letter of 12 October 1714, Remond states that he has read Longobardi's *Religion Treatise* and asks for Leibniz' opinion on it.[2] He appears to raise the possibility of Leibniz composing a formal treatise when he mentions having read Nicholas Malebranche's *Entretien d'un philosophe chrétien et d'un philosophe chinois sur l'existence et la nature de Dieu* (A conversation between a Christian philosopher and a Chinese philosopher on the existence and nature of God) of 1708. When Remond repeats his request for an opinion from Leibniz on the Longobardi treatise, Leibniz replies that he has not yet seen the treatise by Longobardi and Malebranche.[3] Consequently, with his letter of 4 September 1715, Remond sends copies of Longobardi's *Religion Treatise,* Malebranche's *Conversation,* and Sainte-Marie's *Mission Treatise* to Leibniz.

In a letter of 4 November 1715,[4] Leibniz refers to the Longobardi and Sainte-Marie treatises Remond had sent him, but he gives no signs of actually composing the treatise. These signs come in his letter of 17 January 1716, where he speaks of having composed an entire discourse on the theology of the Chinese that touches upon God, spirits, and the soul.[5] Ten days later, Leibniz states that he has finished his *Discourse,* a small treatise which he compares in length to that by Malebranche.[6] In March, however, he is speaking of the need for a bit more work in order to complete the *Discourse.*[7] By November Leibniz was dead, and I have seen no evidence that he ever sent the *Discourse* to Remond. The only extant original appears to be the manuscript written in Leibniz' own hand and presently on file in the Leibniz archives at Hanover.

The *Discourse on the Natural Theology of the Chinese*—also known as the *Letter on Chinese Philosophy*—is a work of thirty-two manuscript pages in folio that compares in length to Leibniz' important *Discourse on Metaphysics.*[8] Leibniz divided the work into four sections that deal with Chinese conceptions of (1) God, (2) the creation by God of matter and spirits, (3) the human soul, its immortality, and its rewards and punishments, and (4) the characters and binary arithmetic of Fu Hsi. The evidence offers some support for concluding that the fourth section was added after a lapse in composition.[9] At any rate, Leibniz' concern with God and God's process of creation is reflected in the fact that these first two sections occupy three-fourths of the total length of the *Discourse.* Christian Kortholt, who edited the first published version of the *Discourse,* made editorial divisions of the work into seventy-five subsections, an arrangement that has been followed by later editors.[10]

Throughout the treatise, the chief protagonists are Frs. Longobardi and Sainte-Marie. Leibniz begins by referring to the fundamental and parallel themes of the Chinese ancients versus the moderns and Ricci versus Longobardi. In contrast to Ricci's "accommodation" theory (*Discourse* 1)[11], which stressed the Chinese ancients and the similarity of their doctrine to the True Law of Christianity, Longobardi emphasized dissimilarities to the True Law he found in the doctrines of contemporary Chinese. Reflecting his sensitivity to politics, Leibniz treats Longobardi's preoccupation with criticizing the contemporary Chinese as a result of the chaos of his age, which has since been pacified with the authority of a new "prince" (that is, the K'ang-hsi emperor) and the many capable people of his court (*Discourse* 1).[12] The reference here is to the chaos of the late Ming period: the dynasty was collapsing under the pressure of internal struggles among cliques and eunuchs and also external pressure from peasant secret societies, pirates on the southeastern coast, and aggressive Manchus on the northern border. The dates of Longobardi's and Sainte-Marie's respective treatises, about 1600 and 1668, parallel the protracted turbulence of the transition from the Ming to the Ch'ing dynasties, which occupied most of the seventeenth century.

In aligning himself with authorities such as Martino Martini who follow Ricci's position, Leibniz notes that they have persisted in the face of opposition not only from other missionaries but also from Chinese mandarins. They have done so not only because of the inherent logic of their argument but also because the Chinese classical texts support their view. (Leibniz notes here that his examination has been limited to doctrine and does not extend to ceremony and cultic rites.) It is here that we come to the fundamental importance of the *Discourse* as a document that records the transmission of concepts from Chinese classical texts directly to a prominent European philosopher via missionary mediaries. The *Discourse* offers an unusual opportunity for evaluating this transmission and assessing early eighteenth century European understanding of Chinese philosophy and religion.

In the *Discourse* 3,[13] Leibniz concedes that since the extracts from Chinese documents available to Europeans are still limited, any judgment of their doctrines must remain provisional. Since Leibniz has drawn his conclusions from Longobardi's and Sainte-Marie's translated extracts, however, and since these extracts have been used to support conclusions contrary to his own, Leibniz notes that Longobardi and Sainte-Marie could hardly be accused of biasing the argument by selecting extracts to flatter Leibniz' argument. Perhaps this approach helps explain why Leibniz does not directly refer to a more complete set of extracts from Chinese classical texts contained in *Confucius Sinarum Philosophus,* a document produced by a group of Jesuits at Paris in 1687. At any rate, Leibniz thinks that Chinese antiquity predates that of Europe and contains a "natural theology" or knowledge of God derived simply from observation of nature, and that this characteristic, together with an admirable moral exterior, has fostered a China that in many ways surpasses Europe.

## The Chinese Sources

In his *Discourse,* Leibniz cites seven Chinese texts: *Book of Changes, Book of History, Book of Odes, Analects, Doctrine of the Mean, Compendium* and *Comprehensive Mirror.*[14] Putting aside the *Book of Changes* and the *Comprehensive Mirror,* to which he makes only passing mention, Leibniz uses the indirect sources of Longobardi's *Religion Treatise* and Sainte-Marie's *Mission Treatise* to draw upon five important Chinese texts. The texts associated with Neo-Confucianism—the *Compendium,* the *Mean,* and the *Analects*—are cited most often. The choices are ironic since Leibniz expresses a strong preference for Chinese antiquity and the older or classical Confucianism.

The *Compendium*—more fully, the *Great Compendium of Natural and Moral Philosophy (Hsing-li ta-ch'üan shu)*—is cited most often by Leibniz. It represents an anthology drawn from the Neo-Confucian school associated with the Sung dynasty (A.D. 960–1280) philosophers Ch'eng I (I-ch'uan, 1033–1108) and Chu Hsi (1130–1200) and symbolizes the Ch'eng-Chu school of the *Hsing-li* (natural and moral, or more literally, human nature and principle) philosophy, from which the complete *Compendium* title derives. The work was compiled in 1415 under the direction of Hu Kuang (1370–1418) at the order of the Yung-lo emperor (r. 1402–1424). The latter's wish to filter out certain politically undesirable elements from Sung Neo-Confucianism had resulted in the production of three new anthologies: (1) the above-cited *Compendium,* (2) the *Ssu-shu ta-ch'üan* (Great compendium of the four books), and (3) *Wu-ching ta-ch'üan* (Great compendium of the five classics). These three, but particularly the *Compendium,* became the basis of all civil service examinations. The *Compendium* is a lengthy compilation of seventy *chüan* (chapters).[15] It is entirely derivative, though selectively so. Yet it is derivative not of the classics themselves but of a definite interpretation—or reinterpretation—of the classics that emphasized the classical texts and fragments known as the Four Books *(Analects, Doctrine of the Mean, Mencius,* and *Great Learning).*

Leibniz goes along with Ricci and those sympathetic to Chinese rites in holding that the modern Chinese are atheistic and only the ancient Chinese and the ancient texts reflected the natural religion. Nevertheless, he cites from the *Compendium* as if it were merely a summary of the classical texts and not itself the product of a much later school of interpretation. Leibniz' confusion on this point may be traceable to his great reliance on the *Religion Treatise* and the *Mission Treatise* for information on Chinese textual matters.

In the *Religion Treatise* 1:2, Longobardi classifies the four kinds of books found in the literati sect of Confucianism. The first includes books by ancient kings and savants such as the *Book of Changes* and the *Book of History.* The second type of work consists of commentaries on these books that subdivide into (1) those of a brief and precise nature that contain the text and a gloss by a single author, for example the *"Zu-Xu"* (presumably the detailed commentary appended to each section of text by Chu Hsi in his arrangement of classics called the Four Books) and (2) the *ta-ch'üan* (great compendium) type, which includes a collection of comments by different authors on a specific subject. The third type of work is said to be a compendium of natural and moral philosophy known as the *hsing-li* (literally, human nature and principle). Longobardi's fourth category includes books by authors who had lived since the burning of the books by Ch'in Shih Huang-ti in 213 B.C.[16]

In the *Mission Treatise* (pp. 2–3) Sainte-Marie gives a concise description of the Chinese classics. He refers to the Five Classics *(Book of Changes, Book of History, Book of Odes, Spring and Autumn Annals,* and *Record of Rites)* as the five doctrinal works of Confucianism edited by Confucius. He compares the Chinese reverence toward the Four Books *(Great Learning, Doctrine of the Mean, Analects,* and *Mencius)* to the Christian veneration of the four Gospels. Next, Sainte-Marie refers to the *Tasiven Singli, (Hsing-li ta-ch'üan),* which he refers to as a work compiled over 300 years before, although it was closer to 250 years. Sainte-Marie emphasizes the anthologylike nature of the *Compendium* and the

theory of its being a mere collection of previously scattered interpretations. Longobardi had also stressed the remarkable accord on
points of doctrine to be found among authors of the literati sect.

From a marginal notation made by Leibniz in his copy of the
*Religion Treatise*[17] and by his references there to Sainte-Marie's
descriptions, we know that he accepted the classifications of these
missionary interpreters. Here he outlines a division into four main
types that correspond to those of Longobardi as supplemented by
Sainte-Marie. In his *Discourse,* Leibniz makes abundant use of
Longobardi's translations from the *Compendium,* and thus he
would seem to accept the notion that this compendium represents a
collection of views continuous with and in agreement with the
beliefs of Chinese antiquity. In fact, they are from a much later
school of Confucianism that had a very specific interpretation of
Chinese antiquity and the classics. But *if* the differences in interpretation between the original Confucian classics and the commentaries by the Sung school of Neo-Confucianism were minimal—a
highly debatable claim—then such a compendium of views subscribed to by the entire sect of literati would appear possible.

Leibniz may have followed this line of thought, and this may explain why he shows so little hesitation in citing the *Compendium* to
help explain a classical passage. In this practice, he is merely following Longobardi. However, Leibniz disagrees with many of Longobardi's interpretations—both in terms of the Chinese rites and in
the meaning of key Chinese terminology. Specifically, while Leibniz believed there was a need to distinguish between the ancient and
modern Chinese as natural religionists and atheists, respectively,
Longobardi believed that the entire tradition was atheistic. Given
such a premise, Longobardi would be led to minimize textual differences between the various schools and to minimize also any differences in points of view presented in the original classics contra-
dicting those of the *Compendium.* Something similar might be said
of Sainte-Marie. But from the Chinese point of view, the differences were considerable. The energy and feeling with which the literati engaged in differences over interpreting these classics indicated
how unreal the Chinese would have considered any such notion of
exegetical uniformity. Yet one's view of a problem can very often

depend on one's position. In his failure to take these differences into account, Leibniz fell victim to his reliance on secondary sources. The problem here appears to be not so much that Longobardi and Sainte-Marie were wrong as that Leibniz was confused over where he stood. In his interpretation of the Chinese texts, he was in fact seeing things from a point of view basically different from that of these Chinese interpreters.

The *Compendium* is actually a product of neither the ancients (the alleged natural religionists) nor the modern literati (the alleged atheists) but of an intermediate group.[18] Yet Leibniz makes no real distinction between the classical Confucianism of the ancients and the Neo-Confucianism of the intermediate group. He treats both views as synonymous and contrasts them with the contemporary Chinese view. He appears to be unaware that this treatment somewhat contradicts his position that only the Chinese of antiquity produced a form of natural religion from which later practitioners deviated. Only the books produced in this period, that is, those that came to be called the Chinese classics, preserve traces of this natural religion.

To the extent that the Neo-Confucian philosophy was created by men who followed nearly 1300 years after the end of Chinese antiquity—for our purposes, the end of antiquity is the close of the Chou dynasty at about 250 B.C.—Neo-Confucianism does not reflect natural religion. But to the extent that the Neo-Confucian philosophy was a reinterpretation based on the classical texts, elements of natural religion are preserved. Since Leibniz depends upon distinctly Neo-Confucian terms such as *li* (principle), *ch'i* (material force), and *t'ai-chi* (ultimate maximization) as well as terms drawn from the classical corpus such as *shang-ti* (King-on-high or God), *tao* (the Way), and *kuei-shen* (spirits), it would seem that both the classical Confucian and the Neo-Confucian interpretations are necessary to his presentation.

### Li, the First Principle

The fundamental Chinese term in the *Discourse* is *li*, which Leibniz interprets as a first principle. It is this important Chinese term that Leibniz saw as the foundation stone for ecumenical accord between

China and the West. He defines the term at an early point in the *Discourse* 4[19] by saying:

> The first principle of the Chinese is called *li (Religion Treatise* 2:1*)*, that is, *Reason* or the foundation of all nature *(Religion Treatise* 5:1*)*, the most universal reason and substance *(Religion Treatise* 11:2*)*; there is nothing greater nor better than *li (Religion Treatise* 11:10*)*. This great and universal cause is pure, still, subtle, without body and without shape, and can be known only through understanding *(Religion Treatise* 5:1*)*.

Leibniz' description of the first principle of the universe as "still" *(quiéte)* brings to mind descriptions of God found in both the mystical poetry of T. S. Eliot and the philosophy of Aristotle. While Eliot's *Four Quartets* refers to the "still point of the turning world,"[20] Aristotle's *Metaphysics* describes an "Unmoved Mover."[21] Both are descriptions of God as the real or apparent paradox of a force that activates and yet remains unactivated or still.

In comparing this interpretation with Chinese expositors of *li*, one finds differences in emphasis as well as fundamental similarities. For instance, the approach of the foremost Neo- Confucianist, Chu Hsi, uses quiescence as a description of one aspect of the phenomenal world. Instead of having quiescence describe the first principle and activity describe the first principle's productions, quiesence *(ch'ing)* and activity *(tung)* are used along with *yin* and *yang* as complementary pairs to describe these productions. These complementary pairs compose the material force *(ch'i)*, the complementary element to the First Principle *(li)*.[22] This interpretation differs from that of Leibniz in reflecting less of a stress on *li* as a first principle and more of a stress on *li* as a complementary force. On the other hand, Chu Hsi does recognize a logically prior aspect of *li*. Furthermore, *t'ai-chi*, which Chu Hsi partially equates with *li*,[23] has the aspect of a Supreme Ultimate or Supreme Pole whose metaphysical significance bears a similarity to Eliot's "still point." In *Hsing-li* Neo-Confucianism, *t'ai-chi* contains both quiescence and activity and so parallels the paradoxical containment found in Eliot's "still point" and Aristotle's "Unmoved Mover."

Though the term *li* is not philosophically significant in the original classics, it appears to have had the early meaning of ordering or patterning. Later, Han dynasty scholars stressed the etymological interpretation of *li* as containing the semantic particle for jade, *yü,* and the phonetic-semantic particle *li*[a], which refers to an inner sense as, for example, in the lining of clothing, *li*[b]. *Li* combines these senses to refer to the inside of jade as in the sense of natural grain or a system of veins, which the jade cutter must ascertain and follow in making an effective break. This organic sense of the internal structure that determines a thing's nature and content was emphasized by the Sung Neo-Confucianists when they incorporated *li* into their metaphysics.[24]

One of several parallels between Leibniz and Chinese philosophy appears in connection with this etymological significance of *li*. In 1700, a French translation of John Locke's *Essay Concerning Human Understanding* (London, 1690) came into Leibniz' hands. This became the basis of a critique by Leibniz entitled *Nouveaux Essais de l'Entendement humain* (New essays concerning human understanding), written by 1704 but unpublished until 1765.[25] In the *New Essays,* Leibniz rejects Locke's comparison of the soul, a term including much of our modern notion of the mind, to the Aristotelian *tabula rasa.* Instead of a blank tablet or completely uniform block of marble, Leibniz uses the metaphor of a "block of marble that has veins." He states:

> For if the soul resembled these blank tablets, truths would be in us as the figure of Hercules is in the marble, when the marble is wholly indifferent to the reception of this figure or some other. But if there were veins in the block which should indicate the figure of Hercules rather than other figures, this block would be more determined thereto, and Hercules would be in it as in some sense innate, although it would be needful to labor to discover these veins, to clear them by polishing, and by cutting away what prevents them from appearing.[26]

This is very close to the sense in which the *Hsing-li* school uses the term *li,* and it is confirmed by an instance from a favored Neo-Confucian text, *Mencius* 6:1.1, in which it is said that man's moral cultivation must follow the inherent nature of man just as the carving of utensils must follow the organic or natural grain of the willow.

Of the Chinese texts that Leibniz relies upon in developing his interpretation, only the *Compendium* presents *li* in its metaphysical maturity, for only the *Compendium* among all these texts is fully reflective of the *Hsing-li* school. Only in that school did *li* reach full development, even though it must be reemphasized that the school always took certain Chinese classics as its basic texts. Though *li* rarely appears in these classics—and when it does it has little philosophical significance—it was believed that *li* was implied by these works and that such a term as *tao* (the Way) could be taken as an approximate equivalent.

Leibniz did not have direct access to the Chinese originals, yet Longobardi's *Religion Treatise* and Sainte-Marie's *Mission Treatise* contain lengthy quotations and paraphrases from these texts, which Leibniz used as indirect sources. Longobardi and Sainte-Marie wrote their treatises with the specific purpose of rejecting any sympathetic interpretation of the Chinese rites toward ancestors and Confucius, as well as discarding any equivalences between Chinese and Christian religious concepts. Leibniz, of course, opposed their positions, but he was able to use their work as source material for deriving opposite conclusions.

While Longobardi and Sainte-Marie argued that Chinese philosophical concepts were ultimately materialistic, Leibniz stressed a spiritual guiding force that in its different aspects may be called *li* (principle), *t'ai-chi* (Ultimate Maximization), *tao* (the Way), or *shang-ti* (King-on-high). To emphasize that the direction and production of phenomena lie not in things themselves but in *li*, Leibniz in the *Discourse* 4²⁷ quotes almost directly from Sainte-Marie in the *Mission Treatise* (p. 73), which in turn draws from the *Compendium* (bk. 26, p. 8a).²⁸ (Longobardi gives a fairly careful paraphrase of this same *Compendium* passage in the *Religion Treatise* 13:5.) An examination of the *Compendium* passage shows Sainte-Marie to be neither quoting nor giving even a close paraphrase so much as presenting an interpretation. Sainte-Marie in the *Mission Treatise* (p. 73) describes the *Compendium* (bk. 26, p. 8b) as maintaining that cosmic generation "is not at all in the disposition of things nor does it depend on them, but that it consists and resides in this *li;* that it predominates over everything; that it is in everything, governs and produces everything in the absolute matter of Heaven and Earth." But this is a misleading interpretation that overemphasizes *li* at the expense of the complementary *li-ch'i.* The *Com-*

*pendium* (bk. 26, p. 9a) makes specific reference to this complementary and to the necessary presence of both *li* and *ch'i*. The implications of this essential complementary ingredient of the *Hsing-li* school are something that Sainte-Marie and Longobardi never fully face. Rather, they deemphasize such an approach and tend to treat the two as different manifestations of the same element—that is, *ch'i* as "air" and *li* as "prime matter." But in the *Hsing-li* school's view, *li* and *ch'i* are not both material elements. *Ch'i* is a material force, but *li*, while clearly not material, is said to be normally unable to subsist independently of the material element, *ch'i*. *Li* rather represents principle, a component that orders the chaotic *ch'i*.

What allows Longobardi's and Sainte-Marie's views some measure of plausibility is their concession that *li* appears superficially to be both rational and spiritual and that only deeper investigation will show it to be ultimately material. In such a way, Leibniz explains *li* by emphasizing the Neo-Confucian view that "All things are one" (*Discourse* 21–22)[29] and holds that both Longobardi and Sainte-Marie express this view, although it would seem that their presentations of this notion are far less explicit than that of Leibniz. On the other hand, Leibniz (*Discourse* 26)[30] follows Longobardi's interpretation (*Religion Treatise* 13:6) of the *Compendium* (bk. 1, pp. 31a–b) by stating that *li*, which Leibniz—not Longobardi—equates with reason, dominates worldy phenomena and needs nothing from them. The *Compendium* passage consists entirely of commentary based on correlating the Five Phases[31] *(wu hsing)* with the directions and seasons and generally stresses the orderly unfolding of universal processes. From the Chinese sources, Leibniz seems to have derived, rather than quoted or even paraphrased, the notion the *li* governs worldly phenomena while being fully independent of influence from these phenomena.

### *Li* and the Monads

It is not certain that *li* was as independent of *ch'i* in the Neo-Confucian conception as Leibniz sees it, but it is clear in Leibniz' philosophy that the monads are entirely unaffected by the activity of phenomenal forces. The monads translate the progress of the phenomenal world without being affected by it. Nor do the monads affect one another; they are said to be windowless. They are likened by Leibniz to a series of clocks that manage to keep time without being connected. The Leibnizian notion of "preestablished harmony" guarantees accord between monads without any need of either interaction betweens the two or outside intervention by a supernatural force. The content of the monads is predetermined by a subject-predicate logic in which all the predicates are contained within the subject.[32]

More specifically, each monad is characterized by a "complete concept" within which all its predicates and rules of development are contained. Consequently, were one able—as is God—to determine a given complete concept, then the particular monad's future development could be completely foreseen by logical derivation. It was on the basis of comparing an infinite number of complete concepts that God chose those of our particular world to actualize on the grounds that while it was not completely perfect, it contained the greatest amount of perfection possible or was the "best of all possible worlds." The Leibnizian concept of reality always begins with logic and metaphysics, from which one works into progressively more exterior ontological orders. And this correspondence and harmony between the various orders come from the Leibnizian notion of a derivative (i.e., more exterior) level of reality being "well-founded" upon a higher (i.e., more interior) realm.

Leibniz emphasizes the internal nature of *li* and draws from Longobardi's interpretation (*Religion Treatise* 13:5) of the *Compendium* (bk. 26, p. 8a). This interior aspect has a certain affinity with Leibniz' conception of the monads. For example the *Monadology* no. 11 states: "The natural changes of the monads must result from an *internal principle,* since no external cause could influence their interior."[33] Leibniz conceived of existence as made up of individual units. The function of the monads was to join these units with the realm of logic and with statements about universals. In the process of translating individual units into a more interior representation, any given monad will present a living mirror of the universe. In terms of physical theory, when Leibniz translates monadic perceptions into lower ontological levels, physics is expanded beyond the Cartesian components of extension and impenetrability to include natural inertia.[34] This is a fundamental alteration of a physics of inert substance into a physics of force.

Leibniz summarized his position of physical theory in regard to Cartesianism in a letter to Bouvet of 2 December 1697. The context is a discussion of what form of philosophy—Leibniz' universal perspective prevents him from calling it "Western philosophy"— should be introduced to the Chinese as a means of preparing them to receive "the true religion," that is, Christianity. While recognizing that some Europeans would hope to abolish the "philosophy of the schools" (that is, Scholasticism, or modified Aristotelianism) and replace it with Cartesianism, Leibniz thinks that the application of certain insights of modern philosophy to the philosophy of the ancients could suitably enrich the latter and prepare it as a vehicle for teaching the Chinese. In a letter to Bouvet, Leibniz had referred to his intense debates with Cartesians:

> And I have demonstrated to them by means of mathematics that they themselves do not at all have the true laws of nature and that in order to have them, it is necessary to consider in nature not only matter, but also force, and that the forms of the ancients or entelechies are nothing but forces. And by this means I have faith in rehabilitating the philosophy of the ancients.[35]

Leibniz reiterates this theme in his letter to Bouvet of 1703 when he aligns his position with that of the ancients and opposes the "material philosophy of the moderns," that is, the Cartesians. Leibniz regards force as the essence of corporeal substance and again asserts the identity of force with the entelechy of the ancients.[36] "Entelechy" and "substantial form" were two of Leibniz' alternative terms for designating the monad.

The term "monad" does not even occur in the *Discourse,* though the concept is present. This is surprising only if one fails to realize that "monad" was only one of a number of terms for designating this central element of Leibniz' philosophy. In his first formulation of this concept—in the *Discourse on Metaphysics* (1686)—Leibniz refers to it as "individual substance." Prior to 1696, Leibniz used the term "monad" infrequently. He clearly prefers the word in the popularized summary of his philosophy entitled the *Monadology* (1714); however, he continued to use several designations for the concept.[37] A grasp of the monad is necessary to understand Leibniz' interpretation of Chinese natural theology and, particularly, his interpretation of the relationship between the Neo-Confucian *li* and *ch'i* and the issue of the relationship of parts to the whole. For example, see the *Discourse* 7, 13, and 26.[38] Leibniz frequently uses 'entelechy" to designate the monad. This term appears, in singular and plural forms, in the *Discourse* 14, 19, 21, and 38.[39] "Spirit" and "soul," terms that Leibniz sometimes uses to refer to the monad, occur throughout the *Discourse*.

In his short piece *De primae philosophiae emendatione, et de notione substantiae* (On the improvement of first philosophy [metaphysics], and the notion of substance)[40] of 1694, Leibniz invokes the notion of force (Latin: *vis* or *virtus*; German: *Kraft*) to offer a new and, he believes, more fruitful definition of substance. He clearly states that force is inherent in all substances—physical as well as spiritual. Consequently, the notion of force becomes a link between the metaphysical and physical realms. To what extent does this metaphysical view compare to the Neo-Confucian view of *li* and its complementary, *ch'i*?

In a letter to De Volder in 1703, Leibniz refers to (1) the primitive entelechy or soul (primitive active force) and (2) primary matter (primitive passive force) as two aspects that together compose a monad.[41] Since the monad is on a metaphysical level and these notions of the soul and primary matter are on a phenomenal level, *li* would compare to metaphysical reality and *ch'i* to phenomenal reality. The Neo-Confucian view of *ch'i* accords with Leibniz' rejection of inert matter as a phenomenal explanation and with the emphasis upon force as a primary component. In addition to impenetrability and extension, Leibnizian primitive force is characterized by inertia. This is not an inert element but a force in a state of resistance to motion. Complementary to this is the first entelechy, or primitive moving force, which joins with extension (the purely geometrical) and with mass (the purely material) and acts. This primitive active force is known as a soul or substantial form, depending on whether the given entity is living or nonliving.[42] Consequently, on a metaphysical level there are monads and perceptions, of a clear and confused type, respectively. Corresponding to this is the abstract level of phenomenality where there are corporeal substances that duplicate a twofold breakdown into the complementaries, primitive active force and primitive passive force. In turn, corresponding to this is the observable level of phenomenality containing bodies that continue the twofold division into derivative active and passive forces.

*Ch'i* is conceived of as an activated and fluid form of matter, perhaps best described as having the breathlike connotations of ether or pneuma—that is to say, without direction. The direction is provided by *li,* and taken together, *li* and *ch'i* provide the component aspects of any given element. In the *Monadology* no. 63, Leibniz reaffirms the relationship set forth in his letter to De Volder: "The body [i.e., primitive passive force] belonging to a monad which is its entelechy or its soul constitutes, together with this entelechy [i.e., primitive active force] what may be called a *living unit* and together with this soul what may be called an animal." In comparing *li* to the monadic level and *ch'i* to the phenomenal level, or primitive passive force and primitive active force and their observable derivations, one need not say that the Leibnizian concept of reality necessarily conflicts with the Neo-Confucian notion. Admittedly, while *li* is abstract and logically precedes *ch'i,* which is phenomenal, the notion of Neo-Confucian organicism provides only an implicit parallel to phenomenal and real realms in Leibnizian notions of preestablished harmony and "well-founding"; that is, the appearances of the phenomenal realm are derivative from the more real monadic realm.[43] Furthermore, the Neo-Confucian analysis of *ch'i* stops short of that found in the Leibnizian scheme of the phenomenal level. Yet Leibniz himself thought there were considerable similarities.

The obstacles to coming to a firm conclusion on the degree of similarity or dissimilarity between Neo-Confucianism and Leibniz' philosophy bring us to the problem of different directions in philosophical development. From the Neo-Confucian point of view, intellectual analysis was prerequisite to spiritual cultivation and such analysis would be evaluated in terms of its degree of contribution to the advancement of the practitioner's spiritual, moral, and social cultivation.

It is in this area that the cultivation of reality appears as a flux in which the fluid etherlike nature of *ch'i* as a phenomenal essence has a metaphysical parallel in the vital and changing organic conception of *li*. But the flux is also experiential. The natural metaphors of the venation in *li* and the pliable bamboo as both social and artistic paradigms represent a coherent experience in which one divines with the *Book of Changes* in a manner more introspective than that of going to a fortune-teller to hear what the future will bring.

Actually, the fixed answers associated with the limited number of divinable hexagram possibilities may not *tell* the questioner anything. The process demands intense introspection. The responsiveness of the answer in the *Book of Changes* will vary with the depth of the question asked, although at times the particular hexagram form will involve an extensive reply. One divines for oneself in order to better discern the direction of events (that is, the conflux of *ch'i* and *li*) and slide more smoothly into that particular flow. The content of the divination's answer is far less significant than the manner in which one harmonizes oneself with the direction of the flow. The Confucian gentleman does not rage against his fate. Nor does he passively accept it. The process of harmonizing one's body and will with the direction of one's fate requires an intensive personal and spiritual cultivation. Ideally, one's exterior should in the process emanate a certain tranquillity, which is frequently mistaken for passivity. Such is hardly the case, even though the concentration of activity in such a situation tends to be far more interior than exterior.

This is a philosophy of delicate balance and far-reaching complexity, even though it may be quite different from that practiced by Leibniz. Since the respective philosophies involve different methods and aims, the differences in results are quite understandable. These results do not in themselves reflect differences in quality, but the degree to which they accomplish the aims of the particular philosophy invites comparison in terms of their respective successes.

## The One and the Many

Of equal significance to Leibniz' own philosophy is his emphasis on passages from Neo-Confucian texts that describe the dual aspect of *li* as both universal and particular, of both one and many. This aspect can be signified as the *Li* (universal)–*li* (particular) relationship. In the *Discourse* 21–22[44], Leibniz cites the Chinese statement that "All things are one," and in the *Discourse* 26[45] he refers to the

*Li-li* relationship, drawing upon Longobardi's interpretation (*Religion Treatise* 13:10) of a passage in the *Compendium* (bk. 26, pp. 1b–2a). Longobardi is generally accurate in paraphrasing the passage in terms of the dual aspect of *li* or *t'ai-chi*. *Li* is manifested as both one thing and many parts—that is, having a universal as well as a particular aspect. The *t'ai-chi* is also described as both a substance and a universal spirit of everything as well as a substance and particular spirit of each thing.

Leibniz rejects interpreting the *Compendium* passage as meaning that the *li* literally has parts, on the grounds that a thing composed of parts does not constitute a true unity. Rather, as a pile of sand or an army, it has only the semblance of unity. Leibniz holds that the reference to the parts of the *t'ai-chi* can only be a figurative manner of speaking, in the same way we may say that souls would be "parts" of the Divinity. Here we see the concern that led Leibniz to reject the notion of atoms (discrete and uniform material units) in favor of monads (organically connected and unique spiritual units).

Leibniz' interpretation of this Chinese notion of a universal-particular relationship is an essential part of the Leibnizian philosophy and appears in the *Monadology* no. 13:

> This particular [trait of what is changing] must comprehend a multiplicity in the unity, that is, in the simple. For since all natural change proceeds by degrees, something changes and something remains. Consequently, there must be in the simple substance a plurality of affections and relations, though it has no parts.

Further, *Monadology* no.62 states:

> Thus, every created monad represents the whole universe; nevertheless, it represents more distinctly the body which is particularly attached to it and of which it is the entelechy. And since this body expresses the whole universe through the interconnection of all the matter in the plenum, the soul, too, represents the whole universe by representing this body which in a particular manner belongs to it.

Leibniz says that there is a connection between the more exterior element of body and the more interior element of monad by which the latter represents the body. Insofar as the body is particular, the monad represents the body. But since the body is connected with all other bodies, the monad also represents all other bodies or mirrors the universe. In its role as entelechy or actualizer of this potential body, the monad must be the source for representing these particular and universal aspects and therefore it must itself bear particular and universal relationships to other monads. Leibniz insists that parts do not exist, so the relationship must be an organic hierarchy of monads leading up to the supreme monad, which is sometimes referred to as God.

We have here a description that could be equally applied to the Neo-Confucian notion of *li,* which bears both particular and universal aspects in ordering, and consequently, in actualizing the material force, *ch'i.* The particular *li* relates to a universal *Li,* which in cosmological manifestations is referred to as *t'ai-chi* and in moral manifestations as the *tao.* Yet these similarities do not guarantee an accord that carries down into the deeper levels of Leibniz' monads and the Neo-Confucian *li-ch'i* relationship. In all, given the secondary and imcomplete nature of Leibniz' sources of Chinese philosophy, we are faced with the remarkable degree of similarity he was able to postulate. How does one explain it? Leibniz felt that such similarities were spontaneously generated. We cannot ignore the fact that his interpretations of similarities between *li* and the monads, of elements of natural religion common to Europe and China, and of the binary basis of the *Book of Changes* all contain errors, some of which are apparent to even a novice of modern sinology. Yet these errors do not diminish the validity of Leibniz' other perceptions of similarities, which will be presented and summarized in course. Nor do they diminish the possibility that something in the nature of man or his situation determined the emergence of these similarities.

### The Primal Pair: *Li* and *Ch'i*

Leibniz in the *Discourse* 15–17[46] disputes Longobardi's identification of *li* with the European scholastics' formless prime matter. First, he believes that the classical passages presented by Longobardi define *li* as a source, spiritual in essence, from which all things and activities of the world emanate. Leibniz considers Longobardi's attempt to prove his identification of *li* with prime matter to involve a forced list of reasons (found in the *Religion Treatise* 14:19) that conflict with the Chinese textual passages. Longobardi begins the list by arguing that *li* cannot be truly spiritual since it cannot subsist by itself but has need of "primeval air" *(ch'i)* and compares this to the term *coava*. The reference here is probably to the Latin term *caelum,* which is connected with the Latin *cavus* (hollow) and means the air associated with the sky or heaven. In the *Discourse* $15^{47}$, Leibniz expresses doubt over whether the Chinese formally state that *li* cannot subsist without "primeval air." Instead, he explains their meaning by saying that the need for "primeval air" or prime matter refers to the times when *li* manifests itself among things, that *li* cannot be its own agent but has need of prime matter for its actualization. The Neo-Confucian texts refer to this prime matter as *ch'i,* which would be more accurately translated as "material force."

Actually the Neo-Confucian texts do state that *li* and *ch'i* are unable to function separately. Yet they also speak of *li* as prior in a logical, rather than temporal, sense.[48] Since he makes no reference to other textual sources, Leibniz would appear to base his explanation of the need of *li* for *ch'i* on his own conception of how the interior (that is, rational) realms of the monads have need of force in order to express the monads' temporally simultaneous origin of *li* for *ch'i*. In doing this, however, he neglects the logical priority of *li*. It must be admitted that Leibniz carries this priority further than most contemporary interpreters of Neo-Confucianism, but the unsatisfactory nature of such contemporary explanations may stem from an unresolved tension in Chu Hsi's own philosophy—that is his expression of a temporal co-origin of *li* and *ch'i* on the one hand and the logical priority of *li* on the other.

This tension is clearly expressed in the *Mission Treatise* (pp. 80–81), where Sainte-Marie cites the *Compendium* (bk. 26, pp. 8b–9a) to the effect that *li* and *t'ai-chi* have a priority over *ch'i* that consists of "nature or of origin" and not of time. Sainte-Marie compares this distinction to the one made by St. Augustine in the *Confessions* 12:19 between the first form and unformed or prime matter. However, a look at this *Compendium* passage will show that Sainte-Marie's comparision of *li* and *ch'i* to the Augustinian distinctions between form and the formless and the mutable and immutable is invalid. Augustine's passage in the *Confessions* quite clearly refers to God's direction of the relationship between form and matter. In comparing this to *li* and *ch'i,* Sainte-Marie omits the directional component provided by God and correlates form and matter with *li* and *ch'i*. But this omission makes for an unsatisfactory comparison since the Chinese clearly include a guiding principle in *li*. Furthermore, Leibniz is not arguing that there is a Chinese concept of God in addition to *li* and *ch'i*, as Sainte-Marie's Augustinian comparison would seem to imply. He is saying that *li* contains a type of priority that enables its universal, as opposed to its particular, aspect to be equated with God.

The *Compendium* itself (bk. 26, p. 8b) contains a terse reference to the priority of *li*: "Before there is Heaven and Earth and the myriad things, there first is *li*. But this *li* cannot be suspended in midair in the middle of something." In effect, *li* has a type of priority, but it needs some material force (i.e., *ch'i*) in which to be realized. Consequently, there follows a strong emphasis on the lack of any priority between the two. Rather, Chou Tun-i's "Diagram of the *t'ai-chi*" is quoted to the effect that *li* and *ch'i* are held to be prior and posterior in the way that movement and quiescence or *yang* and *yin* are prior and posterior; that is, they function in a reciprocal manner. Motion precedes quiescence, which in turn precedes motion, which in turn precedes quiescence, and so forth. In sum, we come to know from this passage far more about *li's* coequal status with *ch'i* than about *li's* prior aspect over *ch'i*. In other texts, Chu Hsi speaks more extensively on the priority of *li*, yet the nature of the priority seems always to express a certain ambiguity, perhaps reflecting a certain irresolution in Chu Hsi's own mind.

Longobardi's second argument in the *Religion Treatise* 14:19 for saying that *li* is equivalent to prime matter is that *li* considered by itself is inanimate, lifeless, without determination, and without intelligence. Sainte-Marie in the *Mission Treatise* (pp. 81–82) concurs in this view of Longobardi's and for support cites the *Analects* 15:28, where it states that the *tao*—*tao* being taken as equivalent to *li*—is incapable of knowing man, but man is capable of knowing the *tao*.[49] The tendency to equate *tao* with *li* was a forced identity that resulted from an incomplete understanding of these Chinese terms. *Tao* has a long history, which predates *li*, and has many different applications in Chinese philosophy. One may go only as far as saying that in the Neo-Confucian context *tao* and *li* may represent different manifestations of the same Absolute. It is this Neo-Confucian concept of the proximity of the two terms that Western missionaries and interpreters such as Leibniz seized on and emphasized. In so doing, they indiscriminately mixed non-Neo-Confucian with Neo-Confucian passages in a manner that would make a modern scholar blush.

But there is more to be said on the notion taken from *Analects* 15:28 that while *tao* cannot know man, man can know *tao*. Eager to participate in the authority of Matteo Ricci's views, which he manages to do at several points in the *Mission Treatise,* Sainte-Marie refers to Ricci's citation of this *Analects* passage and the view that while man can comprehend *li, li* cannot comprehend man, though it would be capable of doing so were it equivalent to God and the Creator.

Although giving no evidence of other access to the *Analects,*[50] Leibniz in the *Discourse* 16[51] expresses doubts about the precision of Sainte-Marie's interpretation of this passage. Specifically, Leibniz wishes to know more precisely of what Confucius was speaking—first principles? laws in the abstract?—and he suggests that if it is the latter, the meaning may be that the law being abstract and universal in its application knows no individual man. Modern translators such as James Legge and Arthur Waley have interpreted this passage more literally than the early missionaries and have spoken of man as being capable of enlarging the *tao* (Waley: "Way"; Legge: "Principles *which he follows*") but of the *tao* as being incapable of enlarging man. Chu Hsi's commentary on this passage in his *Lun-yü chi-chu* (Collected commentaries on the *Analects*) does not contradict the more modern interpretation, but it does support the fathers' rendering by quoting Chang Tsai as saying: "The mind is capable of exhaustively investigating human nature. Man is able to enlarge [his knowledge of] the *tao*. But human nature does not know how to investigate the mind. So the *tao* cannot enlarge man."[52] The reference is not simply to knowing, but to a type of knowing that leads to moral action. As such, it is a type of knowing unique to man and could hardly be applied to a supreme conception—whether the context be Confucianism or Christianity. Consequently, it would seem that Sainte-Marie has

misinterpreted the passage or perhaps followed a misinterpretation
by Ricci.

## Space and the Great Void

In the *Discourse* 7[53], Leibniz draws upon Longobardi's interpretation of *li* to relate the Chinese concept of space to his own view. In
the latter, which is well defined in Leibniz' correspondence with the
Newtonian apologist Samuel Clarke, space is treated not as a substance but as an order.[54] To support this interpretation, Leibniz
borrows from a list of attributes in the *Religion Treatise* 14:1-20, in
which Longobardi calls the Chinese first principle *(li)* a great
vacuum or space in the sense of an immense capacity, as well as a
sovereign plenitude that contains everything and excludes a vacuum. Among Longobardi's long list of attributes of the Chinese first
principle is a claim in the *Religion Treatise* 14:4 that the Chinese
call their first principle a "great vacuum (or void) and an immense
capacity because in this universal essence all the particular essences
are contained." This containment is compared to the water of
many rivers being contained in and receiving their force from one
spring or to the fruit, flowers, branches, and trunk of a tree that are
contained in the root. Further, in the *Religion Treatise* 14:8,
Longobardi states that the Chinese call their first principle a great
vacuum "because it can receive in itself all things, and that there
would be nothing beyond its limits." But in the *Religion Treatise*
14:14, Longobardi describes the Chinese as calling this first principle a "sovereign solidity of plenitude because the nature and
universal entity fills everything and is the same being with all
things." Longobardi maintains that *The Mean* (chaps. 20-25) supports this claim and holds that the "universal matter" of the first
principle pervades both within and without the universe bestowing
being of both a physical and moral nature upon all things.

The distinction Leibniz draws here seems to be between the
potential and the actual. He refers to capacity for manifestation
versus manifestation of the plenitude, yet he also speaks of the containment of particular essences within a universal essence. Leibniz
proceeds to relate this interpretation to an explanation of the im-
mensity of God as being without, as well as within something and

cites the inventor of the vacuum machine, a "M. Guerike," who believed that space appertained to God.

With the mention of Otto von Guericke of Magdeburg (1602–1686), who invented the air pump in 1645, Leibniz refers to his physical theories. In his fifth letter (18 August 1716) no. 33 of the correspondence with Clarke, which incidentally was written during the same year as the *Discourse,* Leibniz rejects the Newtonian assumption of Clarke that time and space bear an absolute reality and asserts instead that they are ideal constructions of the mind.[55] Similarly, in no. 34 of the same letter, Leibniz rejects the notion of Clarke's construction of Guericke's air pump as representing the creation of a perfect vacuum or space without matter. (Leibniz is said to have corresponded with Guericke on the air pump in 1671 and 1672.[56]) In this, he aligns himself with the Aristotelians and Cartesians who also reject a true vacuum, as they rejected the work attributed to Galileo's pupil Torricelli (1608–1647), who used mercury to empty the air from a glass tube. Rather, Leibniz interprets Guericke's pumping of air out of the receiver as having created not a total absence of matter in space but a "more subtle" air within the receiver than existed in the surrounding air of the room. In a manner typical of Leibniz' tendency toward infinite continua of gradation, he has attempted here to transform a postulated absolute absence into an absence of degree.

Leibniz' rejection of a vacuum is related to his rejection of the Newtonian claim, made through Clarke, of space as absolute and real. Leibniz cannot accept this claim and its close counterpart of treating space as an attribute of God. (Newton had referred to space as the "Sensorium of God.") In his third letter to Clarke (25 February 1716), nos. 2–3, he rejects both claims as contrary to his Principle of Sufficient Reason, to which Clarke presumably assented. Leibniz argues that since space is said to consist of parts, it cannot belong to God, who has no parts.[57] Leibniz returns to the notion of space having parts in his fifth letter, no. 52, where he interprets change, which both Leibniz and Clarke agree is necessary to Design.[58] Whereas Clarke views change as the movement of a finite material universe in real space, Leibniz thinks the universe must be infinite and treats change as an alteration among relationships in which space is an order of relations rather than absolute reality. In no. 54 of the same letter, Leibniz answers an objection that his views are not amenable to treatment by mathematics, an essential tool of the new natural philosophy by saying that time and space mean situation and order, that is, relations, and that relations may be treated quantitatively.

Leibniz uses an explanation in the *Discourse* 7[59] similar to the one that appears in the Leibniz-Clarke correspondence. He suggests viewing space not in terms of substance, with parts existing external to other parts, but as the order of things emerging from God with everything belonging to any given moment. The Leibnizian parallel is the notion of connection as unique monadic units, each occupying slightly different positions in a continuum or order. With regard to this view of time, consider Leibniz' rejection of absolute time in the fifth letter to Clarke, no. 55, where Leibniz dismisses any talk of the world being created sooner than it was as nonsensical. Such a view makes time "absolute, independent upon God; whereas time does only coexist with creatures, and is only conceived by the order and quantity of their changes."[60]

From the preceding discussion it becomes clear that Leibniz cannot interpret the Chinese vacuum to be a perfect vacuum in the sense of being totally devoid of matter. For Leibniz, there can be no such thing as a perfect vacuum. But the reference to the vacuum seems to have some meaning acceptable to Leibniz, and perhaps the key to it lies in the relationship of the vacuum to the complementary notion of sovereign plenitude. *The Mean* (chaps. 20–25) is cited by Longobardi (*Religion Treatise* 14:14) in reference to explaining this notion of plenitude. And even limited to plenitude, they seem only implicitly supportive. *The Mean* passages refer not to *li* but to *tao,* which Leibniz' interpreters regard as an acceptable equivalent of the first principle. (It is doubtful whether the Chinese themselves would have agreed to this degree of equating *tao* with *li.*)

Chu Hsi's commentary in his *Chung-yung chang-chü* (Commentary on The Mean)[61] on these passages from *The Mean* refers to *li* several times, although the context is somewhat different. *The Mean* text emphasizes the process of spiritual cultivation involving Sincerity and the related distinctions between *hsing* (inherent nature) and *chiao* (teaching), between the Way of Heaven and the Way of man. Longobardi's reference to the bestowal of physical and moral being is supported in *The Mean* (chaps. 22) where a progression, common in School of Principle writings, is outlined. In this progression, one moves from one stage to another: from attaining Sincerity to comprehension of one's personal nature, to comprehension of human nature, to comprehension of the nature of things, to the ability to aid in the transformations of Heaven and Earth, and finally, to the formation of a trinity with Heaven and Earth. Moral knowledge and physical knowledge are mutually absorbed by this advance toward wisdom.

Longobardi's interpretation of the first principle as a natural and universal entity filling the universe, both within and without, is partially supported by *The Mean* (chap. 25) where Sincerity is described as the completion of things as well as the completion of the self. Completing the self is referred to as Humanity *(jen*b*)* and completing things as Knowledge. By means of these virtues of inherent nature, the *tao* without is harmonized with the *tao* within. Chu Hsi's commentary emphasizes this external-internal aspect by holding that Sincerity is the completion of the self and things. Humanity *(jen*b*)* is the preservation of substance, and Knowledge is the manifestation of function. Chu Hsi holds that these elements all have a firm existence in one's inherent nature and lack any distinction between inner and outer in the sense that inner attainments are necessarily manifested in external phenomena. The implication here is not simply that inner experience is manifested outwardly, but that morality has both an inner and exterior dimension that can be transformed into a harmony between man and the cosmos.

The most direct support for Longobardi's interpretation comes from *The Mean* (chap. 25). This chapter emphasizes the connection between the moral quality of Sincerity and the physical quality of material generation and cosmic extension. The Way of Heaven and Earth is summarized as being without duplication in the generation of multiplicity and suggests a parallel to Leibniz' identity of indiscernibles in which he infers from the Principle of Sufficient Reason that "there cannot be in nature two real beings absolutely indiscernible because if there were, God and nature would go against reason, in treating the one otherwise than the other. And so

God does not produce two portions of matter perfectly equal and similar."[62] The chapter states that what concentrates before our eyes is the singleness of a bright light that generates and extends as all the forms of light in the world and beyond the world as sun, moon, stars, and so forth. What concentrates before us as the singleness of a clump of earth generates and extends to bear the weight of mountains and contain rivers and seas. What concentrates as a stone generates and extends as the products of grass and trees, the abode of animals, and storehouse of gems. What concentrates as a cup of water generates and extends to encompass all forms of aquatic life and articles of value.

But while these passages from *The Mean* may support the notion of a sovereign plenitude, they only imply the notion of a complementary relationship between a vacuum and plenitude. The implicit nature of such a complementary in *The Mean* could help explain its popularity as a Neo-Confucian text in that such a complementary began to be emphasized with the rise of Neo-Confucianism in the early part of the Sung dynasty (960–1280). Consequently, explicit support might be found in the extensive passages of the *Compendium*. The evidence at hand does not confirm that Leibniz found it there through his indirect sources, but whether he was relying on secondary sources or primarily projecting its existence into Chinese philosophy from his own philosophy, the evidence for the existence of a complementary relationship between a vacuum and plenitude in Sung Neo-Confucian thinkers is quite firm.

The notion of a sovereign plenitude is found in Chou Tun-i's "diagram of the *t'ai-chi*" *(T'ai-chi t'u-shuo)*, which is quoted in the *Compendium*. The first sentence is *"Wu-chi erh t'ai-chi"* or "Under the circumstances of there being *wu-chi* (maximization of nothingness), there is *t'ai-chi* (maximization of everything)." The statement presents two maximized situations that exist simultaneously; hence, the diagram symbolizes the statement with a circle (see Diagram 2). But both the circle and Chou's explanation imply something more than simply simultaneous existence. Rather, they seem to describe two different representations of some underlying unity.

For elucidation, one might turn to the other elements in Chou's

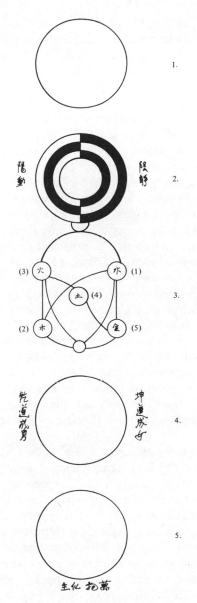

1.

陽
動                                    陰
                                     靜

2.

(3) 火        水 (1)

          土 (4)                      3.

(2) 木        金 (5)

乾                                    坤
道                                    道
成                                    成
男                                    女

4.

5.

生化 抱萬

Diagram 2.    Diagram of the *t'ai-chi* (*t'ai-chi t'u-shuo).*

explanation of the diagram of the *t'ai-chi*. Other component complementaries include *yin* and *yang*, *ch'ing* (quiescence) and *tung* (motion), *ch'ien* (the first hexagram or creative force) and *k'un* (the second hexagram or receptive force), male and female. Though citing polar extremes, Chou is concerned with the whole and connects these extremes as elements in a type of organic tension. The point of connection is associated with the term *chi*, which refers to the ridgepole in a house or the celestial pole connecting the emperor's throne with the pole star. In both cases, the pole represents the center of focus, a point into which all forces—whether of a house or a universe—converge and from which they emerge. Viewed as the point of convergence, the point represents the supreme nadir or maximization of nothingness for all universal process, that is, *wu-chi*. But viewed as the point of emergence, this same point represents the supreme source of potential or the maximization of everything, *t'ai-chi*. Viewed from the perspective of potential development, the point of initial emergence represents the point of maximal unfolding.

One of the reasons why Chou Tun-i and his contemporary Shao Yung are associated with the same Neo-Confucian school is because of their agreement on the *wu-chi–t'ai-chi* complementarity. Though Shao substitutes *t'ai-hsü* for *t'ai-chi*, Shao's complementarity seems to duplicate the relationship of Chou's *wu-chi–t'ai-chi*. For example, Shao states: "With the *t'ai-hsü* (supreme or maximized potential), there mutually acts the *wu-chi* (minimized potential or maximized actuality); therefore, Heaven cannot be exhausted."[63]

As with Chou's *wu-chi* and *t'ai-chi*, Shao's *wu-chi* and *t'ai-hsü* represent two ways of looking at the same point—that is, from the perspective of convergence *(wu-chi)* or emergence *(t'ai-hsü)*. While *wu-chi* represents the absence or exhaustion of potential, *t'ai-hsü* represents the maximized potential. The term *hsü* means vacuous or empty of actuality but pregnant with potential yet to be actualized. To emphasize its specific kind of emptiness, *hsü* is contrasted with *k'ung*, which refers to emptiness of both actuality and potentiality. Shao states that "the *Book of Changes* speaks of *hsü* [empty of actuality], but does not speak of *wu* [nonbeing]. It speaks of concealment, but does not speak of *k'ung* [empty of both actuality and potentiality]."[64]

Chang Tsai (1020–1077), another Neo-Confucian philosopher frequently quoted in the *Compendium,* appears to have a more sophisticated conception of a vacuum-plenitude complementarity in which the vacuum or void *(hsü)* is identified with Chang's conception of material force *(ch'i).* In making a point that bears upon this discussion, the contemporary scholar T'ang Chün-i holds that Chang Tsai rejects the Newtonian position of matter in an infinite vacuum and instead agrees that Chang sees the void of a thing as lying within the thing itself rather than without. Employing the continual flux of process, as opposed to inert matter, the concrete materiality of *ch'i* of one thing makes contact with another by means of this void within (i.e. potential aspect) enabling it to transcend its corporeal limits (i.e., actualized aspect) and interact and consequently transform itself into something else.[65]

It is worth noting that the early Sung Neo-Confucianists such as Chou Tun-i, Shao Yung, and Chang Tsai were more influenced by Taoism than was Chu Hsi. The notion of a void is quite prevalent in each of their philosophies. The term *wu-chi* was probably taken from chapter 28 of the *Lao Tzu.* Chu Hsi sought to minimize the Taoist influence and so made certain reinterpretations and additions to Chou Tun-i's explanation of the *t'ai-chi* diagram. Primary among these was his emphasis on the term *t'ai-chi* over that of *wu-chi* and his consequent identification of *li* (principle) with *t'ai-chi.* This identification is not present in Chou Tun-i's philosophy.[66]

We have already noted Leibniz' rejection of Cartesian extension as overly inert and his emphasis upon treating matter as reducible not to discrete, inert atomic units of matter but to units of force called monads. Yet while the monad may be defined as force, monads do not manifest themselves in the phenomenal world. Rather, they are interior, not in the sense of being physically inside but in the sense that Chang Tsai's void exists inside the actualized manifestation of *ch'i* as potential. Where Leibniz appears to differ from the Chinese concept is in his emphasis on the predetermined aspect of the monads. The absence of an equivalent logical interest in China, combined with the presence of a highly developed tradition of spiritual cultivation that had no such highly developed counterpart in Europe, contributed to this difference. While the techniques of logic work to isolate and freeze certain elements, those of spiritual cultivation must deal with the continual flux and vicissitudes of the human experience.

# 5
# The Discourse on Chinese Philosophy: Part II

## Spiritual Substances

The *Discourse on the Natural Theology of The Chinese* presents the Chinese doctrine on spiritual substances as a subject of fundamental importance and intimately related to the doctrine of *li*. Leibniz does not view the Chinese doctrine on spirits as a separate theological matter, but as part of the philosophical doctrine. As with Leibniz' treatment of so many Chinese matters, we have here an interpretation of Chinese philosophy that parallels his own approach to Western philosophy. A fundamental question is: How valid are these similarities that Leibniz perceived?

Contrary to some opinions,[1] I do not see the evidence to support the view that Chinese philosophy was influential in shaping Leibniz' own philosophy. Leibniz' early correspondence with Grimaldi shows just how undeveloped his knowledge of China was in the year 1689, and this was three or more years after the first formulation of his mature philosophy in the *Discourse on Metaphysics* (1686). The initiation of the correspondence with Bouvet in 1697, following the writing of the *Novissima Sinica,* marks the beginning of a deeper knowledge of China. By this time, Leibniz was moving outward toward an application of his system with practical consequences. In the relationship with China, he saw a chance for such an application.

It is too simple to say that his motivation, whether philosophical, political, or religious, predetermined the nature of his interpretation of Chinese philosophy. The motivation was there and forms part of the picture, but it is not dominant. The purer forms of objectivity do not always aid an investigation to the degree that is often assumed. While more superficial predisposing molds of thought usually hinder the process, predisposing forms of thought of a more profound level of awareness can aid an investigation. This, of course, assumes that truth is not infinitely malleable and that Leibniz brought a depth of awareness to his investigation of Chinese philosophy that gave him insights he might otherwise not have seen. In short, the fact that Leibniz carried a relatively mature conception of his own thought into his study of China both distorted and deepened his interpretation of Chinese philosophy. Had the positive motivation—one could call it prejudicial in terms of its subjectivity—not been present, he would probably not have become involved with interpreting Chinese philosophy.

Leibniz is aware of the problematic nature of the question of whether the Chinese recognize spiritual substances. After giving the matter a great deal of thought, he states in the *Discourse* 2[2] that the Chinese *have* recognized spiritual substances; however, they do not usually separate spiritual substances from matter. Leibniz recognizes that even though this notion differs from the dominant Christian view of his day that separates spiritual substance from matter, it is a fact that several ancient church fathers believed that angels have bodies. Furthermore, Leibniz himself believes that "the rational soul is never entirely stripped of all matter." This view is part of Leibniz' conception of reality approached, as described in the previous chapter, from different levels. On the metaphysical level, there are monads; on the abstract phenomenal level are forces; on the observed phenomenal level are bodies. The notion of force is the link between the monad and the body and is not unlike the connection between the Neo-Confucian *ch'i* (material force) and *li*. *Ch'i* is logically subordinate to *li* just as force and body are in some sense logically subordinate to the monad.

Leibniz is aware of the pertinence of *li* and *ch'i* to the argument and cites the Neo-Confucian concept as definitive in setting forth the view of the Chinese link between God, as the soul of the world, and matter. Nevertheless, he again demonstrates his confusion of later Neo-Confucian philosophy with the classical and ancient Chinese philosophies by attributing the concept of *li* as first principle and *ch'i* as its production to the "most ancient authors of China." Clearly, the full conception of *li* and *ch'i* was not explicitly developed until the eleventh and twelfth centuries A.D., even though much of the theory may have been implicit in earlier Chinese notions.

Leibniz describes the Chinese tendency to link matter with spiritual substance by citing their attribution of spirits to elements, streams, and mountains. He explains that by means of this attribution, the Chinese bestow the force of action—Leibniz interprets *li* as the First Action—upon these things. Leibniz compares this to the attribution by the ancient Christian fathers of "subtle and ethereal bodies" to genies and angels. While Leibniz recognizes that this attribution is probably erroneous, it would not subvert an acceptance of Christianity. Leibniz notes that the scholastic influence has led some to concur with Aristotle that certain intelligences govern the celestial spheres, and he compares this to the Chinese view that their ancestors and great men are among these types of spirits and are similar to angels. Among those who have held such views, both in China and in Europe, the attribution of bodies to these genies or angels by no means excludes the attribution of spiritual substances, or rational souls. Consequently, Leibniz concludes the *Discourse* 2[3] by denying the position of Longobardi and Sainte-Marie that the Chinese attribution of bodies to their spirits means that they deny the existence of spiritual substances.

In the *Discourse* 14[4], Leibniz draws from Longobardi's interpretation (*Religion Treatise* 12:7-8) of the *Compendium* (bk. 28, pp. 2b-3a) to discuss the relationship of Chinese spirits to *li*.[5] Though Longobardi's translation appears to be adequate, something should be said here of the highly controversial nature of certain Chinese terms in translation. Since some of the terms Longobardi is translating remain problematical in meaning, any translation represents an interpretation as well as a translation. For instance, a fairly literal translation of the passage at hand might be: "Someone asked whether spirits are simply material force *(ch'i)*.

And Chu Hsi answered that within this material force there is something akin to spiritual substance *(shen-ling)*. Longobardi translates the same passage as: "Someone asks: Are spirits air *[ch'i]*? And he [Chu Hsi] answers that it would seem perhaps that they are force, vigor and activity *[shen-ling]* which is in the air rather than the air itself." In sum, Longobardi's rendering represents a debatable possibility.

Chu-tzu (that is, Chu Hsi) is said to claim that spirits are called *li;* however, Leibniz recognizes an ambiguity by which *li* is sometimes grasped by the supreme spirit and sometimes through all the spirit, that is, spiritual substance. Leibniz suggests that etymologically *li* signifies "reason" or "rule," which is, in fact, somewhat similar to the etymological interpretation of "patterning" that the Chinese attribute to *li*. Continuing with Longobardi's rendering of the Chinese text, Leibniz deduces that all spirits are species of *li* in the sense that *li* constitutes the substance and universal activity of all things. Leibniz notes that the Chinese distinguish the *li* of the air from the matter of the air, in which circumstance *li* signifies not prime spiritual substance, but spiritual substance in general. Leibniz equates this spiritual substance with "Entelechy, that is, that this is endowed with the activity and perception or rule of action like Souls." Both the term "entelechy" and the definition correspond to one form of the Leibnizian monad.[6]

This identification with the monad is further strengthened when Leibniz goes on to interpret the Chinese passage in the *Compendium* (bk. 28, p. 3a) that treats differences as a matter of relative degree of grossness or extension of the material. He explains this in terms of a scale of perfection in which *li* or spirit is joined to matter of varying degrees of grossness and extension. Leibniz judges that the Chinese author, in seeking to explain differences in spirits in terms of the medium of matter, its degree of grossness or extension, shows that he has not sufficiently penetrated the issue. In this respect, the Chinese author shows a certain similarity to many European philosophers. Leibniz believes that the failure is one of not perceiving the preestablished harmony of all things. The attempt to find differences in varying degrees of grossness or extension, although not incorrect in itself, fails to penetrate far enough.

In Leibniz' view, the real differences emerge from an interior dimension, which the degree of grossness or extension of matter merely reflects. This interior dimension structures things into a hierarchy in which they are graded according to their degree of perception and consciousness. At the bottom of the hierarchy are inert objects to which we might attribute "bare monads." Moving up the scale to plants and animals, we have a dominant monad that reflects an increase in psychological, perceptional, and conscious powers and is called a "soul." With man and other higher intelligences, the dominant monad increases its ability to the point of being able to reason and consequently acquire a sense of morality. These dominant monads are called "spirits."[7] Finally, God represents the supreme monad. Not all Leibniz scholars accept the view that God is a monad.[8] In Leibniz' interpretation of the Chinese concept of spirits, he implies an equation between the supreme *li* and the supreme monad and calls both of them God. So without specifically saying that God is a supreme monad, Leibniz' argument in the *Discourse* supports such a view.

## Spirits and Sacrifice

The connection between *li* and sacrifice is brought out when Leibniz (*Discourse* 54[9]) cites Longobardi's translation (*Religion Treatise* 12:2-3) of the *Compendium* (bk. 28, pp. 37a–37b). In the passage, the Neo-Confucian philosopher Ch'eng I rejects as highly ignorant any appeal to the temple idols of the forest and earth for rain on the grounds that reason and observation of the relations and proportions of things will show it is the vapors of mountains and streams that produce rain and consequently it is the spirits of the mountains and streams to which one should direct his appeals. Only in this way will there be an accord with the spirits or universal spirit *shangti* or *li,* the supreme reason governing all. This represents a critical reference by Ch'eng I to Chinese folk religion, possibly intermingled with traces of Taoism and Buddhism.

Most Neo-Confucianists professed, as did Ricci, a highly critical attitude toward Buddhism. But several of these same Neo-Confucianists, for example, Chu Hsi and Chang Tsai, understood and admired a great deal in Buddhism. The contradiction in their outlook was partially stimulated by their perception of Buddhism as a form of competition for their own beliefs. In their tendency to be stimulated into criticism of Buddhism out of a sense of competition, they seem to have been joined by Matteo Ricci. Leibniz accepts this rendering by Longobardi, up to the point where Longobardi holds that the Chinese would regard the spirits of the mountains and streams as consisting not of a spiritual substance but of material air *(ch'i)*. Leibniz seems quite justified in rejecting Longobardi's position. In the Neo-Confucian view, *ch'i* nearly always requires the concomitant presence of *li*.

Longobardi's skill as a translator is demonstrated in a long paragraph translated from the *Compendium* (bk. 28, p. 38b) in the *Religion Treatise* 12:9 and cited by Leibniz in the *Discourse* 51.[10] (Sainte-Marie gives a loose paraphrase of this passage in the *Mission Treatise*, p. 30.) While Longobardi uses the passage to reemphasize his view of the ultimately material basis of Chinese spirits, Leibniz uses the passage to confirm the existence of a Chinese concept of spirits as ultimately spiritual. The passage is a quotation from Chu Hsi, who holds that were there no spirits, the ancients would not have carried out the seven days of sexual abstinence and the three days of fasting prior to certain types of sacrifices. In assigning particular objects of sacrifice to different levels of society, Chu Hsi may have struck a chord sympathetic to Leibniz' hierarchic but organic monadic scheme. The emperor sacrifices to Heaven and Earth, the feudal lords (Longobardi: "princes and dukes") to the mountains and streams, and the great ministers (Longobardi: "lords") to the five sacrifices (i.e., various household spirits). Further on in this section of the *Compendium,* schools and universities are said to sacrifice to Confucius, and there is an enumeration of other groups and their objects of sacrifice, down to the sacrifices of the common people to their ancestors.[11]

Longobardi draws from this same section of the *Compendium* to show a certain depth of appreciation, which while not equal to that of Ricci or other Jesuits, is considerably above that of Sainte-Marie. The latter's *Mission Treatise* frequently reads like a detailed travel journal in which his observations of Chinese religious practices, including sacrifice, have been carefully recorded. But his appreciation of the inner aspects of Confucian rites is so meager and unsympathetic that his accounts suffer to the point of being mere records of external detail that fail to grasp the inner significance and frequently mislead. On the other hand, his translations of Chinese texts have a certain accuracy. Longobardi, who is more familiar than Sainte-Marie with the classical texts—the core of the Confucian tradition—shows some awareness of this inner dimension. This awareness is reflected in the *Compendium* (bk. 28, pp. 38b–39a), translated by Longobardi in the *Religion Treatise* 12:10 and cited by Leibniz in the *Discourse* 52[12].

In this passage, a disciple asks Chu Hsi whether one sacrifices in order to demonstrate the proper inner state of reverence or because *ch'i* ("air") comes to receive the offering. In answering, Chu Hsi attempts a middle path that will encourage people to sacrifice and yet show that the nature of spirits cannot be depicted by the imagination. Consequently, he says that if nothing comes to receive the sacrifice, there is no reason to sacrifice, yet credulity is strained by any notion of an ethereal carriage descending to receive the sacrifice. It is quite possible that Longobardi's treatment of spirits as material was strengthened by Chu Hsi's reference to the spirits by the term *ch'i*. But, as is made clear many times in the texts by Chu Hsi, *ch'i* never stands without *li,* except in the abstract, and Chu Hsi must have been using the term *ch'i* in a looser sense than as the complementary to *li.*

There is, however, another thing about Chu Hsi's answer that is atypical of both classical Confucianism and Neo-Confucianism— the lack of emphasis on the cultivation of inner reverence. Such a cultivation was present, for example, in the previously cited passage from the *Compendium* in which several days of sexual abstinence and fasting prepared the inner state of the person for the sacrifice. This imbalance is partially rectified in the *Compendium* (bk. 28, pp. 39a–39b), from which passages are translated in the *Religion Treatise* 12:12 and described in the *Mission Treatise* (pp. 30–32), where a certain necessity of accord between the "air" of the sacrificer and the object of the sacrifice is discussed. The tendency to become entangled in investigation of the nature of spirits and the consequent detraction from the cultivation of inner reverence and morally informed action were a great concern expressed by Confucius in the *Analects*. Perhaps we should now turn to Confucius' view of spirits.

### Confucius' View of Spirits

In the *Discourse* 48[13], Leibniz takes up the famous sinological question of whether Confucius was agnostic, along with the very terse evidence given in the *Analects*. Leibniz detects a division between the Chinese literati who seek to explain the ways of Heaven and Earth completely in terms of natural causes and the general populace who explain their world in terms of the supernatural, and spirits that act as variations of a *deus ex machina*. Leibniz believes that the literati's path would better enable them to understand recent European advances reducing natural phenomena to mathematical causes and distinguishing between macrocosm and microcosm. But such causes would not be understood as emanating from any sort of supernatural machine.

This view is consistent with Leibniz' conviction that the advances of European natural philosophy are reconcilable with a Christian, though not necessarily with *any* Christian, concept of God. While God was not fully intelligible to man, he was partially open to man's understanding, and open to the extent that worldly phenomena could be comprehended without resorting to any supernatural device. (One of Leibniz' reasons for rejecting Newton's theory of gravitation was that he thought the theory would require the perpetual miracle—that is, the unexplained force—of action at a distance.) Nevertheless, the difficulties of such comprehension were great, and Leibniz believes that Confucius' reticence on the subject of spirits can be traced to his concern that only those sufficiently advanced in wisdom could comprehend such matters.

In such a way, Leibniz explains Confucius' reluctance as described in the *Analects* 5:12,[14] where the disciple Tzu-kung complains of his failure to get the master to speak on human nature and the "natural state" of Heaven. Leibniz then paraphrases the *Analects* 6:20, stating that the good manner of governing the people is by doing so in a way that honors the spirits while maintaining a distance from them. Leibniz next cites the *Analects* 7:20, where Confucius is said to have affected a great silence on four things—one of which was spirit(s). Finally, Leibniz cites the *Analects* 11:11 and interprets it to mean that Confucius sought to free himself from the constant questioning of his disciples on matters of the spirits, the rational soul, and life after death by formulating a general rule confining them to affairs of this life while restricting them from matters of spirits and the dead.

Longobardi provides Leibniz with accurate translations or paraphrases of the *Analects* passages cited above. Yet Longobardi offers no compelling reasons for Confucius' reticence on matters of spirits, the rational soul, and life after death. Lonogbardi's suggestion that Confucius' reticence was due to the secrecy of an esoteric doctrine is an insufficient motive. In the *Discourse* 49,[15] Leibniz briefly raises the possibility that Confucius was ignorant of spiritual matters, but he does not appear to regard the suggestion very seriously. In the *Discourse* 50,[16] however, he regards more seriously the possibility that Confucius' silence on spiritual matters may have been similar to that of authors who urge that God and the spiritual realm be revered without discussing and disputing their nature and manner of operation. This notion would represent an emphasis on spiritual cultivation that operates in the immediate present. As such, the emphasis on this life is dictated not by agnosticism but by the functional needs of the process of spiritual cultivation beginning with the present moment, with the *now* of experience. Given such a need, speculations about spirits and life after death represent intellectual distractions from the immediate path. This is an essential point to which I return in the concluding chapter.

In the *Discourse* 29[17], Leibniz discusses the Chinese association of *li* with *t'ien* (Heaven). Leibniz argues that Heaven should not be understood in its physical sense, but in the sense of a supreme deity as described in the *Mission Treatise* (pp. 12-13). In this work, Sainte-Marie links the Chinese Heaven with the same place where European pagans used to locate their supreme deity Jupiter, and he stresses Heaven as the absolute deity for the Chinese. Leibniz cites Longobardi who, in listing the attributes of the first principle of the Chinese, says that they call it *li* (*Religion Treatise* 14:1) and locate it in Heaven (*Religion Treatise* 14:10) because the sky is qualitatively the best part of the universe. Leibniz presses the association between *li* and Heaven by drawing from the description attributed to the *Analects* 2:5 praising both *li* and Heaven as principles of incomparable essence and without equal in the universe.

Though Leibniz does not cite it as such, the source of his reference to the *Analects* is probably the *Religion Treatise* 14:17, where Longobardi discusses the Chinese use of *shang-ti* (King-on-high), *t'ien* (Heaven), and *li* as near-synonyms. In contrast to Leibniz, however, Longobardi specifies in the following section that the similarities between these synonyms and the Christian God are only apparent and dissolve when *li* is seen in its true essence as prime matter. There is, however, a textual problem in that the references by both Longobardi and Leibniz to the *Analects* 2:5 appear in error since this passage contains no reference to *t'ien, li,* or *shang-ti.* Though the passage does contain a reference to another *li*d (Propriety, Ritual), which Chu Hsi's commentary treats as the *li* (principles) of externals, the contents seem clearly unrelated to the point Longobardi makes.

Rather than *Analects* 2:5, a possible source of the reference is *Analects* 5:12, where the term *t'ien-tao* appears in the text.[18] This term is a binomial composed of "Heaven" and the "Way" and may be rendered as the "Heavenly Way"; however, Longobardi may have inferred, not without some basis, that such a juxtaposition implies some sense of identity between the two terms. Since *tao* has been used elsewhere by Longobardi as a synonym for *li* and since Chu Hsi's commentary on this passage—to which Longobardi was quite possibly exposed—defines *t'ien-tao* as "the natural basic substance of Heavenly Principle,"[19] the result may have been a derivation on Longobardi's part of a close association between *li* and Heaven.

But there is an additional complication. As with the *Analects* 15:28, in which there were differences between missionary and modern translations, there would seem to be differences in the interpretation of 5:12. In his translation notes, James Legge points out the difficulties involved in both passages. Both Chu Hsi and modern interpreters treat the passage as referring to Confucius' willingness to speak on personal manifestations of goodness but reticence to discuss man's nature and the Way of Heaven. Could the missionaries have interpreted this reticence as a manifestation of respect and reverence? (A similar interpretation is possible for the *Analects* 6:20, where Confucius speaks of revering the spirits while keeping one's distance from them.) Could this reticence in some way represent praise toward matters of Heaven, *tao,* and *li,* as well as toward human nature?

## The Chinese Concept of Soul

In the *Discourse* 20[20], Leibniz criticizes Longobardi in the *Religion Treatise* 14:19 for interpreting the *Compendium* (bks. 26 and 34) as evidence for the belief that the world contains nothing really spiritual, but that all is ultimately material.[21] Since specific passages from the *Compendium* are not cited, it is difficult to check the direct accuracy of Leibniz' interpretation, but there seems to be an organic basis in Neo-Confucian cosmology for his claim that particular souls are not reducible to discrete elements of matter, that is, material atoms, but are "all united of body." Knowingly or unknowingly, Leibniz also interprets the Chinese view in accordance with his own view when he claims that the Chinese hold that the soul after death would not be stripped of all "organized matter" or "fashioning air." The notion that death represents mere diminution of growth for the soul, and birth a hastening of growth, can be found in the *Monadology* no. 73.

The distinction between a lighter and heavier soul is prominent in Chinese religion. In the *Discourse* 59[22] Leibniz describes the death of the legendary King Yao in terms of the separation of a lighter from a heavier soul. The source is traced back through the *Religion Treatise* 15:4 to the *Book of History* ("bk. 1, p. 16"), but the closest equivalent is found in the *Book of History* II, i, III, 13, which speaks of the death of King Yao but does not support Leibniz' description of higher and lower souls. However, Legge's commentary on this passage cites Chu Hsi as making such a distinction. There are other bases on which to make this distinction, and Longobardi cites two of them in the *Religion Treatise* 15. First, in the *Religion Treatise* 15:5, he refers to the *Compendium* (bk. 28, p. 41a), where Ch'eng I is loosely quoted as saying that when a man dies, the heaven and earth separate; the pure air, which is the human entity, returns to heaven and the corporeality, or the earthly entity, returns to earth. The other basis of support comes from the *Book of Odes* III, l, i, l ("bk. 6, p.1"), cited twice by Leibniz, who draws from both Longobardi and Sainte-Marie and presents King Wen, rather than Yao, in such a situation.

In the *Discourse* 58[23], Leibniz raises the difficult problem of communicating to the Chinese the true meaning of the Christian soul. As is often the case in cultural transmission, certain indigenous terms were used to ease the entry of foreign concepts into the native tongue. The initial usefulness of such native terms fades, however, as the secondary stages of the transmission approach and demand a precision and clarity in terminology for which the native near-equivalents no longer suffice. A similar situation occurred with the introduction of Buddhism to China in the early centuries of the first millennium A.D., when the *ko-i* method of seeking native Chinese equivalents for Buddhist terminology lost its initial effectiveness and was eventually rejected with a growth in linguistic, doctrinal, and spiritual knowledge.

Leibniz offers Longobardi's citation of "Dr. Paul's" (Hsü's) expression of confusion in regard to Chinese near-equivalents of the Christian soul, such as *ling-hun* (that which subsists after the death of the body) and *yu-hun* (wandering soul). The term *ling-hun* is associated with the *Book of Odes* III, 1, i, 1, where the ancient founder of the Chou dynasty, King Wen, is said to have received the Mandate of Heaven for the new dynasty and is described as rising and descending at the left and right sides of God *(ti)*. Leibniz' source is the *Religion Treatise* 15:5–7, where we find the above-cited reference to the *Compendium* (bk. 28, p. 41a) describing the separation of celestial and earthly components at death and Longobardi's attempts to distinguish between "air" and the soul, two elements frequently confused by the Chinese. Longobardi does this by citing the *Book of Odes* III, 1, i, 1, where it is said that King Wen rises and descends at the side of the King-on-high. He holds that it is not a soul that rises (i.e., lives after death) but rather a manifestation of "celestial air" that persists after the death of the person. Longobardi explains the description of rising and falling near the King-on-high as a reference to the unordered and random movement of this air that pervades the universe. It may be an indication of his materialistic interpretation that Longobardi refers to the soul which separates from the body as *yu-hun* (wandering soul or ghost) and omits mention of *ling-hun* (spiritual soul), which Leibniz uses in describing this passage.

Following a materialistic interpretation, Longobardi holds that this chaotic air associated with the "soul" is governed by the body and the chaotic air of heaven is ordered by heavenly bodies. Longobardi reasserts that the Chinese attribute immortality only to *li* (universal substance), which both pervades and follows after all passing phenomena. All this *li* is in Longobardi's view, of course, not spiritual but consists of prime matter.

In the *Discourse* 65[24], Leibniz again discusses the *Book of Odes* III, 1, i, 1; but in this instance he draws upon Sainte-Marie's interpretation of the passage in the *Mission Treatise* (p. 27). In arguing that the ancient Chinese professed the immortality of the soul, Leibniz holds that the ancient doctrine speaks of souls receiving rewards and punishment after death. Furthermore, Leibniz argues that even though contemporary Confucianists tend to mock notions of an afterlife—they in fact treat them as Buddhist vulgarities—these same Chinese recognize a supreme source of wisdom and justice which, Leibniz feels, logically extends to the world of spirits and souls. Leibniz argues that this system of a cosmic monarch would, like that of the monarch of man, require rewards and punishment for the preservation of order. Leibniz sees the ancient Chinese making the same recognition and casting *shang-ti* as a dispenser of justice. Leibniz cites Sainte-Marie's description of the *Book of Odes* III, 1, i, 1 in the *Mission Treatise* (p. 27), setting forth the rewards of virtuous kings who after their death rise to assist the King-on-high. Further, Leibniz argues that the same passage describes kings rising to Heaven and descending to Earth, and he interprets this in a manner similar to Sainte-Marie—namely, that this represents the process by which kings can aid the living.

## Metaphysics versus Spiritual Cultivation

In the *Mission Treatise* (pp. 69–70), Sainte-Marie cites Confucius as saying in *The Mean* that *t'ien-tao,* which Sainte-Marie equates with *li,* certainly governs Heaven in its courses and natural operations and, furthermore, that *li* constitutes its own truth, its own law, and infallible regularity. Leibniz in the *Discourse* 29[25] accepts this explanation of *t'ien-tao* (Heavenly Tao, principle), in part, on the basis of Sainte-Marie's attribution of such a definition to Confucius in *The Mean*.

As with most of Leibniz' judgments of the validity of a particular secondary interpretation by Sainte-Marie or Longobardi, the acceptance or rejection is made not so much on external familiarity with the original text as on grounds of logic and internal consistency. When Leibniz does make a positive judgment, however, he feels that the text will support him. Examination shows that such support is not always clear-cut, even though in this case Leibniz' acceptance of Sainte-Marie's interpretation appears to be on consistent grounds.[26]

If Sainte-Marie's reference to *t'ien-tao* may be taken as a very loose paraphrase rather than a close translation, then a possible source is *The Mean* (chap. 20) in conjunction with Chu Hsi's commentary on this passage. *The Mean* text reads:

> Sincerity is the Way of Heaven *(t'ien chih tao)*. The process of becoming sincere is the Way of man. Sincerity does not strive and yet is at the Mean. It is not conscious and yet succeeds. It follows and is enveloped in the Way. This is sagehood. In the process of becoming Sincere, one grasps the good and firmly holds on to it.

Chu Hsi comments on this passage as follows:

> The above passage presents and discusses the Sincere person. Sincerity as genuine reality and lack of deception is what is meant by the natural condition of Heavenly Principle *(t'ien-li)*. The process of becoming sincere implies that though one has not yet reached the stage of being genuinely real and without deception, yet he has the desire to be so. This is what is meant by the proper condition of human affairs. The power-virtue of sagehood is the fulfillment of Heavenly Principle. If one who is genuinely real and without deception does not wait for conscious deliberation, but follows and is enveloped in the Way, this then is the Way of Heaven *(t'ien chih tao)*.[27]

This commentary provides a foundation on which to associate *t'ien-tao* with *li* as well as some basis for Sainte-Marie's description of *li*, which Leibniz accepts. But if this is the textual basis for Sainte-Marie's reference, to the extent that he fails to refer to Sincerity he misses the essential meaning and essential religious aspect of Confucianism. Consequently, he continues to be limited to the outer manifestation of the Confucian rites as well as being limited in the depth of knowledge of Chinese religion he is able to communicate to Leibniz. While Leibniz seems to have had some remarkable insights into the metaphysical nature of Neo-Confucian philosophy, the highly developed spiritual cultivation of classical Confucianism and Neo-Confucianism largely eluded him.

The notion of Sincerity appears in reference to Leibniz' use of *The Mean*. In discussing spirits (*Discourse* 43[28]), Leibniz maintains that Sainte-Marie had misunderstood Confucius' meaning on the connection between spirits and things. The separation of the two elements occurs not, as Sainte-Marie holds, because the Chinese believe that spirits disintegrate but because *things* perish, a fact that Longobardi seems to have grasped. Leibniz demonstrates Longobardi's comprehension of this point by citing the latter's interpretation of *The Mean* (chap. 16), where according to Leibniz it is held that spirits constitute part of the being of things from which they are separated only when the things—*not* the spirits—are destroyed.[29]

Leibniz then gives his own interpretation that Confucius' use of spirits as parts of things does not include all spirits and further that the notion of "part" as related to spirits refers to something internal to a thing and "requisite to its substance or conservation." This is similar to the notion of connection that appears in Leibniz' conception of monadic parts. In the latter, unique monadic units are connected by a preestablished inner harmony by which each monad reflects all other monads. The Chinese "things" to which the spirit is necessarily connected assumes a *yang* and then a *yin* stage, moves and then is quiet, flows and then ebbs, and then repeats the entire process. The Leibnizian parallel is the monad's material manifestation whose flow and ebb is defined as an increase (commonly associated with birth) and diminution (commonly associated with death).

In one of Leibniz' sources of interpretation of *The Mean* (chap. 16), Longobardi (*Religion Treatise* 11:17) poses and answers the question as to whether the sacrificer directs his actions toward the spiritual component of something or to the thing itself. First of all,

Longobardi correctly stresses that there is a great amount of tradition involved and the emphasis on authority has blurred the consciousness of the situation. The sacrifices involve customs handed down from antiquity, and their value is, to a great extent, derived from this transmission. Longobardi then notes that most capable scholars see *li* and *ch'i* in the objects of their sacrifice. Here Longobardi cites *The Mean* (chap. 16), where he holds that Confucius explained spirits as parts composing the being of a thing, the objects of great inner and external forms of reverence. Leibniz, however, diverges from Longobardi when the latter explains in the *Religion Treatise* 10:3 that the being of the thing constituting spirit refers to the essence of the material rather than to its spiritual nature. Picking up on *The Mean* (chap. 16) treatment of *kuei-shan* as two different manifestations of *ch'i*, Longobardi concludes that the Chinese concept of spirits does not fully qualify as a spiritual concept familiar to the West but is inseparable from the materiality associated with *ch'i*.[30]

As for the text of *The Mean* (chap. 16), it is a short chapter that emphasizes the subtlety of *kuei-shen* (spirits) and the difficulty of perceiving them and, by implication, the difficulty of distinguishing them from things.[31] Their subtle nature requires caution in one's treatment of them. Fasting, sexual abstinence, and careful observance of dress are employed in cultivating the proper attitude toward spirits. Sincerity is meant to be both the result and the medium for contact with spirits since it is one of the ways in which these subtle spiritual elements manifest themselves.

Leibniz' interpretation of the Chinese concept of spirits seems a possible derivation from *The Mean* text and commentary by Chu Hsi, as passed on to Leibniz by Longobardi. However, the difficulty of calling it a fully accurate or even probable derivation is complicated by the fact that it is based on lines of development that the Chinese text and commentary merely infer but never actually develop. Consequently, evaluation in terms of the accuracy or inaccuracy of Leibniz' and, to a certain extent, Longobardi's intepretations involves no direct referent, only an implied one. Leibniz, for instance, interprets the Chinese spirits as an essential component of the substance of a given thing. The Chinese text and commentary may imply this, but explicitly the stress is not nearly so much metaphysical as experiential. The Confucian concern is with the perception and understanding of the location of spirits, or the spiritual, as a step toward making proper contact and attaining the fruits of such contact. This should not be interpreted in such a coarse external sense as Sainte-Marie tends to do. Leibniz' interest in the Chinese text is intellectual and political, though he openly professes a religious concern. The Chinese interest, on the other hand, is a very immediate spiritual concern to which metaphysics is the handmaiden.

The *Discourse* 66[32] gives an instance of how dependent Leibniz can be upon his secondary sources for information on Chinese practices. In this passage, Leibniz discusses the Chinese cult of ancestors, said to have been passed down from the ancient Chinese of the third millennium b.c. The cult involves the formal expression of gratitude by the living toward the dead, the recompense of Heaven, and the stimulation of the living to act in a way that will gain posterity for them through cultic worship. Leibniz makes note of an additional theme in ancestor worship whereby the spirits of virtuous ancestors acquire access to the "Monarch of the Universe" (i.e. God) and consequently the power to reward their descendants.

Leibniz refers to Confucius' honoring of Shun (legendary reign: 2255–2204 b.c.) as the founder of the cult of ancestors and to his tracing of the prosperity of the realm to this cult. (According to traditional Chinese legendary sources, Shun is said to have passed his authority on to Yü who by passing it on to his own son initiated a genealogical line that became the first Chinese dynasty, the Hsia.) Leibniz describes Confucius as praising the ancient kings (Yao, Shun, and Yü) as models for posterity and asserting that he who would completely comprehend the cult of Heaven and Earth and the reasons for sacrifices to one's ancestors will achieve peace, prosperity, and good government.

As sources for this information, Leibniz cites chapters from *The Mean*.[33] He apparently relied upon Sainte-Marie, who in the *Mission Treatise* (pp. 21–24) presents an almost direct and generally accurate translation of *The Mean* (chaps. 17–19). But in his interpretive summary of these chapters, Sainte-Marie errs by stressing Confucius' belief in the happiness of the realm as dependent on the external element of ancestral protection, whereas the Confucian emphasis was in fact on the inner element of reverence and its connection to external action informed by this reverence.

## Correspondences between Western and Chinese Philosophy

Central to Leibniz' ecumenical plan was the belief in the existence of correspondences between Western and ancient Chinese cultures, of which he hypothesized the following:

1. That there are correspondences between the diagrams of the *Book of Changes* and Leibniz' binary mathematics.
2. That Confucian and Leibnizian philosophy express a similar relationship between interior and exterior dimensions. (This relationship could be described as between the dimensions of the Chinese *li* and phenomena and between the dimensions of Leibnizian monads and phenomena, of which the essential intermediaries are *ch'i* and *vis viva,* respectively, both involving the notion of physical force.)
3. That the metaphysical connection between *li* and the monads participates in an organic whole that connects unique units but is without separable parts.
4. That part of this connection is accomplished through a mirroring process.
5. That *li* and the monads are each of a particular and a universal variety, the latter denoted by *t'ai-chi* and God, respectively.
6. That *li* and the monads are both ultimately rational and spiritual in essence and that both bear a type of logical priority toward their phenomenal representations.
7. That *t'ai-chi* represents an immense capacity that, translated from a metaphysical to a physical level, contains all elements and excludes the possibility of a vacuum.
8. That *t'ai-chi* most essentially represents an order of relations and that this compares to the Leibnizian notion of space, which rejects a vacuum, or any notion of space or time, as absolutely real. *T'ai-chi* instead represents, on its most basic level, an order of relations.
9. That there is an affinity between Chinese and Christian con-

cepts of spirituality and that the Chinese sacrifices reflect in their order and hierarchy a rationality similar to that of Christianity.

10. That *shang-ti, t'ien,* and *li* are near-equivalents of the Christian concept of God and that *t'ai-chi, li,* and *ch'i,* taken together, correspond to the Christian Trinity.

11. That the Chinese have a notion of an ethereal soul as distinct from a material soul and that this ethereal soul, sometimes called *ling-hun,* is close to the notion of a spiritual soul in Christianity.

12. That the Chinese have a doctrine of reward and punishment after death in which *shang-ti* is the dispenser of justice and that this implies both the Christian concept of the immortality of the soul and divine justice.

This is a substantial list of correspondences and contains considerable validity. Yet it failed to establish a lasting basis for accord. The effort was hindered not so much by the lack of potential bases for ecumenical accord as by a certain predisposing motivation present in the ecumenical outlook of Leibniz himself. This failure is pursued in the next two chapters.

# 6
# *The Failure of Leibniz' Philosophy*

## Failure in Both China and Europe

Jesuit maneuvering and the growth of anti-Jesuit feeling in Europe fed the Rites Controversy to the point that the European debate interfered with the functioning of the missionaries in China. Prior to the mission of the papal legate, Charles de Tournon, to China in 1704–1710, the debate over the Chinese rites had been only a moderate obstacle to the work of the mission. But after the disastrous encounter of the K'ang-hsi emperor with Tournon and his supporter Maigrot in 1706, the fortunes of the mission deteriorated.

A letter to Des Bosses of 1710[1] shows that Leibniz was critical both of Tournon's lack of circumspection and reverence for the K'ang-hsi emperor and also of the "two decrees" that Tournon formally released. Leibniz' reference here is probably to the Decree of 1704 issued by the Roman Inquisition and confirmed by Pope Clement XI (20 November 1704). This decree forbade *shang-ti* and *t'ien* and approved *t'ien-chu;* it forbade church tablets with the term *ching t'ien* and forbade Christians any role in the sacrifices to ancestors or to Confucius; moreover, it proscribed ancestral tablets with characters calling the throne the seat of the spirit of the deceased, allowing only a tablet with the name of the dead.

The second decree Leibniz refers to is probably Tournon's "Decree of Nanking" (7 February 1707), which was promulgated largely in response to the K'ang-hsi emperor's decree of December

1706. The emperor's decree had ordered Maigrot and other missionaries banned from the empire and had punished several Chinese associated with the Tournon legation. Furthermore, the K'ang-hsi emperor had ordered that all missionaries be required to obtain an imperial *piao* (permit), which would be issued only on the condition that they promised to abide by the practices of Matteo Ricci. Tournon's decree reaffirmed the condemnations of the Decree of 1704, in addition to taking the extreme step of threatening violators with excommunication.

The papal bulls *Ex illa die* (1715) and *Ex quo singulari* (1742) officially ended the controversy and left the Chinese offended by the pagan status to which Rome had relegated them. In 1724, the Yung Cheng emperor (r. 1723–1735) revoked the Toleration Edict of 1692 and broadened the recent edicts against Christianity made by his late father, the K'ang-hsi emperor.[2] The attempted worldwide suppression of the Society of Jesus in 1773 further crippled the missionary effort in China until its resurgence in the nineteenth century under primarily Protestant auspices. The decline of the China mission contributed to the decline of Leibniz' hopes for accord.

In addition to the attention directed toward China, Leibniz' irenics involved an active and prolific correspondence within Europe. But the auspicious beginnings for the ecumenical cause that Leibniz had experienced soon after his arrival at Hanover in 1677 gradually gave way to impasses in negotiations. From 1680 to 1693 Leibniz corresponded with Ernst, landgrave of Hessen-Rheinfels, and from 1690 to 1693 with Mons. Paul Pellison, court historian to Louis XIV, both men Roman Catholic converts from Calvinism. The results were no more fruitful, however, than those from the correspondence with Bossuet, bishop of Meaux, carried on in 1678–1693 and again in 1699–1702.

The Leibniz-Bossuet correspondence has been viewed as a classic debate that recapitulates more than a century of irenic discussion. In it, the learned and renowned theologian Bossuet defended the positions of the Council of Trent against those of the Augsburg Confession. The arguments for the Augsburg Confession were offered by the brilliant but youthful Leibniz, who had access to the splendid library at Hanover, which included a Bible with Luther's own annotations.[3] Increasingly, an awareness of the width of the

chasm separating them was heightened by the worsening of Protes-
tant-Catholic relations following the revocation of the Edict of
Nantes in 1685. It would be inadequate, however, to say that events
of history were the primary cause of the failure of Leibnizian ecumenism. Fundamental and perhaps irreconcilable differences in
principles were also involved. And, at least in regard to Leibniz'
hopes for China, a full explanation requires that one look into elements in Leibniz' own philosophy and perspective, views that were
shared by certain Jesuits and contributed to the failure of philosophical religion as a basis for accord.

## The Tension in Leibniz' Philosophy

Ironically, Leibniz' attempts to reconcile the increasing divorce of
reason from faith led to a synthesis so completely rational and lacking in direct spiritual practice that his ultimate contribution was to
the further secularization of European thought.[4] Here we encounter an irresolvable tension within Leibnizian philosophy. In
one direction there is a search for union between China and Europe, and between Catholicism and Protestantism, in a medium
that seems fully religious. Simultaneously, in another direction, the
tendency toward reducing religious actions to intellectual functions
works to exclude a vital element of religion. This tension, intrinsic
in Leibniz' philosophy, was a fundamental cause of the failure of
his ecumenism.

Nicholas Rescher's generally commendable study of Leibniz'
philosophy refers to the tension within Leibnizian ethics, which was
on the one hand "apparently theocentric" in origin and on the
other directed toward completely secular aims.[5] Rescher attempts
to resolve the tension by treating the doing of God's will as a fully
humanistic enterprise to the point that any active concern for God
can be left behind in the pursuit of secular goals. Goodness becomes a function of knowledge since it is *right action* that best
serves man and knowledge, rather than "faith, inspiration, or
goodwill" that best fosters the right sort of action.

Such a severe separation of religious components from knowledge treats religion as highly impractical. This position conflicts
with the utilitarian character that is part of nearly every vital religion and in which transcendental elements are normally goals but

rarely the immediate means to be applied. Leibniz neglects—a neglect that Rescher is competent in reproducing—the recognition that the sick are best served by a knowledge that is at one with the spirit. But does Leibniz neglect this connection as fully as it would appear? In regard to a tension involving forces pushing in opposing directions, Rescher describes the force in Leibnizian philosophy that is pushing toward secularity, but he tells us very little about the force that seeks to foster a strong spiritual faith and bond with God.

Since there are few radical breaks in Leibniz' writings or in the methods by which he comes to the conclusions those writings express, we may be justified in looking to the early years of Leibniz' studies for evidence of this emerging tension. One suggestion traces a definite tension between Aristotelian and Platonic-Pythagorean influences back to his student days at Leipzig. The Aristotelian influence is reflected in his *De principio individui* (Principle of individuation) (1663) and the Platonic-Pythagorean influence in *De arte combinatoria*—also known as *Ars combinatoria* (Combinatory art) (1666).[6] But this suggestion must be tempered by the possibility that *De principio individui,* as his bachelor's thesis, may have reflected academic demands as well as an inclination on Leibniz' part toward Aristotelianism. Furthermore, *De arte combinatoria* is a considerably more substantial work than his thesis.

It is generally recognized that Pythagoreanism sought to discern the harmonic mathematical relations existing in the external world, but it is insufficiently stressed that Pythagoreanism originally involved a brotherhood and that this outer discernment was to be related to an inner discernment in an attempt to create a spiritual harmony between the two, with geometry and mathematics as merging instruments.[7] Leibniz was introduced to this influence after 1663 by Erhard Weigel of Jena, who opened a private school of Youth and Virtue *(Jugend und Tugenschule)* to confirm the practical role of mathematics. As part of the curriculum, Weigel taught calculus as a moral discipline.[8]

Through Weigel, Leibniz was introduced to the combinatory art of Raymond Lull, which involved a series of nine concepts and questions placed on a wheel of seven concentric disks and mechanically manipulated to yield answers. Lull's answers were far less influential than his method, which affected Gassendi, Giordano Bruno, Thomas Hobbes, and eventually Leibniz.[9] Leibniz refers to Lull's work and its connection with that of Gassendi, Bruno, Kircher, and Hobbes in De arte combinatoria.[10] Yet the tension between philosophical and religious concerns in Leibniz is such that a contemporary study of Leibniz' De arte combinatoria can treat Weigel purely in terms of his intellectual achievements as a rather mediocre mathematician while avoiding significant reference to his Platonic-Pythagorean tendencies and the work of Raymond Lull.[11]

In formulating his later notion of universal science based upon an art of characteristic symbols in Scientia Generalis. Characteristica (A universal science: characteristic), Leibniz recalls how he anticipated the discovery of his youthful De arte combinatoria and compares this Universal Characteristic or calculus of symbols to a Cabala of mystical words or arithmetic of Pythagorean numbers.[12] Leibniz confirms the persistence of Pythagoreanism in his mature work and its connection with his religious motives in several passages in the Theodicy.

In Theodicy no. 181, he speaks of ethical virtues, for example, piety, sobriety, justice, and chastity, and how they were virtues prior to God's choosing to bring them from the status of a possible to an actual world. Virtues are so because the nature of rational creatures guarantees their constitution prior to any choice by God. Leibniz compares this situation to the Pythagorean notions of proportion and harmony inherent in the ideal state of music and therefore already determined prior to their actualization in the playing of music.[13] In Theodicy no. 208, Leibniz refers to the Pythagorean characteristics of simplicity and harmony while describing the basis on which God chooses to actualize possible elements. God's choice is made on the basis of what is conducive to the greatest harmony, to that quality which is "the most productive in proportion to the simplicity of ways and means."

An additional confirmation of Leibniz' connecting Pythagorean elements with religion comes in reference to his discussion of the Chinese in his preface to the Novissima Sinica. Leibniz attributes the Chinese failure to attain the Western equivalent of success in certain areas of the sciences to the absence of what he calls the "two eyes" of Europeans. The first is geometry, in which the K'ang-hsi emperor's children and, to a lesser extent, the emperor himself were being instructed by Bouvet. The Pythagorean elements are clearly present in Leibniz' declaration that geometry is what Plato taught as the only entry into "the mysteries of the sciences." The second eye was "First Philosophy," by which Leibniz means the science that leads to an understanding of the spirit, or the "true religion."[14]

It would be restrictive to say that Leibniz proposed no forms of religious practice. Like Weigel, Leibniz treats mathematical and intellectual pursuits as moral exercises. He could do so because all knowledge was a knowledge of God and his methods. Men could know in the same way that God knew, except in a much more limited way: God could perform the infinite analysis required of factual truths, while man could not. Consequently, truth in the Leibnizian view acquires a moral tone. For Leibniz, knowing was accompanied by a certain religious awe and possibly a feeling of transcendence. This notion bears a certain similarity to the Chinese linking of knowledge and morality.

But Leibniz gives little evidence of accepting the basic premise in religious practice that the intellect is not identical with the spirit. This premise maintains that the intellect, like the body and emotions, has its separate relationship to the spirit, at least until one reaches the higher stages of spiritual advancement, where there is a unification of previously separate elements and a greater sense of wholeness. We cannot doubt that Leibniz manifests a strong element of unity in his views, and to the extent that such unifying tendencies are associated with religious motives, Leibniz was deeply religious. But when we come to the religious motive of dissolving subject and object distinctions to form the unity of the One, we are confronted with a fundamental position of logic in the Leibnizian philosophy.

The distinction between subject and object or between "I" and "thou" is bred of discrimination, which is a tool of the intellect. The distinction cannot be dissolved by merely intellectual means, which in this case can be partially identified with individual means. Rather, the dissolution must be accomplished by methods whose aim is to transform the normally hostile condition between reason and emotion into a harmony between wisdom and compassion. These methods involve breaking down the barriers of ego by advancing in a particular form of spiritual cultivation in which discipline is essential. The disciplinary method may involve meditation, prayer, fasting, abstinence, regularity, tranquillity, charity, self-flagellation, manual labor, or some other form of daily practice. All involve cultivation of a less discursive type of knowledge.

The literate mind often goes astray in its analysis of such practices when it regards them as nonintellectual and therefore unable to attain a high degree of inner consistency. Yet progress in spiritual discipline normally involves progressive stages of coherency holding between a vast array of seemingly unrelated elements. The ability of these nondiscursive forms of knowledge to deal with complexity is comparable to that of discursive knowledge. However, the emphasis upon the qualities of simplicity and harmony, connected in the preceding discussion with Pythagoreanism, is even greater than in the discursive forms.

Perhaps what distinguishes Leibniz' interest in simplicity and harmony from a more religious concern centers on the differing natures of the respective approaches. Even if Leibniz' particular form of subject-predicate logic is not the essential ingredient of Leibnizian philosophy to the degree that Couturat and Russell have maintained, this logic is nevertheless an important ingredient.[15] A view of the world that derives from a breakdown into subject and predicate would seem to be more discriminating than unifying. Yet the existence of logic did not necessarily lead to the degeneration of spiritual cultivation in Buddhism.[16] Buddhism contains a large number of deeply cultivated spiritual disciplines. Leibnizian philosophy does not.

In all fairness, we must go back to the Christian tradition, from which Leibniz draws. In comparison with Buddhism or other Chinese philosophies, the mainstream of the Christian tradition contained a far less developed meditative discipline, leaving the realm of meditation to the informal and individual approaches of the Christian mystics. On the other hand, meditation and contemplation are not the sole paths of spiritual cultivation, and we cannot say that Leibniz' religious motives were impractical, for his ecumenism was intended to serve a very real spiritual need in seventeenth- and eighteenth-century Europe.

## Leibniz' Spiritual Understanding

It is tempting to criticize modern interpreters of Leibnizian philosophy who regard his religious elements as incidental, but one cause for such interpretations can be traced to Leibniz himself. He was unquestionably concerned with God and with constructing a theodicy (i.e., a justification for God's tolerance of evil), but his concern was so dominated by rationality that the truly spiritual elements may have been smothered. It is typical of Leibniz that his youthful plan for a Christian apologia entitled *Demonstrationes Catholicae* (Catholic demonstrations) sought church reunion and conversion of the world to Christianity through the primary means of logical demonstration.[17]

We know very little about Leibniz' conventional spiritual practices. Biographical accounts tell us that by the end of his life, Leibniz' infrequent church attendance and rejection of communion fostered the general view that he was an unbeliever. Such a view conflicts with what we know of him and yet it may tell us something about his lack of less intellectually oriented practices. God was essential for Leibniz because he was the guarantor of truth, but spiritual cultivation was in Leibniz' view synonymous with intellectual cultivation. In the most highly cultivated of religious people we find a dissolution of what less advanced practitioners perceive as barriers between the intellect and spirit. We must try to determine whether Leibniz reflects such a union that may have been misread by later interpreters, or whether Leibniz himself read into the essence of religion something overly intellectual.

Some recognize that among the various types of mystical experience there exists an experience associated with our analytic powers.[18] In this instance, a chain of rational thoughts culminates in a "contemplative insight." There is reason to believe that Leibniz did experience such contemplative insights, particularly since his work was directed more toward perceiving similarities than differences and more toward unity than division. The unifying impulse, of itself, seems to reflect a religious temperament.

It might be just such a contemplative insight that is described by

R. W. Meyer in reference to Leibniz' early life. At that time, Leibniz is said to have had an illumination that strengthened his faith by making him capable of a new experience of God and a realization that the world is created by the act of the spirit. This insight was first formulated in *Hypothesis physica nova* (New physical hypothesis), written when Leibniz was 25 years of age, and it became a main theme of all his later philosophical writing. Leibniz compares his insight to something that Platonists undoubtedly experienced, but unlike Platonists and the mystics of Henry More's type who saw the act of the spirit as intuitive and suddenly creative, Leibniz regarded it as a reflective experience. In Meyer's view, Leibniz' mathematics enabled him to replace the identity of a mystical and intuitive nature with a new notion of identity in which systems of relations become representative of one another.[19] It was this notion of correspondence that culminated in the conception of the monads.

It is possible to see in the development of the Protestant ethos of activity a link between the change from a practical, discipline-oriented Christianity to a more occasional Christianity. Instead of daily life in the service of religion, there emerged an increasing tendency toward daily life in the service of secular aims or, perhaps more accurately, daily life in the service of itself. Leibniz seems to have participated in one strand of that developing secular ethos. For Leibniz, God's function was seen not so much in terms of salvation or spiritual advancement as in terms of truth. While salvation and spiritual progress both involve truth, in these perspectives truth represents only one of several equally important concerns. But for Leibniz the pursuit and determination of truth constituted an activity worthy in itself, much as the Protestant work ethic came eventually to value daily activity and secular success for their own sakes.

This high valuation of knowledge and truth can be linked with a highly rationalized image of God in which the objective nature of truth is guaranteed by a God constantly thinking these truths. Leibniz' adoption of the theological concept of truth (i.e., the notion of truth as divine thought) placed him within a tradition in Western thought going back to the Platonic doctrine of ideas. The precision of God's thought is equivalent to calculation. To the extent that we can cultivate precision in our own disciplines and move toward calculation, we not only approach God but in fact become at one with God. We can never equal God's capacity to deal with the infinite analysis of contingent truths, but we can develop our abilities in certain areas and in those limited areas we will "calculate" in the same manner as God.

Leibniz' separation of the realms of physics from metaphysics, or of extension and organic bodies from forms and souls, is well summarized in his *Animadversiones in partem generalem principiorum Cartesianorum* (Critical remarks concerning the general part of Descartes' principles) no. 64.[20] The separation is the product of a brilliant insight and diverts the increasing pressure of secular questions on the body of Christian theology. With Leibniz' division, it simply makes no sense to try and answer questions of the dynamics of organic bodies within the realm of souls, for the latter is an area of metaphysics and therefore operates by laws of reason whereas the physical realm functions by laws of necessity. But in a way Leibniz' insights were too intellectually brilliant and proved too restrictive of the realm of souls and spirits. In effect it isolated this realm while advancing the investigation of the realm of extension. The advancement of the natural sciences has been almost entirely within this area, while interest in the realm of the souls has ebbed because of the seeming lack of practical relevance such an area might offer. The path of religion was to be increasingly otherworldly.

Leibniz' admiration for the Jesuit order was instrumental in leading him to formulate plans for new approaches to truth, which for him were synonymous with serving the greater glory of God. In 1678, Leibniz proposed the establishment of an order of charity, a Societas Theophilorum (Society for the learning of God) to engage in areas of study that the Jesuits had neglected, even while living in close fraternity with the Jesuits.[21] In its avoidance of scholastic elements and emphasis upon studying the mysteries of nature, free cures for the ill, education of youth, and particularly in the area of *Theologia mystica,* Leibniz' proposal seems really to be for a study society rather than a spiritual brotherhood.

This emphasis would appear to have been strengthened as Leibniz transferred his later interests from a religious order to the

founding of academies, an interest that fell short of immediate ful-
fillment in Dresden, St. Petersburg, and Vienna but succeeded in
Berlin. The academy he founded there was geared to serve the
needs of a learning whose advancement depended upon an international correspondence among scholars. Both the precise sciences
and Leibniz' intellectual glorification of God involved a discursive
type of knowledge that thrives upon communication, in contrast to
a spiritual discipline more in need of solitude.

The harmony of Leibniz' philosophy was specifically aimed at
countering the chaos of his time. Yet he was ineffectual in con-
tributing to the advancement of religion, and this failure has turned
out to be one of the great ironies of Leibnizian philosophy. Perhaps
he was victimized by forces beyond his control, such as the
secularizing tendencies of knowledge. These may have oriented his
view of religious practice toward the pursuit of more precise
methods of knowing, which glorified God. A second possibility is
that his interest was not so much directed toward religion as toward
the political achievement of social peace, in which he saw religion
as a chief means to an end. But this would involve attributing more
deception to Leibniz' discussion of theological principles in his
irenic negotiations than seems justified. Perhaps his legal disposition and training strengthened his inherent tendencies toward viewing the world in terms of law.

Another possibility for explaining Leibniz' failure to advance the
religious cause is that his comprehension of religious experience
was a good deal more shallow than has been thought. The man was
an intellectual giant, but his spiritual sense may have been the weak
counterpart within him. His desire for position and his tendency
toward pettiness, of the sort exhibited in the Leibniz-Newton dispute over the invention of the calculus, are not necessarily reflective
of Russell's concept, dividing a man into public and private sides.[22]
Such a division may attribute too much consciousness on Leibniz'
part and may be too condemning of something that probably
comes closer to mere human weakness. Using a less critical interpretation than Russell's, one might see Leibniz as a man whose
moral and spiritual aptitude simply did not keep pace with his intellectual abilities. Though his intentions seem sufficiently genuine, he
was obviously no religious sage, as the failure of the religious side

of his philosophy amply confirms. Yet by most modern Western criteria, he would be judged a genius. The importance of analyzing this judgment in such detail lies in the possibility of what it might tell us about ourselves. While extensive and carefully executed studies may reflect our expertise in evaluating the intellectual achievements of a man, our inability and perhaps our reluctance to judge his spiritual achievements may reflect our own weaknesses as well as his.

## Sin as Intellectual Deprivation

In his religious treatise, the *Theodicy* no. 20, Leibniz maintains that evil did not originate in the way the ancients said, namely, through matter uncreated and independent of God. Rather, evil originated from an ideal conception of man in which sin exists as an original imperfection prior to any act of sinning. (Since sin exists as a deprivation, it has no efficient cause, although its ideal cause is embodied in the previous.) Leibniz' conception of sin is not radically new, but he does give a unique focus to comprehension of the nature of sin through analysis. In the process, what suffers is the understanding of sin that comes through experiencing both sin and its converse, goodness. Though Leibniz clearly did not spend all his time isolated in a remote study, he seems to have carried with him everywhere a spiritual outlook weakly informed by practical experience and to have seen the world through consistently analytic eyes.

Leibniz extends this conception of sin as deprivation to cover malice, error, and ignorance, mental aberrations such as one may experience in intellectualizing. For instance, the perception from a distance of a square tower as round involves a privation of the truth (*Theodicy* no. 32), for it remains actually a square tower. We may be able to correct this privation through reflection. In effect, Leibniz expands the concept of sin as deprivation to include intellectualization and then proceeds to emphasize the intellectualization. If Leibniz' intention was consistently practical and oriented toward resolving the cultural and spiritual anxiety of his age, then his achievements in mathematics, logic, and metaphysics—however great in their own right—failed to resolve that anxiety. It is true that certain of his discoveries did have a practical application—for instance, his mathematics and logic.[23] But rather than glorifying God, their application made it easier for men to forget about God.

## Discursive versus Spiritual Languages

Leibniz spent a considerable amount of time dealing with the particularly Christian dilemmas of God and whether he exists, to what extent his will is arbitrary or dictated by the nature of necessity, his relationship to truth, and so forth. But I would suggest that such problems contribute very little to religious practice. On the contrary, posing such questions reflects a wrongheaded approach in which one will inevitably end up uncertain and in contradiction with spiritual truths. Must we know whether God acts arbitrarily or through necessity? Must we know whether God even exists in order to pursue a path of spiritual cultivation? Such questions only arise when one loses the commitment of the spirit and begins to pursue isolated questions of the mind.

Reliance solely upon discursive methods of knowledge cannot produce a certainty upon which one can base a religious practice and faith. The discursive method, characterized by a logically ordered progression from premises to conclusions, carries an inherent thrust toward knowledge of an ever more refined and intricate sort. This method may be used in conjunction with religious practice to further the ends of both, but as an end in itself it subverts the formation of a basic commitment to spiritual practice. It does not foster such fundamentals of spiritual cultivation as tranquillity, detachment, joyous acceptance of the moment, obedience, action, compassion, and diminishment of the self. Frequently, it tends to foster the reverse of these things.

Leibniz did not agree to this separation of the discursive from the spiritual methods of knowing. But while he maintained that they are one, the influence of his philosophy has been to advance the discursive at the expense of the spiritual. Do I misinterpret Leibniz? We must concede that the unifying element is present and operative in his philosophy, but is this presence sufficient to constitute a genuine appreciation of the religious path? Or could the Pythagorean components in Leibnizian philosophy offer an escape from this sort of criticism?

The Pythagorean impulse is at bottom a religious one because it seeks through mathematics to reconcile external harmonies with internal ones. Leibniz' Pythagorean affinities appear in an argument (*Theodicy* no. 181) that is fundamental to the task of his theodicy—that is, to show that God's acts and therefore God's justice are not merely dispensed by arbitrary action on God's part but by a necessity built into the nature of things. Virtues are chosen to be realized by God precisely because of the possibility of perfection or the prevention of imperfection inherent in the nature of these elements. This means that their virtuous natures are just as incapable of being arbitrary as the rules of musical proportion and harmony may be arbitrary prior to being actualized in a musical performance. Just as proportion and harmony are part of the ideal state of music prior to its actualization, so too is the furtherance of perfection intrinsic in the ideal state of a particular virtue prior to its actualization by God. Furthermore, Leibniz holds that the virtues of rational creatures are similarly inherent in the ideal state of such creatures prior to actualization.

From the preceding discussion, we can conclude that just as with rules of musical harmony and proportion, virtues are arbitrary for neither God nor man. The rightness of such elements resides in their nature and fosters harmony between the inner and outer realms of experience by removing any relativity associated with choice. Choice becomes not a matter of choosing from among a variety of elements but simply a matter of acting or not acting upon a particular element, depending on the nature of the particular virtue. By understanding the nature of something—and Leibniz clearly emphasized this stage of the process—one reduces the number of choices to these two possibilities and thereby reduces the opportunities for dissension and disharmony.

In this light, knowing oneself becomes a religious precept with a very specific meaning. In the process of knowing oneself, one comes to understand the necessity of one's own nature and thereby directs oneself to the particular path needed to satisfy this necessity. To this extent, at least, Leibniz did understand something of the process of spiritual practice, and to this extent criticism must be tempered.

### Leibniz' Option for a God of Knowledge

When in *Theodicy* no. 78 Leibniz explains why God created the world, hubris is quietly passing in the guise of humility. Leibniz says that God created the world "solely to manifest and communicate his perfections in the way that was most efficacious, and most worthy of his greatness, his wisdom and his goodness." But to know God's motive for creating the world is not essential to spiritual practice. What is more important to understand is *how* to make one's path. Instead of beginning with the humble self, Leibniz attempts to imitate the thought of God—admittedly in a less extensive manner than God—and to understand what God did and why he did it. One wonders to what extent the interest in God and his reality was based upon a human projection, that is, God as the perfect man, the man who excels in all ways in which man falls short. From such a perspective, the motive of supreme wisdom that Leibniz attributes to God is full of hubris and gets around to compassion in a very abstract and indirect manner.

The fundamental characteristic of Leibniz' God is not supreme compassion that waits on the struggle until all men have been saved. Nor is it the supreme power of a God that, as the Newtonians argued, miraculously intervenes to make adjustments in the world. Rather, Leibniz' God is fundamentally characterized by supreme wisdom. God's compassion becomes inseparably mixed with his wisdom when he chooses, from among infinite possibilities, the best possible world to actualize. This essentially intellectual choice yields a world with the greatest possible amount of goodness. The divine attribute of power is similarly overshadowed by that of wisdom in that God's choice is limited to the given possibilities. His power consists of choosing to actualize one of these worlds, but it does not extend to creating an even better, much less a perfect, world. Furthermore, since God foresees all possibilities and chooses once and for all, Leibniz argues that God does not intervene in the world's consequent unfolding.

When Leibniz discusses how God chooses the best possible sequence of events for this world only after having compared it with all other possible sequences, and states that certain men continue to live in sin and damnation (*Theodicy* no. 84), he relieves God of the responsibility for saving all men by emphasizing the necessity of the reality to which even God is bound. An essential difference between us as humans and God is that God understands this necessity, whereas men must remain deluded enough to believe that a truly good God would not rest until all men were saved. Leibniz reemphasizes the dominance of God's intellect in the *Theodicy* no. 147 when he describes God's bestowal of intelligence upon man as the bestowal of "an image of Divinity." Men play out their intellectual essence of Divinity as little gods in their microcosmic world. There is no mention of compassion.

In the *Monadology* no. 83, Leibniz distinguishes between "ordinary souls" and "spirits." The latter are animals who attain the rank of human nature in terms of the respective qualities of their reflecting power. While ordinary souls are living mirrors of the universe, spirits go beyond this to mirror God and thereby become capable of imitating some aspects of God and acting as minor deities. What is apparent here is Leibniz' tendency to view things in terms of gradations; in this instance we approach the top of the monadic hierarchy to God. The gradations seem to lack any gap and continue into the infinite. It is essentially a ladder of knowledge, open and accessible to the climber. It may be here that one can pinpoint the hubris that pervades Leibniz' system and eats away at his religious efforts. The notion of a progressive approach to God is not unusual in religions. But such an approach normally contains an intense spiritual and moral cultivation. Yet Leibniz fails to supply this, or at least his system has failed to provide it for later men.

In the Leibnizian heritage, God becomes completely defined in terms of the totality of his knowledge. God's omnipotence is a function of his intellect; the power of love is neither recognized nor cultivated. But the most vitiating force of all is the human pride that lends itself to deification. Suppose that man can imitate God by knowing as God knows but on a less comprehensive scale. In reference to this supposition, Galileo spells out what Leibniz implies—namely, that men may know less comprehensively than God, but in the areas they do know, for example, in mathematics, men know *as well as* God.[24]

It is interesting to note that contemporary China indicts much of the intellectual inquiry of the West as the product of the self-serving interests of a particular class. Whether one agrees with this sort of Marxist analysis or not, one cannot ignore the direction the Chinese have set for themselves: cultural and moral life is founded on the fundamental premise of the intellectuals serving and learning from the masses.[25] Clearly, times have changed in China. Yet the Chinese remain as convinced now as they were before that the moral dimension of truth is clear and vital. Are we really more aware of this dimension than was Leibniz?

# 7
# Spiritual and Moral Cultivation as a Basis for Accord

## The Jesuit Approach in China

What were the motives of the Jesuit effort in China? In trying to disentangle the reality from the heated propositions made over centuries of debate about Jesuitical methods, one cannot elude the probability that the Jesuits were strongly motivated by a proselytizing and chauvinistic spirit. But this spirit is more present in some Jesuits than in others. Longóbardi and Sainte-Marie seem to have been far more touched by it than was Ricci. Yet Ricci and Bouvet were not without their biases. Longobardi made a blanket criticism of Chinese culture, while Ricci was very apologetic of the Confucianists but unfairly harsh toward the Buddhists and Taoists. Longobardi saw practically nothing in Chinese culture that could facilitate the introduction of Christianity, while Ricci believed that Confucianism could be amalgamated with Christianity. Bouvet concurs with Ricci's position that the ancient Chinese were not atheistic and superstitious, regardless of how much the modern Chinese seemed to fit into these categories. Yet Ricci cultivated contemporary Chinese literati culture, whereas Bouvet showed little interest in the Chinese scholarship of his day.

Bouvet does not seek Ricci's solution of maintaining Confucianism as the social element in a future Christian-Confucian amalgam. Instead he analyzes the ancient culture in terms of Fu Hsi's numerology of the *Book of Changes* diagrams, trusting them to explain the bases of all sciences. In this regard, Bouvet sees the ancient heritage not simply as Chinese but as a universal heritage whose ideas are reflected as much in Pythagoreanism-Platonism as in the ancient doctrine of Fu Hsi, long since lost in China. To the extent that Bouvet sees this heritage as universal rather than the property of any one race or nation, his outlook is ecumenical. But since few contemporary Chinese shared either this interpretation of their past or the specific spiritual practices of Christianity embodying this interpretation, the foundations for a lasting accord between Europe and China were not established.

There also seems to have been another motive present in Bouvet's thinking. Elsewhere,[1] I have suggested that what motivated seventeenth- and eighteenth-century Europeans to ask whether Chinese civilization contained indigenous equivalents of Christianity bears a striking similarity to the motivations of post–World War II Western sinologists who asked whether Chinese civilization contained an indigenous form of science. In both cases, there is an implication that the inquiry was brought on, at least in part, by a growing hesitation and doubt concerning fundamental beliefs and practices of Western culture. By finding equivalences abroad, one adds much needed confirmation to wavering convictions toward things at home. In itself, such a philosophical and spiritual quest might appear superficially to be concerned merely with manifestations of confidence. But these projections onto the rest of the world of what is happening at home can also express deep doubts couched in face-saving terms.

But even granting the motivation of hesitation and doubt in one's own beliefs, what then is the method and content used in resolving this doubt? In Bouvet's case, one encounters a basic concern with the fundamentals of religion that transcends division by sects. Compared side by side, the strong barriers existing in Longobardi's mind between the saved and the heathen give way to the milder and more expedient lines in Ricci's mind, which in turn give way to the surprisingly open and creative space of Bouvet's outlook. Within this open area are the fundamentals of a *Book of Changes* numerology that is neither Chinese nor restricted to Pythagoreanism-Platonism but contains ancient and universal knowledge and religious truths of timeless relevance.

The great Rites Controversy between Europe and China in the

years 1610 to 1742 was brought on by a number of reasons, some of them quite political. But these reasons generally manifested the basic complaint against the Jesuit missionaries for their tendency to compromise Christian doctrine and ritual with beliefs and practices of the indigenous culture. One of the less subtle explanations of this compromising tendency was to attribute it to a power-thirsty drive on the Jesuits' part that led these missionaries to emphasize skills that could be exploited politically.

But there are other, more reasonable, approaches. For instance, there is a view of missionary practice which holds that Christianity cannot be assimilated by a non-Western country unless it is blended with practices and doctrines containing the cultural or national essence of that land. This was a characteristically Jesuit view. No matter how difficult such an essence might be to define, it was regarded as real. The assumption was that it included far more than the abstractions of scholars and involved concrete phenomena that could be ascertained only through long and direct experience with the native culture. The spirit of this approach remains part of the perspective of a number of contemporary Jesuits.[2]

## Common Ground between Christianity and Confucianism
### *The Connection between Morality and Truth*

A similarity between Christianity and Confucianism is found in the connection between morality and truth. Confucianism repeatedly blends morality and truths of nature in what a superficial reader of the texts might call a confusion of the two. But confusion hardly applies to the deeper understanding that Confucian philosophy has traditionally borne in relation to its Western counterparts. In Confucianism, morality is melded with the truth of the natural world and blended with the seeking of truth in an individual man. Traditionally, only a moral man was fully entitled to the description of "learned." Our tendency to scoff at this as nothing more than a mouthed ideal misses a connection that the Chinese were quite clear about and still are.

The modern West has seen the rise of technical experts whose expertise is judged quite apart from their qualities as good men; perhaps this is because we have become preoccupied with external knowledge. But when we come to knowledge that involves our inner selves, a dynamic connection emerges between the kind of person we are and what we can know. For an openly immoral Chinese to present himself as an exemplary Confucianist would simply be absurd, although certainly history contains instances of such absurdity. The continuation of this moral thread in contemporary China was apparent in the role of morality and confessions of guilt in the Great Proletarian Cultural Revolution of 1966–1967. The specific content of the Chinese terms has altered, but the insights into the connection between morality and knowledge remain.

Yet the West cannot be completely devoid of insight into this connection if there is any validity to the Christian view that sees truth as the "fruit of faith and charity."[3] By means of faith and charity, one experiences a love that enlightens the intelligence and gives a new understanding different from that produced by discursive reason alone. By means of the practice and experience of the spirit—whether it be Christian contemplation or charity, Confucian "watchfulness while being alone" *(shen-tu)* or Benevolence *(jen)*,[4] Buddhist meditation or compassion—intellectual knowledge is altered in a way that is beyond the reach of the spiritually unpracticed.

## The Flux

A basic insight of the religions of China, and of a great deal of religious experience, is the realization of a flux in which nothing remains unchanged even for a moment. The assimilation of the given moment or the "now" as one of the essentials of religious experience involves a joyous acceptance of this flux. Leibnizian philosophy combats Locke's notions of a passive materialism by asserting the continuous activity of both the soul and the body.[5] The body is never without motion, nor is the soul ever without perceptions. The perpetual activity of the body relates to Leibniz' physics and his notion of force *(vis viva),* while his assertion of the perpetual activity of the soul in terms of continuous perception bears affinity to modern psychological notions of the unconscious. All perceivable material is retained in the mind, though some perceptions are too feeble to be clearly distinguished from the continual flow of other perceptions.

Leibniz wishes his denial of the passivity of the soul to have no bearing upon the doctrine of the immortality of the soul, yet he concedes that "if the soul is passive, it is also without life, and it seems that it can be immortal only by grace and by miracle."[6] But while Leibniz disapproves of using the means of grace or a miracle to prove the immortality of the soul, he believes that the soul is active and has life and immortality. His refusal to mix theological reasons with philosophical reasons is based on solid logical grounds, but logical elements in philosophy and theology are insufficient to take us into the integrating core of religious experience, and this insufficiency was what weakened his attempt at accord.

In the *New Essays,*[7] Leibniz refers to the disagreement between Locke and the bishop of Worcester, who thought Locke's doctrine of ideas threatened Christianity—though Leibniz doubts that it did. Locke held that the ends of religion and morals were served by proving the soul to be immortal, although not necessarily immaterial, while the bishop thought the soul could best be proved immortal by means of its immaterial nature. Leibniz then adds his comments to the debate. What concerns us are not the details of the debate but the seriousness with which Leibniz and others entertain the threat posed to Christianity by intellectual understanding. In contrast, the beliefs of a Confucianist tended to be confirmed more by their practical than their theoretical efficacy. Admittedly, such standards involve internal criteria more than external debate, yet it would be deceiving oneself to identify interior criteria with mere subjectivity. The practice of a belief does not resolve itself into an objective-subjective dichotomy.

## The Internal Discipline

Though contemplative and meditative techniques have rarely played a dominant role in Christianity, they have always been present somewhere in the background and have occasionally been highly significant in the lives of individual Christians. In offering an ecumenical stepping-stone, William Johnston speaks of how the Zen meditative technique can be used by Christians who are potential contemplatives. They must not smother the tiny flame of love with discursive thinking, but must be "silent, empty and expectant."[8] Such a position is quite removed from the approaches of both Leibniz and Bouvet, and of many of the Jesuit missionaries.

To explain why both the earlier Jesuits and Leibniz could not perceive the forms of spiritual cultivation present in China as a basis for accord, one might return to the notion of seventeenth- and eighteenth-century Europe, which was doubting many of its own beliefs and seeking to reverse this debilitating tendency by finding equivalences for these beliefs in China. It is not the turning eastward that is crucial but the specific manner in which the turn is made. Instead of turning within for confirmation from some inner light, these Westerners sought confirmation in China, but the nature of the search largely predetermined what they found.

The motivation involved tended to supply its own interpretations, emphasizing the external culture of China and failing to penetrate the deeper dimensions, such as spiritual and moral cultivation. The hexagrams of the *Book of Changes* contain a technique of cultivation that was practiced by many Confucianists, but Bouvet and Leibniz dismissed this dimension of the *Changes* as superstitious divination. In emphasizing external manipulation of the diagrams to achieve their binary progression, Bouvet and Leibniz neglected the interior aspect of the Pythagorean impulse. More faithful to this interior aspect, the Confucian gentleman used divination to cultivate harmony with his circumstances and did not seek external knowledge. In modern times the West has once more looked eastward, but now attention is focused on elements of spiritual cultivation because something in the Western perspective has changed.

### Religion as Spiritual Cultivation

There is a certain confusion concerning the relationship of the immortality of the soul to religion. This confusion arises, in part, from an unfamiliarity with the beginnings of the religious impulse in circumstances where fundamentals are often unexciting. One of these fundamentals involves a daily discipline that for most devotees contains far more routine and dull practice than anything associated with the stimulation of mystical experience. Of course, there are exceptions: there are those who are drawn to religion through initial experience with the intensity and insight that is termed fully mystical. But for the most part, the early years of religious discipline are far more routine.

Too often it is thought that the aim of religious life is the mystical experience. The novice meditator looks for enlightenment in a sudden rush of light and weightlessness during a meditative session; the supplicant looks for a "sign" as an answer to his prayers; and both become disillusioned if there is none. But all this misses the point because the true aim of these practices is what they may cultivate within us. One of the fruits of such cultivation is a tranquillity based on acceptance of the moment—the *now*. This acceptance is accompanied by an absence of desire to move either forward in search of the future or backward in search of recreating the past. It is not passivity bred of fear for the future; nor is it the product of an intellectual insight. Rather, it is the result of a daily effort to apply that insight toward the stilling of excessive ego. And this tranquillity is not attained until its positive value is experienced and begins to counteract the negative effect of withdrawal from excessive gratification of ego.

The acceptance of the now is the acceptance of each moment in the realization that the moment is our only reality. The future represents a mere anticipation and the past is a recollection, whether experienced directly or through another, as in transmitted tradition or history. The acceptance of the moment is marked by a mild form of joy. This quiet happiness differs as much from the overpowering feeling of ecstasy as it does from the liberation attained through resignation.

Cultivation of the spirit through specific practices alters the content of discursive truth and enables one to attain a new and higher type of knowledge we may call wisdom. The practices are applied through a discipline that mortifies the self—that is, controls inordinate desires and passions through their denial and through the expansion and deepening of interior experience. The latter area is that of the "inner light," which when properly tapped through a full sense of harmony can be a source of strength and sustenance. The specific content of the discipline may vary according to the needs of the person, but the practices are frequently very physical as well as intellectual and meditative. We may meet with differences when we begin to discuss specific religious contexts for cultivating the spirit through practice, and their comprehension may require direct experience rather than mere explanation. We can see, however, that notions such as wisdom, power, and compassion are common to religious elements as seemingly diverse as Christian Godliness or the Buddha nature and are also present in Confucianism.

## Spiritual Cultivation in Confucianism

In his *Discourse* 46,[9] Leibniz responds to Longobardi's indictment of both ancient and modern Chinese as atheistic. Leibniz interprets Confucius as saying that the object of proper worship of the Spirit of Heaven, the seasons, the mountains, and other inanimate things should be the Sovereign Spirit, *shang-ti, t'ai-chi,* and *li.* Yet he suggests that Confucius chose not to explain the spirits of natural things because he thought that the people were incapable of comprehending such an explanation. In the *Discourse* 50,[10] Leibniz states that though he would have preferred to have Confucius clarify his religious views, the absence of investigation into the nature and operations of spirits does not necessarily make one an atheist, for certainly such a corresponding lack of interest can be found among Christians. Leibniz contends that so long as one does not dispute the existence of the spirits and so long as one honors spirits and practices virtue for the pleasure of the spirits, one can surely escape the label of atheist.

Leibniz appears not to realize that most of the time Confucius was speaking not to gatherings of people but to his disciples, who supposedly would be able to grasp things better than those of commoner mind. The notion of spiritual cultivation might offer a meaningful explanation of Confucius' reluctance to discuss spirits and life after death. Given such a notion, one could begin with one's self and one's own life rather than by contemplating spirits and death, things far removed from more basic concerns. Spiritual cultivation can begin with these immediate concerns, but Leibniz gives little evidence of an awareness or appreciation of a spiritual discipline, at least of the type present in Confucian tradition.

The joyous acceptance of the now is contained in Confucianism. For example, the well-known Chinese historical consciousness need not be explained as a yearning to return to the golden age of the legendary emperors Yao and Shun. It can be seen as a heightening awareness of continuity with the past and as a basis for accepting one's limited moment in the present. This joyous acceptance of the now would seem to occur in the classic most basic to the Confucian tradition, the *Analects,* particularly in section 6:9 where Confucius praises the ability of his disciple Hui (Yen-tzu) to remain joyous and unperturbed by a lack of food, drink, and comfortable surroundings. A similar ability to accept waiting is attributed to both Hui and Confucius himself in *Analects* 7:10. Such a joyous acceptance implies a highly cultivated inner life acting as a source of joy in the midst of poor external conditions. The religious discipline aims at bringing on this unperturbed state by cultivating an inner source of sustenance, thereby reducing the need for dependence on one's surroundings. Mencius seems to convey a similar outlook in the *Mencius* 4b:29, where he compares Hui's virtuous behavior to that of the legendary figures Yü and Chi. On the surface, the very active lives of Yü and Chi seem much more positively oriented than the acceptant waiting of Hui, but in Confucian doctrine both types of behavior are appropriate at their respective times. Mencius says that Yü and Chi are acting in an age of peace, whereas Hui and Confucius lived in times of chaos. Confucius devotes considerable attention to the problems of living in times when a gentleman *(chün-tzu)* must know how to wait not with anxious eyes but with a joyous acceptance of the moment.

The joyous acceptance of the moment can act as both result and means. It is the result of detachment from a desire for things that are not to be had. Yet it also acts as a means to happiness which, in turn, reinforces the detachment. A similar phenomenon occurs in *Analects* 7:15, where Confucius is quoted as saying: "He who seeks only coarse food to eat, water to drink and bent arm for pillow, will without looking for it find happiness to boot. Any thought of accepting wealth and rank by means that I know to be wrong is as remote from me as the clouds that float above."[11] Joyous acceptance of the moment and detachment are manifested in the person as tranquillity. Something similar can be found in *Analects* 7:36, where Confucius contrasts the serenity of the gentleman and the fretfulness of the small man. This tranquillity implies an absence of anxiety and fear (*Analects* 12:4).

In *Analects* 7:3 and 6, Confucius voices what might be taken as a prescription for spiritual cultivation: "Not cultivating virtue, not practicing what has been learned, unable to follow righteousness which has been heard, unable to alter what is not good—these are the things I fear." And: "The master said, Set your heart upon the Way, support yourself by its power, lean upon Goodness, seek distraction in the arts."[12] In *Analects* 12:21, the disciple Fan Ch'ih asked Confucius about the best methods for elevating virtue, correcting evils, and distinguishing delusions. For the first, Confucius advises primary attention to service before gain; for the second, rectification by turning within rather than by rectifying others; for the third, the advice is less clear but involves filial piety.

The means of achieving Confucian spiritual cultivation may vary from simple acts of filial piety to a skilled form of meditation, even though Confucius himself stressed forms of ritual, music, and social behavior. Confucius' lack of office in a time of social chaos provided sanction for later Confucianists to retire from public life in periods of either personal or general political turmoil. Mingled with Taoist influences, this practice gave rise to a strong eremitic tradition. Within this tradition, men such as Wu Yü-pi (K'ang-chai) (1391–1469) are said to have tilled their own land and fed their disciples the crops.[13] Fostered by Buddhist and particularly Ch'an meditation and Taoist breath control, Neo-Confucianism came to include a variety of meditative practices including *ching-tso* (quiet-sitting). This practice, however, is not always strictly synonymous with meditation. Poetry and painting as spiritual techniques were also essential to the related *wen-jen* (literati) tradition.

Later Confucianists emphasized these types of spiritual cultivation in an attempt to create a discipline aimed at the development of not only a moral man but also one whose spirit was in harmony with his position in society and the cosmos. Certainly this was an ideal, and its path was strewn with failures. Yet it was a practical ideal and one within reach of the practitioner. Unfortunately, Leibniz failed to perceive it as a basis for accord. The failure seems to have been a product both of his philosophy and the errors of his interpreters, on whom he was dependent for so much of his knowledge of China. Actually, the only interpreter who showed an appreciation for the Confucian spiritual discipline was Ricci.

## Conclusion: Accord for the Present

In the process of seeking an accord between China and the West, a first step is an attempt to reach some understanding of Chinese culture and society. Out of this understanding we can arrive at similarities between Chinese and Western cultures. However, such similarities will not necessarily be equally developed in both cultures. Clearly, even if Leibniz had recognized Chinese spiritual and moral cultivation, he could not have converted the quite different Christian strain of spiritual cultivation into its Chinese equivalent. While accord between two nations or cultures must be founded on some common ground, the ideas and beliefs by which they come to that common ground may differ. Nevertheless, recognition and development of these common points, even if not to the degree of their Chinese counterpart, can enlarge this common ground and enhance the chances for accord. This is why the Jesuits' and Leibniz' failure to recognize and develop Confucian spiritual cultivation weakened their efforts at accord.

On what grounds might an accord be established with China today? Currently, Confucianism and Buddhism are not viable forces on the Chinese mainland. Whether they will have a future role there remains to be seen. However, although the particular forms in which spiritual and moral cultivation were previously manifested are gone, this does not mean that the cultivation itself has disappeared. While Confucian and Maoist ideologies may themselves be irreconcilable, the intense cultivation of morality found in contemporary China has much in common with that recommended in Confucianism. As in the Confucian perspective, issues tend to become moral issues. Education, politics, art, economic policy, natural sciences, technology, literature, philosophy, and agriculture all assume varying degrees of moral coloring. This coloring was abundantly evident in the Great Proletarian Cultural Revolution of 1966–1967 and the Anti-Confucius Campaign of 1973–1974.[14]

There is a tendency among both religious and secular groups of America to approach China today from a strictly humanistic point of view in the belief that humanism alone will suffice as a foundation for meaningful accord. I believe this to be based on too narrow a conception of the Chinese. Although they may practice humanitarian principles, they do not derive their deepest beliefs from humanism. These deeper beliefs are rather derived from the Truth and Goodness they perceive in Marxist-Leninist principles, as interpreted by Mao Tse-tung. At least for the present, Marxist-Leninist principles appear unlikely to generate an equivalent intensity in the United States. It seems quite possible, however, that we could arrive at several forms of spiritual and moral cultivation that might be able to unify the sadly separated dimensions of American knowledge and action.[15]

The attempt to find an indigenous foundation for Christianity in China has been unsuccessful, both in Leibniz' time and in its more recent manifestations.[16] The nineteenth- and twentieth-century Christian missionary experience was a step backward from the seventeenth- and eighteenth-century Jesuit approach. The technological superiority of the modern West convinced the nineteenth- and twentieth-century missionaries that it was far more important to bring "superior" Western religious and cultural forms to the Chinese than to attempt to understand China. In order to go forward, we will have to, in our own age, be at least as observant as Ricci, Bouvet, and Leibniz. In spite of their faults and errors, what these men did accomplish was motivated by deep religious and moral beliefs. To advance from where they left off, our beliefs in *something* will have to be at least as deep as the beliefs of these failed seekers of accord.[17]

# Appendix:
## A Contemporary Western Interpretation
## of the Book of Changes

In addition to comparing Bouvet's and Leibniz' interpretation of the *Book of Changes* to that of certain Chinese commentaries, one might use a recent Western interpretation to bring out several key distinctions. Both Bouvet and Leibniz see the sequence found in the diagrams associated with the *Changes* as a double geometrical progression. A geometrical progression builds upon a sequence in which every number stands to the preceding in the same ratio. In the case of the *Changes* diagrams, the ratio is "double" or 2; that is, each number in the sequence is multiplied by 2 in order to attain the next number. From this point of view, the sequence should be 1, 2, 4, 8, 16, 32, 64, and so forth. This sequence does indeed describe the number of permutations and combinations of diagrams in each given *category* of lines; however, the *lines* of the diagrams increase in an arithmetical progression—that is, each number after the first number in the sequence increases by the addition of the same amount, as in the progression 4, 8, 12, 16, 20. In the case of the number of lines in the diagrams, the specific arithmetical progression is 1, 2, 3, 4, 5, 6, and so forth.

The painter Alfred Jensen has arrived at an arithmetical interpretation of the *Changes* diagrams by using concretely experienced number structures that he believes were prevalent in ancient cultures, antedating the abstract numbers used in mathematics since Euclid (fl. circa 300 B.C.). Jensen believes that the ancient Chinese, Egyptian, Greek, and Mayan cultures "reveal in their building principles concrete, numerically-based art forms." (See Jensen's "The Aperspective Structure of a Square," the catalog from an exhibition at Cordier and Ekstrom, New York, 11 March–4 April 1970.)

Jensen derives a numerical system inseparable from the chromatic values of quantity, quality, intensity, and pigment. Making great use of Pythagoras' theorem that in a right triangle the square of the hypotenuse is equal to the sum of the squares of the two shortest sides, Jensen explains this theorem by exploring the significance of Pythagoras' emphasis on the numbers 9, 16, and 25. He does this by using the theme of the square and subdividing three forms of the latter into equal squares totaling 9 ($3^2$), 16 ($4^2$), and 25 ($5^2$), respectively. Instead of interpreting the numerical sequence of the *Changes* diagrams in terms of the abstract number of a binary progression, as do Leibniz and Bouvet, Jensen interprets them by means of squares, each of which is subdivided into chromatic squares of equal area. The numerical sequence is computed by counting outward from the center square into circumferencing square units composed of smaller squares, each of which differs from the preceding and smaller square unit by the addition of a constant of two squares to each side of the ever-larger square unit. Letting two squares equal one numerical element, an arithmetical progression is formed by a side from each of these squares, which may be represented as 1, 2, 3, 4, and so forth.

As Jensen stresses, his work cannot be understood by an analysis that ignores its totality, as represented in his art. Nor am I able to give a full representation of even this incomplete aspect of his work. What is significant for the purpose at hand is, first, the recognition of the fertile potential of the *Changes* diagrams, whose ability to stimulate those with whom it comes into contact has persisted from Chinese antiquity down to the seventeenth and eighteenth centuries (Bouvet and Leibniz) and into the twentieth (Jensen). Moreover, although differing from Bouvet and Leibniz in calling the *Changes* progression arithmetic rather than geometric, and chromatic rather than abstract, Jensen shares with Bouvet and Leibniz the tendency to see the numerical progression of the *Changes* as a supremely simple key to explaining the principles of ancient sciences. Like Bouvet and Leibniz, Jensen sees through Pythagorean eyes when he believes that this *simplicity* is a long-lost prize that could cut through some of the seeming complexity of modern life. Conversely, one should note that Jensen shares a greater belief in the *Changes'* power of divination than did Bouvet and Leibniz. To this end, he has designed a movable divination board, which he believes duplicates models found in ancient China.

9. The source of this and several of the following details on Leibniz' contact with the China mission is Franz Rudolf Merkel, *G. W. von Leibniz und die China-Mission*. Originally a doctoral dissertation at the University of Göttingen, the work was published but remains inaccessible to most readers. It is, however, a primary study in the area of Leibniz' relations with China and is pregnant with information, especially for the student without access to the voluminous unpublished material in the Leibniz archives at Hanover. The study's usefulness is increased by Merkel's practice of including generous quotations in the original Latin, French, or German from the correspondence between Leibniz and those involved in the China mission.

10. Merkel, *Leibniz und die China-Mission,* p. 15.

11. See Paul Cornelius, *Languages in Seventeenth and Early Eighteenth-Century Imaginary Voyages,* p. 69 et passim.

12. See Walter M. Drzewieniecki, "The Knowledge of China in XVII Century Poland as Reflected in the Correspondence between Leibniz and Kochanski," *Polish Review* 12(3)(1967):53-66.

13. Donald F. Lach, "The Chinese Studies of Andreas Müller," *Journal of the American Oriental Society* 60(4)(1940):564-575. In this article, Lach translates the fourteen questions that Leibniz addressed to Müller.

14. See Merkel, *Leibniz und die China-Mission,* p. 17f and especially p. 25. In referring to Leibniz' letter to the landgrave of Hessen-Rheinfels of 9/10 December 1687, Merkel cites Christoph von Rommel's *Leibniz und Landgraf Ernst von Hessen-Rheinfels,* p. 113f. Also see Merkel, *Leibniz und China,* p. 11.

15. The late English sinologist E. R. Hughes thought that *Confucius Sinarum Philosophus* had a direct influence on Leibniz' philosophy, even though he concedes the difficulty of specifying the influence. See E. R. Hughes, *The Great Learning and Mean in Action,* pp. 12-18.

16. Leibniz' letter to Peter the Great of 1716, translated by Philip P. Wiener, in *Leibniz: Selections;* see especially pp. 598-599. The purpose of this letter was to encourage Peter the Great to establish a Russian academy of arts and sciences on the model of the royal societies of France, England, and Prussia, thereby facilitating international exchange in trade and knowledge between nations and particularly between China and the West. By this time experienced as a long-time councilor to princes, Leibniz is sensitive to the practical motive. He stresses that while the Prussian academy costs little to maintain, the potential profits to be reaped from founding such an academy could be great. Furthermore, he states that by aiding knowledge in this way Peter would be serving the Russians and other Slavic peoples in a manner comparable to that in which Fu Hsi served the Chinese, Hermes Trismegistus served the Egyptians, Zoroaster the northern Asians, Arminus the southern Germans, Odin the northern Germans, and Almanzor the Saracens.

17. See Guhrauer, 2:94f. Also see Kuno Fischer, *Gottfried Wilhelm Leibniz: Leben, Werke und Lehre,* p. 195. Fischer also cites the Bodemann-Leibniz correspondence, *Leibniz Briefwechsel* (hereafter abbreviated *Leibnizbriefe*) 341, p. 934, saying that in addition to meeting the Jesuit Grimaldi in Rome in 1689, Leibniz also made the acquaintance of Giovanni Baptista Tolomei, S. J.

18. Leibniz' letter to Bouvet, 13 December 1707, *Leibnizbriefe* 105, pp. 43b-44b.

19. Leibniz expresses these views in letters to Morell of 11 May 1697 cited in Merkel, *Leibniz und die China-Mission,* p. 36.

20. Ricci's synthesis is discussed in chapter 2.

21. See Ignatius of Loyola, *The Spiritual Exercises.* Several of the views of the Society of Jesus described here are taken from Rene Fülop-Miller's *The Jesuits.*

# Notes

*Chapter 1*

1. The most authoritative biography of Leibniz is that of Gottschalk E. Guhrauer, *Gottfried Wilhelm Freiherr von Leibniz: Eine Biographie.* A popularized and condensed English version of this work is available in John W. Mackie's *Life of Godfrey Wilhelm von Leibnitz.*

2. Leibniz, *Disputatio metaphysica de principio individui,* in Carl I. Gerhardt, *Die philosophischen Schriften von G. W. Leibniz* (hereafter cited as *P. S.* ), 4:15–26.

3. Guhrauer, 1:75–76.

4. Leibniz expressed this plan in several forms. The one most often cited is *Consilium Aegyptiacum* in *Sämtliche Schriften und Briefe* 4(2):215f. The belief current in the early 1800s that Napoleon received the idea for his invasion of Egypt from Leibniz' plan appears unfounded. Napoleon did, however, request and receive a copy of *Consilium Aegyptiacum* after his conquest of Hanover in 1803. See Guhrauer, 1:107–112.

5. For details of Spinola's visits, see G. J. Jordan, *The Reunion of the Churches,* p. 46f.

6. The great debate between Leibniz and Newton and their followers over priority of invention of the infinitesimal calculus seems now to be generally resolved in favor of independent invention. Newton's invention apparently preceded that of Leibniz by a short time, but Leibniz' notation has certain advantages over that of Newton. Louis Trenchard More in the biography *Isaac Newton* devotes a full chapter to the controversy and documents some of the vanity and pettiness that occurred on both sides between the years 1699 and 1718. A less modern treatment of the controversy is offered in Guhrauer, 1:284–320.

7. MS 37, 1810, no. 1, pp. 1a–16b, Niedersächsische Landesbibliothek, Hanover, Germany. An edited version of this manuscript has been published in Christian Kortholt (ed.), *Leibnitii epistolae ad diversos . . .* 2:413–494 and in Ludovici Dutens (ed.), *Leibnitii opera omnia* 4:169–210. More detailed bibliographical information on the *Discourse on the Natural Theology of the Chinese* is given in chapter 4.

8. Guhrauer, 2:328–331.

22. The extensive correspondence of 1686–1690 between Leibniz and Antoine Arnauld, conducted through the intermediary of Ernst, landgrave of Hessen-Rheinfels, is published in Gerhardt, *P. S.* 2:1–138. The correspondence has been translated by H. T. Mason as *The Leibniz-Arnauld Correspondence* (Manchester, 1967). The correspondence was initiated by the landgrave, a converted Catholic who sought the aid of the aged but learned Arnauld in the attempt to convert this young, promising Lutheran.

23. Charles le Gobien, S. J. *Histoire de l'Edit de l'Empereur de la Chine en faveur de la Religion Chrestienne*, pp. 127–137.

24. See Arnold H. Rowbotham, *Missionary and Mandarin in China*, chap. 10, for a fairly extensive discussion of this stage of the controversy.

25. Leibniz expresses concern over the danger of harsh papal rulings to the China mission in several letters to Des Bosses, who was in close touch with developments in Rome. These letters include those of 24 April 1710, 2 July 1710, 5 February 1712, 26 May 1712, and 24 December 1715 and appear in Gerhardt, *P. S.* 2:392f.

26. Hughes, pp. 12–18.

27. I am certainly not the first to make the point about the onset of Leibniz' mature philosophy occurring before his more substantive contacts with Chinese culture. Nor am I the first to characterize the relationship of Chinese ideas to Leibniz' philosophy as corroborative rather than formative. For example, both these ideas are briefly referred to in a footnote by Joseph Needham, *Science and Civilization in China* 2:504, even though Needham himself leans toward a formative hypothesis. Still, I believe the reasons that led me to similar conclusions were largely of my own derivation. These conclusions were confirmed by unpublished letters in the Leibniz archives at Hanover, several of which are discussed in following chapters.

28. See Leroy Loemker, "A Note on the Origin and Problem of Leibniz's Discourse of 1686," *Journal of the History of Ideas* 8(1947):449–466.

29. Needham, 2:496–505.

30. *Discourse* MS, p. 7b.

31. *Discourse* MS, pp. 6a and 8a.


## Chapter 2

1. The praise of Ricci as a student in science and mathematics comes from Louis J. Gallagher, S. J., in the preface to his translation of Ricci's journals under the title *China in the Sixteenth Century: The Journals of Matthew Ricci, 1583–1610*. The comments on Ricci's teacher Clavius and his relationship to Galileo are taken in part from Giorgio de Santillana's *The Crime of Galileo*, p. 23f., and Ludovico Geymonet's biographical study, *Galileo Galilei*, pp. 10 and 45.

2. The two-page discussion in Latin of bk. 1, chap. 8 of Trigault's edition of Matteo Ricci's journals may or may not be authored by Leibniz. The main body of the writing is not in Leibniz' hand, but there are marginal notations in a cramped calligraphy similar to that of Leibniz. Whether this is one of the instances among Leibniz' papers where he has added later notations to a secretary's copy of his original draft, I am unable to say. See Leibniz MS 37, 1810, no. 4, pp. 1a–1b, Niedersächsische Landesbibliothek, Hanover. According to the Leibniz Gesellschaft staff, a copy of *De Christiana expeditione apud Sinas* may be found in the Landesbibliothek at Hanover, but it was not part of Leibniz' personal library

3. Ricci, *Journals*, pp. 88–89.

4. Ricci distinguishes between *t'ai-chi* and God in his treatise *T'ien-chu shih-i* (The true meaning of God), chap. 1, pp. 19a-19b. (See bibliographical information on *T'ien-chu shih-i* in note 9 below.) Joseph de Prémare's identification of the Neo-Confucian *wu-chi* with God is presented in his *Lettre sur le monotheisme des chinois*. For a discussion of Prémare's position, see David E. Mungello, "The Reconciliation of Neo-Confucianism with Christianity in the Writings of Joseph de Prémare, S. J.," *Philosophy East and West* 26(4)(1976):389-410.

5. Defining the Jesuit vocation as *contemplativus in actione* (contemplation in action) stems from a tradition that originated with the sixteenth-century *Spiritual Exercises* of St. Ignatius, founder of the Society of Jesus. This emphasis remains in the order today, as testified to by the statement on the Jesuit vocation made on 13 June 1969 by James L. Connor, S. J., of the Maryland Province.

6. Ricci, *Journals,* pp. 233 and 402.

7. Ricci, *Journals,* p. 450. The *Journals* do not specify the title of the work on moral maxims, but the reference is probably to the *Erh-shih-wu yen* (Twenty-five maxims). See Pfister, *Notices biographiques et bibliographiques sur les Jésuites de l'ancienne mission de Chine, 1552-1773.* Variétés sinologiques, nos. 59-60, vol. 2, pp. 35-36.

8. Ricci, *Journals,* pp. 352 and 434. Hsü Kuang-ch'i collaborated with Ricci to translate works on Western hydraulics, astronomy, geography, mathematics, and geometry. One of the most significant of these was a partial translation of Euclid's *Elements,* published as *Chi-ho yüan-pen* (Principles of geometry). In regard to the Buddhist commitment of Feng Mu-kang, see Ricci, *Journals,* p. 357. (Michael) Yang T'ing-yün is described as a formerly devout Buddhist in Arthur Hummel, ed., *Eminent Chinese of the Ch'ing Period (1644-1912),* pp. 453 and 894.

9. Li Ma-t'ou [Matteo Ricci], *T'ien-chu shih-i* (The true meaning of God). This was one of the most influential works written in Chinese by a missionary. The process of writing the book seems to have been a protracted one with Ricci receiving considerable assistance in content and proper literary phrasing from Hsü Kuang-ch'i and other Christian literati. This extended process of revision is reflected in the lack of accord on dates of publication given by scholars. The work was composed apparently in the 1590s and was published in several editions between 1595 and 1607. It was translated into Japanese in 1604 and later into Korean and possibly other languages. A French translation entitled *"Entretiens d'un Lettré chinois et d'un Docteur européen sur la vraie idée de Dieu"* appeared in *Lettres édifiants et curieuses écrites des Missions étrangères* 14:66-248. In the particular edition before me, there are prefaces written by Feng Ying-ching (dated 1601) and Li Chih-tsao (date indiscernible) and Li Ma-t'ou (dated 1604). Hsü Kuang-ch'i is also said to have written a preface, but it does not appear in this edition. An early edition of the work has the variant title of *T'ien-hsüeh shih-i* (The true meaning of God's teaching).

10. Ricci, *Journals,* p. 448.

11. *T'ien-chu shih-i,* chap. 1, p. 17a.

12. Ricci's comments on transmigration appear in his *Journals,* p. 448. Leibniz' rejection of transmigration is found in his *New Essays Concerning Human Understanding,* pp. 20-21. The latter work represents a translation of the fifth volume of Gerhardt's edition of Leibniz, *Philosophischen Schriften.*

13. See, in particular, Ricci, *Journals,* pp. 337-343 and 399-405. In their reverence toward Amitabha (the Buddha of the Western Paradise) and in their frequent invocation of his name, the followers of Amitabha Buddha may have appeared theistic, but closer examination yields conflicting interpretations. The Ch'an Buddhists were originally iconoclasts who destroyed Buddhist images and

minimized theistic treatment of the Buddha. There was a partial blending of the Ch'an and Amitabha sects late in the Ming dynasty. Certainly, one could find instances where doctrine was oversimplified, but to the extent that Ricci was exposed to several of the Buddhist religious leaders, he had opportunities to develop a more discriminating appreciation of Buddhism. It appears that he rejected the opportunities.

14. Paul Demiéville believes that Christianity might have fared better in China if Ricci had sought a reconciliation with Buddhism instead of with Confucianism. Demiéville quotes several Confucianists who perceived a forced logic in Ricci's attempt to align Christianity with Confucianism. In the view of these Confucianists, Christianity had a more natural affinity with Buddhism. Though Demiéville does not note it, the objectivity of these Confucianists' judgment must be balanced against the likely presence of Chinese cultural chauvinism and even xenophobia, phenomena which Ricci knew were more prevalent in some Confucian literati than in others. See Paul Demiéville, "The First Philosphic Contacts between Europe and China," *Diogenes* (Montreal) 58(1967):91–93.

15. Otto Franke, "Li Tschi und Matteo Ricci," *Abhandlungen der Preussischen Akademie der Wissenschaften* (1938)5.

16. Leibniz draws this description of Longobardi from a book by a J. Dezio. See Leibniz' letter to Des Bosses of 7 March 1716 in Gerhardt, *P. S.* 2:512.

17. Ricci, *Journals,* pp. 405f.

18. Des Bosses' letter to Leibniz of 7 March 1716 in Gerhardt, *P. S.* 2:512. The full title of Navarette's work is *Tratados históricos, políticos, ethicos y religiosos de la Monarchia de China* (Historical, political, ethical, and religious treatises on the monarchy of China). Both Navarette and De Cicé were anti-Jesuit.

19. George H. Dunne, S. J., in *Generation of Giants* (pp. 109–112 and 162–164) disagrees with the prominent view that sees Longobardi in great disagreement with Ricci and uncompromising toward the Chinese. On points outside the Rites Controversy, Dunne believes that Longobardi was in harmony with the dominant practices of the Jesuits in China.

20. Thanks to a recent breakthrough made by Henry Rosemont, Jr., I am able to identify Antonio Caballero a Santa Maria with Antoine de Sainte-Marie, author of the *Mission Treatise.* Prior to Rosemont's discovery, it had been customary to treat these two names as if they designated separate people. Consequently, Antoine de Sainte-Marie has been presented as a shadowy figure with little or no biographical detail. The source of the separation apparently dates from the translation of Caballero's *Mission Treatise* from Spanish to French and its publication at Paris in 1703. In the process his name was gallicized into Antoine de Sainte-Marie, and it is in this form that, to my knowledge, students of Leibniz' China studies have referred to him. Likewise, treatments of Antonio Caballero a Santa Maria as a missionary make no reference to his authorship of the *Mission Treatise.* Leibniz, who in his Latin correspondence with Des Bosses referred to Sainte-Marie as "Antonius de S. Maria," appears to have been aware of the identity of the two names.

21. Anastasius Van den Wyngaert, O. F. M. (ed.), *Sinica Franciscana, Relationes et Epistolas Fratrum Minorum* 2:317–332.

22. Dunne, pp. 237–242.

23. The treatise, *T'ien Ju yin* (Christianity and Confucianism compared), has been reprinted with an introduction in *T'ien-chu-chiao tung-ch'uan wen-hsien supien* (Supplementary volumes of records of Christian missionaries in the Far East) 1: XXXVII–XL and 2:981–1043.

24. Father Visdelou supported the cause of the mission of Charles Maillard de

Tournon, papal legate to China in 1704–1710. Tournon came to China for the ostensible purpose of investigating the differences between the various orders, though actually he carried a papal order that was a prejudgment against the Jesuit methods. (See Leibniz' letter to Des Bosses of 2 May 1710 in Gerhardt, *P. S.* 2:403.) Complicating the Jesuit opposition to Tournon were nationalistic factors; for example, the Portuguese Jesuits, particularly Thomas Pereyra (Hsü Erh-sheng, 1645–1708), tended to act more aggressively toward the papal legate than the French because they felt Portuguese status in the mission was threatened by the legate's presence. See Kenneth Latourette, *A History of Christian Missions in China*, pp. 142–143. In a treatment of the Rites Controversy well documented with European-language sources, George H. Dunne, S. J., states that nationalist rivalries far more than interorder competition caused difficulties between Jesuits, Dominicans, and Franciscans in China. (See *Generation of Giants*, p. 236.) Dunne's interpretation may be shaped by his Jesuit perspective. In this vein it is also noteworthy that Dunne minimizes differences between Jesuits such as Longobardi and Ricci and dates the Rites Controversy from the arrival of the Dominican, Francisco Dias [Francisco Díez], and the Franciscan, Francisco de la Madre de Dios [Francisco Bermúdez], in Fukien in 1634. (See Dunne, pp. 245–246.) Also, see Dunne's excellent analysis of the Rites Controversy in terms of documentary sources in chap. 16 (pp. 269–281).

25. Sainte-Marie's *Mission Treatise* is published, with Leibniz' marginal notations, in Christian Kortholt (ed.), *Leibnitii epistolae ad diversos . . . .* 2:267–412. Kortholt's edition of the *Mission Treatise,* in addition to his own pagination, includes the page numbers from the earlier edition from which Leibniz cites in the *Discourse.* For the sake of consistency, all references to the *Mission Treatise* will refer to the page numbers of this earlier edition, which are placed by Kortholt in the margins.

26. The Leibniz-Remond correspondence, which is discussed in chapter 4, indicates that Remond sent Longobardi's *Religion Treatise* and Sainte-Marie's *Mission Treatise* to Leibniz on or about 4 September 1715. (See Remond to Leibniz, 4 September 1715, Gerhardt, *P. S.* 3:651 and Leibniz to Remond, 4 November 1715, Gerhardt, *P. S.* 3:660.) This is corroborated by Leibniz' statement in his letter of 24 December 1715 to Des Bosses that a friend—presumably Remond—had sent him the treatises of both Longobardi and Sainte-Marie. (See Gerhardt, *P. S.* 2:507.) However, Leibniz did possess prior familiarity with both treatises. In a supplement to a letter to Des Bosses of 12 August 1709, Leibniz speaks of reading reviews of both treatises. (See Gerhardt,*P. S.* 2:380–384.)

27. On the subject of Leibniz' use of the Longobardi and Sainte-Marie treatises to write his *Discourse on the Natural Theology of the Chinese,* see Leibniz' letters to Des Bosses of 24 December 1715 and 13 January 1716 and Des Bosses' response of 7 March 1716 (Gerhardt, *P. S.* 2:507–513). Of even more direct relevance are Leibniz' letters to Nicholas Remond of 17 January 1716, 27 January 1716, and 27 March 1716 (Gerhardt, *P. S.* 3:665, 670, 675). The Leibniz-Remond correspondence is discussed in chapter 4.

28. Joseph Needham, *Science and Civilisation in China,* Vol. 4, bk. 2, p. 226, fig. 472.

29. Arnold H. Rowbotham, *Missionary and Mandarin in China,* pp. 233–234. Rowbotham further refers the reader to J. F. Baddeley, *Russia, Mongolia, China,* vol. 2.

30. Leibniz-Grimaldi correspondence file, *Leibnizbriefe* 330, p. 46a. This reference to the "Tribunal in Mathematics" is found among several pages of notes made on Leibniz' conversations with Grimaldi. These are in the form of a draft in

Leibniz' own hand and a copy by a secretary in *Leibnizbriefe* 330, pp. 45a-45b and 46a-47a, respectively.

31. Leibniz to Grimaldi, 19 July 1689, Rome. A draft of this letter in Leibniz' hand and a copy in a secretary's hand can be found in *Leibnizbriefe* 330, pp. 1a-2b and 3a and 5a, respectively. Leibniz wrote letters in French, Latin, and German. His correspondence with Grimaldi is in Latin; the correspondence with Bouvet is in French.

32. Leibniz' renderings of Grimaldi's answers to his list of questions are recorded in a copyist's hand in *Leibnizbriefe* 330, pp. 42a-44a.

33. Joseph Needham, "Chinese Astronomy and the Jesuit Mission: An Encounter of Cultures," China Society Occasional Papers, no. 10, pp. 6f. The contents of this paper are incorporated into vol. 3 of Needham's *Science and Civilisation in China*.

34. Recent studies by both Chinese and American scholars have criticized the Jesuits' introduction of Copernican heliocentric theory into China. The criticism is directed at the theologically motivated obfuscations and distortions in the Jesuit presentation of Copernicanism in China. See Hsi Tse-tsung et al., "Heliocentric Theory in China", *Scientia Sinica* 16(3)(1973):364-376, and Nathan Sivin, "Copernicus in China," *Studia Copernicana* 6(1973):63-122.

The case for criticism is clear, though perhaps not quite so clear as these studies assume. In criticizing the Jesuits for mixing scientific with theological motivations, both studies make dubious assumptions. Indeed, the mixing of scientific motivations with motivations from other realms is present in the Maoist-Marxist viewpoint of the Chinese article itself. In comparison with the Chinese article, Sivin's monograph is technically superior but less sophisticated from an ideological point of view. He either ignores or regards as undesirable the role of such extrascientific factors in the determination of scientific knowledge.

Beyond recognition of the presence of such mixtures is the question of the distance separating scientific truth from other motivating truths, whether in social, ideological, religious, or other realms. The Maoist-Marxist position is sensitive to this aspect in that it concedes a distinction, but then it goes on to say that scientific truth and Maoist-Marxist ideological truth coincide; i.e., the motivations are distinct and yet concur. The Sivin monograph implies that motivating factors outside the realm of the natural sciences contribute very little that is positive to the conclusions of natural science. Sivin's viewpoint deserves our attention. It certainly has been shared by a number of esteemed men of knowledge, including Galileo. Nevertheless, it is but one of several contending viewpoints on the matter. This contention must be balanced against criticism of the Jesuits when making a complete assessment of the validity of the criticism of the Jesuit presentation of Copernicanism in China.

35. Leibniz to Grimaldi, 21? March 1692, *Leibnizbriefe* 330, pp. 39a-39b. This letter has been translated from the original Latin into German by Albert Heinekamp. It is published along with other translations of Leibniz' writings by the Niedersächsische Landesbibliothek as *Leibniz-Faksimiles*, pp. 38-42.

36. This letter from Kepler to Terrentius of 1627 was published in Johannes Terrentius, *Epistolium ex regno Sinarum ad mathematicos Europaeos missum, cum commentatiuncula Johannis Keppleri* (Sagan, Silesia, 1630). Joseph Needham gives further elaboration to what is probably the same letter. He states that Kepler sent this letter to China in 1627 with the Polish Jesuit Michael Boym (Pu Chih-yüan, 1612-1659), who in turn forwarded the letter from Macao to Peking. The contents are said to include a set of Rudolphine (Copernican) Tables. (See Needham, "Chinese Astronomy and the Jesuit Mission," p. 8.) The Rudolphine Tables were

jointly compiled by Tycho Brahe (1546–1601) and Johannes Kepler and were named in honor of their patron, Rudolph II of Prague, emperor of the Holy Roman Empire and king of Bohemia. Also see Nathan Sivin, "Copernicus in China," p. 86.

37. See *Genesis* 10:2–3 and *I Chronicles* 1:5–6.

38. There is a draft of the letter of 20 December 1696 in Leibniz' hand and two copies in the same secretary's hand in *Leibnizbriefe* 330, pp. 15a–18a, 21a–26b, and 28a–33a, respectively. However, there is a postscript in Leibniz' own hand added to one of the copies (p. 26b) that differs from the postscript in the draft (p. 17b) and in the other copy (p. 33a).

39. Latourette, pp. 120–121. Also see Rowbotham, pp. 105–106.

40. Latourette, pp. 111f.

41. See Lawrence D. Kessler, "Joachim Bouvet's *Historical Sketch of the K'ang-hsi Emperor* and Its Influence," unpublished paper, p. 6.

42. Latourette, p. 121.

43. Leibniz-Bouvet correspondence, *Leibnizbriefe* 105, p. 25b.

44. Rowbotham, p. 115.

45. The work *T'ien-hsüeh pen-i* (Fundamentals of divine learning) is attributed to Bouvet. It has a preface written in 1703 by the scholar Han T'an and contains Bouvet's annotation of a selection of quotations from the Chinese classics. The perspective is, of course, Christian and aimed at comparing the Chinese term *t'ien* to the Christian concept of God. The work is said to be based upon an earlier piece by a Chinese convert, Chang Hsing-yüeh (1633–1711). See Arthur H. Hummel, *Eminent Chinese of the Ch'ing Period*, pp. 275–276.

46. Ludovici Dutens, *Leibnitii opera omnia* 4:145–151.

47. Dutens, 4:145.

*Chapter 3*

1. Gorai Kinzō, *Jukyō no Doitsu seiji shisō ni oyoboseru eikyō*.

2. Liu Pai-min, *"Lai-pu-ni-tzu de Chou-i hsüeh,"* pp. 99–116.

3. The chief source for the Leibniz-Bouvet correspondence is the file designated *Leibnizbriefe* 105 at the Niedersächsische Landesbibliothek, Hanover, Germany. However, this file does not contain all the letters in the Leibniz-Bouvet correspondence. Furthermore, it contains material extraneous to the correspondence, as well as occasional duplicates of Leibniz' letters written presumably by a secretary's hand. There is a group project currently under way consisting of Alan Berkowitz (project director), Chris Benoit, and Thatcher Deane that is attempting to transcribe, translate, and annotate the Leibniz-Bouvet correspondence. At the time of this writing, the group has transcribed thirteen letters in French and is in the process of acquiring and transcribing additional letters of Leibniz to Bouvet dated 20 April 1699 and 15 February 1701.

To help clarify the current status and availability of this correspondence, I list below the letters, their date and origin (when available), their source, and the length in pages. Although a number of the letters have been published, I note a publication only if the manuscript form is unavailable. Because Leibniz and Bouvet commonly wrote on both sides of the parchment sheets, and because the pagination assigned by the Hanover archives includes only one number per sheet, I use "a" and "b" to distinguish the different sides of a sheet, citing, for example, pages 24a and 24b. The manuscript sheets are a folio type, that is, large pieces of paper folded once with a resulting two leaves and four pages. The page sizes, which vary, are noted to the nearest quarter of an inch.

(1) Bouvet to Leibniz. 18 October 1697, Fountainbleau, France. *Leibnizbriefe* 105, pp. 1a-1b (two 6 ½'' × 8¾'' manuscript pages).

(2) Leibniz to Bouvet. 2 December 1697, Hanover, Germany. *Leibnizbriefe* 105, pp. 4a-7b (eight 8¼'' × 13'' manuscript pages).

(3) Leibniz to Bouvet. January 1698, Hanover? *Leibnizbriefe* 105, p. 8a (one 5½'' × 8'' manuscript page).

(4) Bouvet to Leibniz. 28 February 1698, La Rochelle, France. *Leibnizbriefe* 105, pp. 9a-12b (eight 6'' × 7¾'' manuscript pages).

(5) Leibniz to Bouvet. 20 April 1699, Wolfenbüttel, Germany. *Leibnizbriefe* 954 (Leibniz-Verjus correspondence file), pp. 26a-27b (four 6½'' × 8'' manuscript pages). Because a brief notation (apparently in Leibniz' own hand) in the marginal heading of this letter designates Verjus as addressee, this letter has been filed with the Leibniz-Verjus correspondence. However, Antoine Verjus, S. J., was the intermediary in the initial Leibniz-Bouvet contact, and it was through Verjus that Leibniz forwarded his letter to Bouvet of 2 December 1697. Consequently, it is possible that the intended addressee of this letter is really Bouvet. Certainly Merkel, who quotes extensively from this letter in *Leibniz und die China-Mission,* pp. 61-62, believes it to be addressed to Bouvet.

(6) Bouvet to Leibniz. 19 September 1699, Peking, China. *Leibnizbriefe* 105, pp. 13a-14b (four 8¾'' × 12¼'' manuscript pages).

(7) Bouvet via Le Gobien to Leibniz. 8 November 1700, Peking, China. Ludovici Dutens (ed.), *Leibnitii opera omnia* 4:146-151 (six printed pages). Also Christian Kortholt (ed.), *Leibniti epistolae ad diversos . . .* 3:5-14.

(8) Leibniz to Bouvet. 15 February 1701, Braunschweig, Germany. *Leibnizbriefe* 728 (Leibniz-Pinsson correspondence file), pp. 94a-96b (six 7¾'' × 13'' manuscript pages).

(9) Bouvet to Leibniz. 4 November 1701, Peking, China. *Leibnizbriefe* 105, pp. 21a-28 (twelve 9½'' × 12'' manuscript pages plus a two-page diagram measuring 7¼'' × 7½'').

(10) Bouvet to Leibniz. 8 November 1702, Peking, China. Dutens, 4:165-168 (four printed pages); also Kortholt, 3:15-22.

(11) Leibniz to Bouvet. 1703?, Hanover? *Leibnizbriefe* 105, pp. 30a-35b (twelve 8¼'' × 13'' manuscript pages).

(12) Leibniz to Bouvet. 28 July 1704, Hanover, Germany. *Leibnizbriefe* 105, pp. 36a-37b (four 6½'' × 8'' manuscript pages).

(13) Leibniz to Bouvet. 18 August 1705, Hanover, Germany. *Leibnizbriefe* 105, pp. 41a-42b (four 4'' × 6¼'' manuscript pages).

(14) Leibniz to Bouvet. Undated (1706?), Hanover? *Leibnizbriefe* 105, pp. 50a-51b (four 6¾'' × 9¾'' manuscript pages). Although the *Leibnizbriefe* 105 pagination places this undated letter after the letter of 13 December 1707, a comparison with Leibniz' discussion of receiving sixteen Chinese volumes from Bouvet, which appears in the opening lines of both this letter and the 1707 letter, gives some indication that this undated letter is earlier. Given this indication, along with Leibniz' tendency in the latter part of the correspondence with Bouvet to write letters on an annual basis (1703?, 1704, 1705, 1707), I would tentatively suggest the year 1706 for this letter.

(15) Leibniz to Bouvet. 13 December 1707, Hanover, Germany. *Leibnizbriefe* 105, pp. 43a-49b (four 6½'' × 8¾'' manuscript pages plus eight 6½'' × 8¾'' manuscript pages containing a list of questions).

4. Thanks to a referral by Thatcher Deane of the Leibniz-Bouvet correspondence project, I can report on at least two letters from China that came to Leibniz' attention after the lapse of the Leibniz-Bouvet correspondence. The letters are unaddressed and unsigned but dated and found in the Leibniz-Francke correspondence file. The first, dated 29 September 1709, is from *"Tartaria magna"* ("Greater Tartary") (*Leibnizbriefe* 282, pp. 15a–21a). The second, dated 27 November 1709 with an appendix dated 1710, is from Peking (*Leibnizbriefe* 282, pp. 22a–25a). These letters in Latin contain news of the Jesuit fathers, including Bouvet, and indicate one of the ways in which Leibniz continued to stay in contact with events of the China mission.

5. See Leibniz' letters to Des Bosses of 4 August 1710 and 8 July 1711 in Gerhardt, *P. S.* 2:410, 424.

6. *Mémoires de Trévoux,* no. 11 (January 1704). The Bouvet to Leibniz letter of 1701 is said to be published also in *Mémoires de l'Académie Royale des Sciences* 3:85f.

7. François la Chaise, S. J., preceded Michel le Tellier, S. J., mentioned in chapter 1, as confessor of Louis XIV. In contrast to the mild, and as some felt, religiously compromising manner of La Chaise, Le Tellier was caustic and unnecessarily harsh in his positions, especially toward the Jansenists. In the respective chronology of their methods, these fathers parallel the progressive worsening of the Rites Controversy and the decline of the China mission.

8. See Donald F. Lach's *The Preface to Leibniz' Novissima Sinica,* pp. 33 and 56.

9. Bouvet's *Portrait historique* has recently been translated into Chinese by Feng Tso-min in a study and translation of Bouvet's work entitled *Ch'ing K'ang Ch'ien liang-ti yü t'ien-chu-chiao ch'uan chiao shih* (The Emperors K'ang-hsi, Ch'ien-lung, and the Catholic missionaries).

10. *Leibnizbriefe* 105, pp. 4a–7b.

11. The standard accounts of the China missions by Latourette and Rowbotham give little description of Bouvet's preparations, but a recent paper by Lawrence Kessler entitled "Joachim Bouvet's *Historical Sketch of the K'ang-hsi Emperor* and Its Influence" gives more detail. As this paper is unpublished, I am indebted to Professor Kessler for sending me a copy.

12. Joseph Henry-Marie de Prémare, S. J., *Selecta quaedam vestigia praecipuorum Christianae Religionis dogmatum, ex antiquis Sinarum libris eruta,* MS at the Bibliothèque Nationale, Paris. This manuscript was later translated into French by Augustin Bonnetty and Paul Perny and published as *Vestiges des principaux dogmes chrétiens tirés des anciens livres chinois* (Vestiges of principal Christian dogmas gathered from ancient Chinese books).

13. Jean-Baptiste Régis, S. J., *I-king, antiquissimus Sinarum liber.* A brief description of the work is given in Pfister, *Notices biographiques* 236:534–535. The *Book of Changes* is one of the most difficult Chinese texts to translate. The difficulty stems in part from the content but also from the archaic nature of some of the language. The original body of the *Changes,* as opposed to its appendices, is regarded by some scholars as the oldest extant Chinese work.

14. Leibniz, *Das Geheimnis des Schöpfung* (The secret of creation), *Neujahrsbrief an den Herzog Rudolph August von Braunschweig-Lüneburg-Wolfenbüttel,* in Loosen and Vonessen, *Zwei Briefe,* pp. 19–23.

15. Here Leibniz is referring to his letter to Grimaldi of 20 December 1696, in which he presents an explanation of his binary system. See *Leibnizbriefe* 330, pp. 15b–16b (Leibniz' draft), pp. 22b–24a (copy), and 29b–30b (copy).

16. Bouvet's letter to Leibniz, 28 February 1698, *Leibnizbriefe* 105, p. 9a.

17. Actually, it was still unknown in Leibniz' time that Hermes Trismegistus was invented by certain second and third century A.D. Romans who identified him with the Egyptian god Thoth, scribe to the gods, measurer of time, inventor of number and language, and god of learning and magic. Consequently, Hermes Trismegistus became known as the founder of alchemy and other occult sciences and the inventor of talismans. He was also associated with the early Judaic prophets, such as Moses. See Frances Yates, *Giordano Bruno and the Hermetic Tradition,* pp. 1–19.

18. The vicariats apostolic were bishoprics created in 1696 by Pope Innocent XII in order to circumvent the Portuguese crown's monopoly over missionary activity in China. The three dioceses of Peking, Nanking, and Macao remained under Portuguese authority, but the rest of China was divided into regions under the authority of individual vicars apostolic who were appointed directly from Rome by the congregation, acting by the authority of the pope.

19. *Leibnizbriefe* 330, pp. 15b–16b, and in corresponding pages in the two copies of this letter.

20. *Leibnizbriefe* 728, pp. 94b–95a.

21. *Leibnizbriefe* 105, pp. 21a–26b. The published version of this letter of 4 November 1701 in Dutens, 4:152–164, has deleted sections totaling one-sixth of the original letter. Dutens' principal omissions are: *Leibnizbriefe* 105, p. 21a (para. 1–3); pp. 24a–24b; and p. 26b (the last eleven lines). The motive for deletion appears to be mainly an editorial desire for greater clarity and readability.

22. The mathematical significance of the *Book of Changes* diagrams, including their parallel to Leibniz' binary mathematics, is discussed in *Leibnizbriefe* 105, pp. 21a–23a.

23. Gerhardt, *P. S.* 2:384.

24. Leibniz, *Explication de l'arithmétique binaire,* in Gerhardt (ed.), *Leibnizens mathematische Schriften* (hereafter cited as *M. S.*), 7:223–227.

25. "Place value" or "value by position" would refer, for example, in the number 5620 to the first figure on the left as representing $10^3$ (10 to the third power); 10 is used because a denary system is involved. Computed, $10^3$ would be $10 \times 10 \times 10 = 1000$ or a four-digit number, i.e., the number of digits in 5620.

The diagrams found in the *Changes* exhibit the same characteristic of place value. For instance, in a given hexagram, the top line might represent $2^5$. Computed, $2^5$ would be $2 \times 2 \times 2 \times 2 \times 2 = 32$, which when translated into the binary progression yields 100 000 or a six-digit number, the total number of lines in the hexagram. The line down from the top of the hexagram might represent $2^4$, which when computed would be $2 \times 2 \times 2 \times 2 = 16$, which when translated into the binary system equals 10 000 or a five-digit number, i.e., the number of lines remaining in the hexagram after the first line is subtracted. The bottom line in the hexagram might represent $2^0$. When computed, $2^0$ would yield 1 or a single-digit number, which is what the place value of the bottom line could represent. Theoretically, one could also reverse this order and treat the bottom line of the hexagram as representing $2^5$ and progressing up to the top line as $2^0$. The order depends upon the direction in which one counts the lines of the hexagrams. While the traditional Chinese method followed the former order, Bouvet and Leibniz were more flexible.

26. Leibniz presents this conception of a Universal Characteristic most fully in *"Scientia Generalis. Characteristica"* in Gerhardt, *P. S.* 7:3–247. A significant though brief segment of this work has been translated into English by Paul and Anne Schrecker as "On the Universal Science: Characteristic" in *Monadology and Other Philosophical Essays,* pp. 11–21.

27. The analysis of the *Book of Changes* diagrams in terms of color is found in *Leibnizbriefe* 105, pp. 22b-23a.

28. *Leibnizbriefe* 105, p. 23b. Frances Yates makes no reference to such a representation of Hermes Trismegistus in her *Giordano Bruno and the Hermetic Tradition*. However, Denis Sinor discusses and presents illustrations of a dog headed figure, not specifically associated with Hermes Trismegistus, in his article "Foreigner-Barbarian-Monster," in Theodore Bowie, ed., *East-West in Art* (Bloomington, Indiana, 1966). On p. 159 of this article, Sinor speaks of this figure as appearing both in the West and in China.

29. *Leibnizbriefe* 105, p. 24a. Compare Bouvet's rendering of this *Li Chi* passage to that in James Legge's translation of *Li Ki*, bk. 7 *(Li Yun)*, iv, 4:386-387.

30. *Leibnizbriefe* 105, p. 24a. Bouvet's reference is apparently to the *Shih chi,* chap. 28, "The treatise on the Feng and Shan sacrifices," where it states:

> A man from Po named Miu Chi . . . instructed the emperor on how to sacrifice to the Great Unity. "The Great Unity," he explained, "is the most honored of the spirits of Heaven and his helpers are the Five Emperors. In ancient times the Son of Heaven sacrificed to the Great Unity each spring and autumn in the southeastern suburbs, offering one set of sacrificial animals each day for seven days. An altar was constructed for the purpose which was open to the spirit roads of the eight directions." [Ssu-ma Ch'ien, *Records of the grand historian of China,* trans. Burton Watson (New York, 1961), vol. 2, p. 40.]

31. *Leibnizbriefe* 105, pp. 24a-24b. This passage is part of over one page of manuscript edited out from the Dutens edition. In its place Dutens, 4:159-160, makes the following transition phrase:

> Le conjecture dont vous me parlez, touchant les caractères, & la langue des Chinois me paroit véritable. Il y a, comme je crois, de l'artifice dans la construction des caractères Chinois; & cet artifice est l'effort d'un sérieux. . . .

Although the view embodied in the omitted passage was radical, the Dutens edition included similar material at the beginning of Bouvet's letter to Leibniz of 8 November 1702 (Dutens, 4:165). Consequently, the reason for the omission is probably as much editorial as the desire to make Bouvet's letter less controversial. Nevertheless, it is well to be aware that in the year 1768 when the Dutens edition was published, the Rites Controversy and the Society of Jesus still aroused strong feelings in Europe.

32. The presence of this dictionary at Le Mans is cited by Henry M. Brock in his article on Bouvet in the *Catholic Encyclopedia* 2:723. Also see Pfister, *Notices biographiques* 171:438, where reference is made to a small Chinese-French dictionary in manuscript form. However, Pfister is uncertain of its location.

33. Cited by Lach, *Preface to Leibniz' Novissima Sinica,* p. 34.

34. See Werner Eichhorn, *Chinese Civilization,* p. 141.

35. Hellmut Wilhelm ("Leibniz and the *I Ching,*" pp. 213-214) disagrees and says that Bouvet's letter of 8 November 1702 can be understood only as a reply to a letter by Leibniz. However, the only extant letter from Leibniz to Bouvet which could possibly fit into that time period is that of *Leibnizbriefe* 105, pp. 30a-35b. This letter is undated; however, the prevailing weight of opinion has assigned the date of 1703. This date has been chosen, in large part, because of Leibniz' statement in the third line of the letter that he had received Bouvet's letter of 4 November 1701 through Le Gobien on 1 April 1703. Following this reasoning, Merkel suggests 1703 (*Leibniz*

*und die China-Mission,* p. 92). Franke, perhaps following Merkel, also assigns 1703 ("Leibniz und China," *Zeitschrift der Deutschen Morgenländischen Gesellschaft* 7 (1928):168). However, Gorai Kinzō suggests the probable dates of 1701 or 1702 (Liu Pai-min, in Li Cheng-kang, *I-hsüeh t'ao-lun chi,* pp. 104–105). Wilhelm feels that Leibniz' reference to "the 1st of April 1703" is erroneous by a year and proposes April 1702 as the date of composition of this letter. I refer to this letter as "1703?". I am indebted to Professor Wilhelm for sending me a copy of his rather inaccessible paper.

36. Bouvet notes as an aside that he has not yet been able to locate a treatise by Kepler in a letter to the Chinese missionary-astronomer, Terrentius, which Leibniz had previously recommended. See Dutens, 4:167.

37. Gerhardt, *M. S.* 7:223–227.

38. Gerhardt, *P. S.* 7:sec. xiv, pp. 198–201.

39. See the appendix for a modern Western interpretation of the *Book of Changes.* This interpretation by a contemporary painter may clarify certain key distinctions.

40. Chu Hsi's stress on the practical aspects of divination in the *Book of Changes* rather than its philosophical implications is immediately evident in his *I-hsüeh ch'i-meng hsü* (Preface to the primer on *Changes*). [See Chu Hsi, *Chu-tzu ta-ch'üan* (Compendium of Master Chu), chap. 76, pp. 17a–17b.] Yet perhaps Hu Shih overemphasized this tendency in Chu Hsi's interpretation when he said that Chu Hsi denied any philosophical significance to the *Changes.* (See Hu Shih, "The Scientific Spirit and Method in Chinese Philosophy," in Charles A. Moore (ed.), *The Chinese Mind,* pp. 120–121. Chu Hsi's *I-hsüeh ch'i-meng* includes expositions of several Shao Yung diagrams, and since Shao's treatment of the *Changes* is extremely philosophical, one wonders whether Hu Shih's minimization of Chu Hsi's interest in the philosophical content of the *Changes* is justified. In fact, as Fung Yu-lan points out (see Fung's *History of Chinese Philosophy* 2:454), we are indebted to Chu Hsi's *I-hsüeh ch'i-meng* for our present knowledge of Shao Yung's diagrams because they are no longer available in Shao's extant writings. This presentation by Chu Hsi was the source for Huang Tsung-hsi's incorporation of Shao's diagrams into his *Sung-Yüan hsüeh-an* (Writings of Sung and Yüan philosophers), chap. 10, 2:219–236.

41. This and several of the following pieces of information on Hu Wei's stay in Peking are taken from the entry on Hu Wei in Hummel's *Eminent Chinese of the Ch'ing Period,* pp. 335–336.

42. See David E. Mungello, "The Reconciliation of Neo-Confucianism with Christianity in the Writings of Joseph de Prémare, *S. J.,*" *Philosophy East and West* 26(4)(1976):389–410.

43. The edition reprinted by the Shang-wu book company in Shanghai, 1935, contains an incorrect depiction of the square arrangement of the Prior to Heaven diagram on p. 156. In contrast to the circular aspect of this diagram, which is accurate, the square aspect contains duplications of certain hexagrams and omissions of others. That the error would belong to the printer rather than the author, Hu Wei, is indicated by the latter's textual references to the correct form of the square arrangement.

44. For the source of the following interpretation of Hu Wei's work, see his *I-t'u ming-pien,* chap. 7, pp. 134 and 136–137.

45. The Leibniz-Des Bosses correspondence is published in Gerhardt, *P.S.* 2:287–521.

46. Longobardi mentions Frs. Pasio, Ruiz, and De Ursis in the opening pages of the *Religion Treatise.* Sabatino de Ursis was an astronomer who participated in the

China mission from 1606 until his death in 1620. He was eventually replaced by Terrentius.

47. Leibniz' letter to Des Bosses of 4 August 1710 in Gerhardt, *P. S.* 2:409–410.

48. Leibniz addresses this complaint directly to Bouvet in two letters. One of the letters is undated but is estimated by this author to be 1706 (see *Leibnizbriefe* 105, p. 50a). The other letter is dated 13 December 1707 (see *Leibnizbriefe* 105, p. 43a). According to a knowledgeable member of the Leibniz Gesellschaft staff, these Chinese volumes were at some time past sent to the university library at Göttingen. The opinion was, unfortunately, that they were probably integrated into the collection without being identified as a gift from Bouvet to Leibniz. Consequently, they may be difficult to locate.

49. *Discourse on the Natural Theology of the Chinese,* MS 37, 1810, no. 1, Niedersächsische Landesbibliothek, Hanover, Germany, p. 15b. Also see sec. 69 in the *Discourse on the Natural Theology of the Chinese* (alternatively titled "Letter on Chinese Philosophy") in Christian Kortholt (ed.), *Leibnitii epistolae ad diversos . . .,* and in Ludovici Dutens (ed.), *Leibnitii opera omnia.*

50. *Discourse* MS, p. 16a. *Discourse* 70 in the Kortholt and Dutens editions.

51. *Discourse* MS, p. 15b. *Discourse* 68 in the Kortholt and Dutens editions.


*Chapter 4*

1. Remond to Leibniz, 2 June 1713, Gerhardt, *P. S.* 3:603–604.

2. Remond to Leibniz, 12 October 1714, Gerhardt, *P. S.* 3:630.

3. Remond to Leibniz, 1 April 1715, Gerhardt, *P. S.* 3:640 and Leibniz to Remond, 22 June 1715, Gerhardt, *P. S.* 3:644.

4. Leibniz to Remond, 4 November 1715, Gerhardt, *P. S.* 3:660.

5. Leibniz to Remond, 17 January 1716, Gerhardt, *P. S.* 3:665.

6. Leibniz to Remond, 27 January 1716, Gerhardt, *P.S.* 3:670.

7. Leibniz to Remond, 27 March 1716, Gerhardt, *P. S.* 3:675.

8. The only known manuscript of Leibniz' treatise on Chinese philosophy is found in the Leibniz archives of the Niedersächsische Landesbibliothek at Hanover, MS 37, no. 1, pp. 1a–16b (thirty-two 8½" × 12¾" manuscript pages). The manuscript consists of a draft in French written on folio pages in Leibniz' own hand and with considerable marginal emendation. The work takes the form of a letter, which was possibly never sent, to Remond. The manuscript itself is untitled but has since been given descriptive titles such as "Lettre de Mr. Leibniz touchant les Chinois" written on a later added title page to the manuscript, or "Lettre de Mons de Leibniz sur la Philosophie chinois a Mons. de Remond" in the Kortholt and Dutens editions. However, Leibniz did refer to the work as the "Discours sur la Theologie naturelle des Chinois" (Discourse on the natural theology of the Chinese) in his letter of 27 January 1716 to Remond (Gerhardt, *P. S.* 3:670) and similarly in his letter of 27 March 1716 to Remond (Gerhardt, *P. S.* 3:675). Leibniz also referred to the work by the Latin title of "Dissertationem de Theologia Sinensium naturali" (Discourse on the natural theology of the Chinese) in his letter of 13 January 1716 to Des Bosses (Gerhardt, *P. S.* 2:508). Consequently, it would seem appropriate to use Leibniz' own designation rather than the more familiar descriptive titles from the Kortholt and Dutens editions.

9. I am indebted to Daniel Cook for suggesting the possibility of the later addition of the fourth section to the *Discourse.* In Leibniz' letters to Remond of 17 January 1716 and 27 January 1716, he refers to three sections on God, Spirits, and the Soul

and indicates that he has completed the *Discourse*. In his letter of 27 March 1716, however, he writes that the treatise needs more work. We might ask whether this additional work involves the addition of the fourth section on Fu Hsi's diagrams and binary arithmetic or whether it simply represents Leibniz' desire to make emendations, of which the manuscript contains numerous instances.

10. See Christian Kortholt, ed., *Leibnitii epistolae ad diversos . . .* (1735) 2:413–494. The Kortholt edition of Leibniz' *Discourse* was reproduced in Ludovici Dutens, ed., *Leibnitii opera omnia* (1768) 4:169–210. Recently a German translation of the work, which uses the Kortholt divisions with occasional further subdivisions, appeared in a French-German bilingual edition by Renate Loosen and Franz Vonessen entitled *Zwei Briefe über das binäre Zahlensystem und die chinesische Philosophie*, pp. 39–132. Since the Loosen-Vonessen work includes manuscript material that the Kortholt and Dutens editions omitted—this material is not extensive—it is the most complete published version of the *Discourse* presently available. It will soon be joined by an English translation of the *Discourse*, with introduction, notes, and commentary, by Daniel J. Cook and Henry Rosemont, Jr. (Society for Asian and Comparative Philosophy monograph 4). Although not bilingual like the Loosen-Vonessen edition, the Cook-Rosemont work expands the introductory and annotative material and attempts to make further improvements in incorporating material from the manuscript. As all four editions use the basic Kortholt divisions, all following textual citations from the *Discourse* will use these divisions to facilitate comparison among the various editions.

11. *Discourse* MS, p. 1a. In this and following citations of Leibniz' *Discourse on the Natural Theology of the Chinese*, the textual citations refer to the seventy-five numerical divisions found in the Kortholt and later editions of the work, while the footnote citations refer to the pagination of the folio sheets of the manuscript in Hanover. In the *Discourse* citations of the *Religion Treatise, Mission Treatise, Compendium*, and *Four Books*, I have taken the liberty of emending unclear, incomplete, and inaccurate citations.

12. *Discourse* MS, p. 1a.

13. *Discourse* MS, p. 1b.

14. The seven Chinese texts cited by Leibniz divide into five classical texts and two texts of lesser antiquity but of near-classical status. The five classics with their Chinese titles are the *Book of Changes (I Ching), Book of History (Shang Shu), Book of Odes (Shih Ching), Analects (Lun Yü)*, and *Doctrine of the Mean (Chung Yung)*. The two works with near-classical status, although separated from the classics by well over a millennium, are the *Comprehensive Mirror (T'ung Chien)* and the *Compendium (Hsing-li ta-ch'üan shu)*.

15. The *chüan* is a traditional Chinese textual unit that is usually longer than a chapter but shorter than a Western-style volume.

16. Longobardi's description represents a relatively accurate classification of Chinese books, except for the misleading distinction between the *ta-ch'üan* commentary and the *hsing-li* compendium. As Longobardi himself correctly notes, the composers of both these categories were the same group of forty-two scholars called together by the Yung-lo emperor. Longobardi's placement of this origin as 2500 years prior to his own time is erroneous for, assuming that Longobardi was writing around 1600, less than 200 years would have already elapsed since the compilation of the *Compendium* in around A.D. 1415. Possibly his separation of *ta-ch'üan* from *hsing-li* merely refers to a distinction within the three collections completed at the Yung-lo emperor's command. These included the *Ssu-shu ta-ch'üan*, the *Wu-ching*

*ta-ch'üan,* and the *Hsing-li ta-ch'üan.* Longobardi's *ta-ch'üan* category may refer to the first two, which involve the classics, while his *hsing-li* division may refer to the third work, which is derivative from the classics.

17. Kortholt, 2:174, and Dutens, 4:95.

18. There is a slim possibility that Leibniz might have accepted Longobardi's erroneous dating of the *Compendium* as over 2500 years old. This would place the *Compendium* on a level of antiquity equal to the other classics. Yet surely he would also have considered the more accurate dating of over 300 years attributed by Sainte-Marie to the *Compendium,* along with the other references to a more accurate dating appearing in the *Religion Treatise* and *Mission Treatise.*

19. *Discourse* MS, p. 1b.

20. T. S. Eliot, *The Four Quartets,* "Burnt Norton," line 62.

21. Aristotle, *Metaphysics,* bk. Lambda.

22. Chu Hsi, *Chu-tzu yü-lei* (Classified conversations of Master Chu), compiled by Chu Hsi's disciples, chap. 1, pp. 1a–3a.

23. Chu Hsi, *Chu-tzu yü-lei,* chap. 1, p. 1b.

24. For more information on the involved development of *li,* see T'ang Chün-i, *Chung-kuo je-hsüeh yüan-lun* (A discussion of fundamentals of Chinese philosophy), 1:1–69. T'ang classifies and discusses in detail six essential meanings of *li.* These are presented in a context of complementaries, which in very rough translation may be rendered as follows: (1) *wen-li* (superstructure-infrastructure), (2) *ming-li* (the nameable–the ineffable), (3) *k'ung-li* (emptiness-absolute), (4) *hsing-li* (physical nature–spiritual nature), (5) *shih-li* (phenomenon-noumenon), and (6) *wu-li* (concrete thing–abstract principle). For a useful article in English on the development of *li,* see Wing-tsit Chan's "The Evolution of the Neo-Confucian Concept *li* as Principle," *Tsing Hua Journal of Chinese Studies,* n.s., 4(2)(1964):123–148.

25. Leibniz, *New Essays;* see Langley's preface, p. xii, and Gerhardt's introduction.

26. Leibniz, *New Essays,* p. 46.

27. *Discourse* MS, p. 1b.

28. Since a page in traditional Chinese printing consists of a double leaf with printing on each side, I have clarified Longobardi's and Leibniz' references to Chinese texts by indicating whether the cited page refers to the "a" or "b" side of the leaf.

29. *Discourse* MS, p. 5a.

30. *Discourse* MS, p. 7a.

31. I am indebted to Nathan Sivin for suggesting that *wu hsing* be translated as "Five Phases" rather than the more common, but less accurate, "Five Elements" or "Five Agents." See Nathan Sivin, "Why the Scientific Revolution Did Not Take Place in China," an address to the Metropolitan New York Section, History of Science Society, 22 April 1975, p. 6 of the transcription.

32. There has been a great deal of discussion and debate since the beginning of the twentieth century over the exact form and role that Leibniz gave to subject-predicate logic in his system. Some of the main differences in interpretation of the role of Leibniz' logic may be found in the following: Louis Couturat, *La logique de Leibniz;* Bertrand Russell, *A Critical Exposition of the Philosophy of Leibniz* (see especially chap. 2 and 3); Nicholas Rescher, *The Philosophy of Leibniz,* pp. 22–34; Gottfried Martin, *Leibniz: Logic and Metaphysics,* p. 85f.

33. All quotations from Leibniz' *Monadology* are taken from the translation by Paul and Anne Schrecker, *Monadology and Other Philosophical Essays.*

34. In my interpretations of Leibniz' physical theory, I am indebted to George Gale's "The Physical Theory of Leibniz," *Studlia Leibnitiana* 2(2)(1970):114–127.

35. Leibniz to Bouvet, 2 December 1967, *Leibnizbriefe* 105, p. 6b.

36. Leibniz to Bouvet, 1703?, *Leibnizbriefe* 105, p. 30b. The draft of the letter in the Hanover archives is undated but estimated to be 1703. This estimate is supported by the opening statement where Leibniz acknowledges receiving Bouvet's important letter from Peking of 4 November 1701 in April of 1703. Bouvet's letter contained the Prior to Heaven diagram of the hexagrams, along with the suggestion of correspondence between the progression of these diagrams and that of Leibniz' binary system. Leibniz has confirmed the suggestion in his own mind, and his letter in both content and length indicates an excitement that would lead one to believe he did not hesitate in responding. This, taken with Leibniz' tendency to reply promptly to Bouvet's letters, makes a 1703 date very plausible. The next letter from Leibniz to Bouvet is dated 28 July 1704.

37. Leibniz' alternative designations for the concept of the monad include "individual substance," "substantial form," "entelechy," and, in more limited circumstances, "soul" or "spirit". See Nicholas Rescher, *The Philosophy of Leibniz,* pp. 20–21, and A. G. Langley's translation of Leibniz' *New Essays Concerning Human Understanding,* p. 101n.

38. *Discourse* MS, pp. 2a–2b, 3b, 7a.

39. *Discourse* MS, pp. 3b, 4b, 5a, 9a.

40. Leibniz, *De primae philosophiae emendatione, et de notione substantiae,* in Gerhardt, *P. S.* 4:468–470.

41. Leibniz' letter to De Volder of 20 June 1703 in Gerhardt, *P. S.* 2:252. I am indebted to Frederick Copelston's *History of Philosophy,* 4:306, for drawing this passage to my attention.

42. Leibniz, *De ipsa natura* (On nature itself), Gerhardt, *P. S.* 6(11):510–511.

43. Rescher, pp. 80–87.

44. *Discourse* MS, p. 5a.

45. *Discourse* MS, p. 7a.

46. *Discourse* MS, pp. 3b–4a.

47. *Discourse* MS, p. 3b.

48. For one such instance of a Neo-Confucian text that discusses *li* in its prior as well as its simultaneous relationships to *ch'i,* see *Chu-tzu yü-lei,* chap. 1, pp. 1a–3a.

49. *Analects* 15:28: "The master said, 'A man can enlarge the principles *which he follows;* those principles do not enlarge the man.' " [As translated by James Legge in *The Chinese Classics,* p. 302.] Alternatively: "The Master said, A man can enlarge his Way; but there is no Way that can enlarge a man." [As translated by Arthur Waley in the *Analects of Confucius,* p. 199.]

50. It is possible that Leibniz had other access to the *Analects* 15:28 through the form of *Confucius Sinarum Philosophus,* but I have found no evidence that he made use of it.

51. *Discourse* MS, p. 4a.

52. Chu Hsi, *Lun yü chi-chu* (1177), published in *Ssu-shu chi-chu* (Collected commentaries on the Four Books), Lun yü, chap. 8, p. 7a.

53. *Discourse* MS, pp. 2a–2b.

54. The Leibniz-Clarke correspondence appears in Gerhardt, *P. S.* 7:347–440, and has been translated by H. G. Alexander as the *Leibniz-Clarke Correspondence.*

55. Gerhardt, *P. S.* 7:394, no. 33; and Alexander, p. 64.

56. Alexander, p. 64n, cites Gerhardt, *P. S.* 1:193, as his source.
57. Gerhardt, *P. S.* 7:373, no. 2–3; and Alexander, p. 25.
58. Gerhardt, *P. S.* 7:403–404, no. 52; and Alexander, pp. 73–74.
59. *Discourse* MS, p. 2b.
60. Gerhardt, *P. S.* 7:404–405, no. 55; and Alexander, p. 75.
61. Chu Hsi, *Chung yung chang-chü* (1184), in *Ssu-shu chi-chu,* Chung yung, chaps. 20–25.
62. Leibniz' fifth letter to Clarke, in Gerhardt, *P. S.* 7:393, no. 21; my translation.
63. Shao Yung, *Huang-chi ching-shih* (Cosmological chronology), chap. 7, p. 22b.
64. Shao Yung, chap 7, p. 23a.
65. T'ang Chün-i's insightful interpretation appears in "Chang Tsai's Theory of Mind and Its Metaphysical Basis," *Philosophy East and West* 6(2)(1956):124.
66. See Wing-tsit Chan, "Chu Hsi's Completion of Neo-Confucianism," *Etudes Song-Sung Studies,* ser. 2, no. 1, pp. 67–70. The Jesuit missionary Joseph de Prémare (1666–1736) makes the interesting argument that *wu-chi* is more fundamental than *t'ai-chi* and that *li* should be identified with *wu-chi* rather than with *t'ai-chi.* See Prémare, *Lettre inédite sur le monothéisme des chinois,* ed. Guillaume Pauthier (Paris, 1861), pp. 12–16.


*Chapter 5*

1. Arguments for the view that Chinese philosophy had a direct influence upon the development of Leibniz' philosophy may be found in E. R. Hughes, *The Great Learning and Mean in Action,* pp. 12–18; Joseph Needham, *Science and Civilisation in China* 2:496–505; and Artur Zempliner, "Gedanken über die erste deutsche Übersetzung von Leibniz' Abhandlung über die chinesische Philosophie," *Studia Leibnitiana* 2(3)(1970):223–231. These views and the question of influence between Leibniz and China were discussed in chapter 1 of the present study.
2. *Discourse* MS, p. 1a.
3. *Discourse* MS, p. 1a.
4. *Discourse* MS, p. 3b.
5. Leibniz mistakenly cites the *Compendium* passage as bk. 28, p. 13. This partially duplicates and partially extends an erroneous citing by Longobardi in the *Religion Treatise* 12:7–8. Longobardi cites two passages. The first is in reference to Chu-tzu and refers to bk. 28, p. 2, which is correct. In the succeeding passage, however, Longobardi cites p. 13 of the same book. Actually, the reference is to p. 3. Leibniz seems to have omitted the reference to p. 2 and copied the incorrect reference to p. 13.
6. At times, Leibniz uses the term "entelechy" to refer to the dominant monad in a monadic aggregate, in which case the reference would seem to be to a "soul" or "spirit." See Nicholas Rescher, *The Philosophy of Leibniz,* pp. 116–120.
7. See Rescher, pp. 118–119.
8. Bertrand Russell, among others, questions whether Leibniz really intended to view God as a monad. See his *Critical Exposition of the Philosophy of Leibniz,* p. 187. See Rescher, p. 21, for an opposing view.
9. *Discourse* MS, p. 11b.
10. *Discourse* MS, p. 11a.
11. Though Longobardi can be skilled as a translator, at times he takes liberties

with the text to the point that the translation cannot be traced to the textual source, even given the citation. Of course, faulty citation is sometimes the cause of this, but not always. One instance occurs in the *Religion Treatise* 12:5 where Longobardi also translates a section from the *Compendium* (bk. 28), which because of the specific reference to "Dr. Chang Zu" would seem to be referring to the Neo-Confucian philosopher Chang Tsai, who is quoted on pp. 37b–38a. Longobardi's translation is: "That the spirits are none other than solidity and plentitude, that is, the substance of *li* joined to its primitive air, which being infinite and immense, extends everywhere." However, an examination of the *Compendium* text shows neither *li* nor *ch'i* ("primitive air") to be present and little apparent basis for such a translation.

12. *Discourse* MS, p. 11b.

13. *Discourse* MS, pp. 10b–11a.

14. Leibniz follows Longobardi's use of a nonstandard system of numbering in which this passage is treated as *Analects* 3:3 rather than the standard 5:12.

15. *Discourse* MS, p. 11a.

16. *Discourse* MS, p. 11a.

17. *Discourse* MS, p. 7b.

18. The confusion of *Analects* 2:5 with *Analects* 5:12 might be accounted for by an error in transposition, that is, by the reversal of the book and chapter numbers and the omission of the numeral 1 from 12. While such a double transposition error of this sort is unlikely, a comparison of the contents of the *Analects* 5:12 offers support for such a possiblity.

19. Chu Hsi, *Lun yü chi-chu,* in *Ssu-shu chi-chu,* Lun yü, chap. 3, p. 5a.

20. *Discourse* MS, pp. 4b–5a.

21. Leibniz criticized Longobardi's failure to cite specific passages—as opposed to whole sections of text—in describing his interpretation.

22. *Discourse* MS, pp. 12b–13a.

23. *Discourse* MS, p. 12b.

24. *Discourse* MS, p. 14b.

25. *Discourse* MS, p. 7b.

26. Unlike Longobardi, who usually cites the section in the quoted Chinese text, Sainte-Marie's normal practice is to refer to the quoted work only by title. In trying to locate the specific passage cited from *The Mean,* several problems arise. First, the term *t'ai-chi* does not appear in *The Mean,* and the few occurrences of *li* (*The Mean,* chaps. 31 and 33) involve little metaphysical significance. The metaphysical term *li-t'ai-chi* was not a familiar combination in the vocabulary of Confucius or his contemporaries. Furthermore, Chu Hsi's commentary on *The Mean* in the *Chung yung chang-chü* contains little discussion of *t'ai-chi.*

27. Chu Hsi, *Chung yung chang-chü,* in *Ssu-shu chi-chu,* Chung yung, chap. 20, p. 19b.

28. *Discourse* MS, p. 9b.

29. The ambiguous nature of the text of *The Mean* (chap. 16) is apparent from the following translation by a contemporary scholar:

> Confucius said, "How abundant is the display of power of spiritual beings! We look for them but do not see them. We listen to them but do not hear them. They form the substance of all things and nothing can be without them. They cause all people in the world to fast and purify themselves and put on the richest dresses to perform sacrifices to them. Like the spread of overflowing water they seem to be above and to be on the left and the right.

The *Book of Odes* [Ode 256] says, 'The coming of spiritual beings cannot be surmised. How much less can we get tired of them?' Such is the manifestation of the subtle. Such is the impossibility of hiding the real *(ch'eng).''* [Wing-tsit Chan, *A Source Book in Chinese Philosophy*, p. 102.]

30. As textual support in addition to *The Mean* (chap. 16), Longobardi also cites the *Compendium* (bk. 28) without giving page citations. There is an extensive discussion of the two manifestations of *ch'i* in the *Compendium* (bk. 28, pp. 5a-6b). Here Chang Tsai is quoted as saying on p. 5b that *kuei-shen* are the inherent capacities of the two *ch'i*. In the next few pages, the two manifestations of *ch'i* are also associated with *yang* and *yin*, expansion and contraction, going and coming, extending and returning, and so forth, though on p. 5a the two *ch'i* are said to be really one. Complementary relationships are developed throughout the chapter.

31. The text of *The Mean* (chap. 16) makes no specific mention of *li* or *ch'i*, but Chu Hsi's commentary in the *Chung yung chang-chü* refers to *kuei* and *shen* as the inherent powers of the two *ch'i*, which are also described as the spiritual beings of *yin* and *yang*, respectively. Familiarity with Chu Hsi's philosophy would enable one to infer a *li* component by viewing *yin* and *yang* in terms of being part of the process dictated by a guiding principle, rather than the complementary aspect of phenomenality associated with *ch'i*. Longobardi does not make this inference but rather emphasizes that the composition of Chinese spirits is exhausted by *ch'i*, from which they are inseparable. For this view, Longobardi relies upon Chu Hsi's commentary, but he seems to apply a very strict interpretation of this commentary—perhaps to support his own views about the lack of equivalence between Chinese and Christian spirits—and to ignore a fundamental tenet of Chu Hsi's philosophy, namely, that *ch'i* components cannot exist in isolation from *li*, though *li* can exist in a certain prior sense to *ch'i*. (In another sense, of course, Longobardi obviates this tenet by treating *li* as consisting of essentially the same essence as *ch'i*.) Consequently, *kuei-shen* could not be exclusively *ch'i*, even though Chu Hsi's commentary specifically emphasizes this aspect in discussing it. Yet because of his interpretation of *li* as materialistic and essentially the same as *ch'i*, Longobardi is able to dismiss the otherwise contradictory implications of his own statement in the *Religion Treatise* 12:8, attributed to the *Compendium* (bk. 28), that spirits are a type of *li*.

32. *Discourse* MS. p. 15a.

33. Leibniz cites *The Mean* (chap. 17 and 18). However, Sainte-Marie mistakenly cites chap. 18 of *The Mean* as chap. ''78,'' and Leibniz, though alert to other textual discrepancies, fails to catch the error and instead reproduces it.

*Chapter 6*

1. Leibniz' letter to Des Bosses of 18 November 1710 in Gerhardt, *P. S.* 2:413.

2. Merkel, *Leibniz und die China-Mission*, pp. 11-12.

3. This is the view expressed by G. J. Jordan in *The Reunion of the Churches*, p. 142f.

4. Leroy E. Loemker's *Struggle for Synthesis* presents another tension in Leibnizian philosophy; he regards Leibniz as a key figure in seventeenth-century European intellectual history who is attempting to synthesize two diverging forces. One is that of the *libertine*, the skeptic of the established orders who recognizes the supremacy of his own individuality and rational powers. The other is that associated with the

*homo honestatis* or *homme honnête* (literally, "virtuous man"), whose essential quality derives from the Stoic virtue of *honestas,* or seeking one's individual freedom as part of a larger order. Loemker describes this latter quality as based upon the Neoplatonic and Stoic doctrine of Logos: each man is a microcosm that reflects the larger world as a macrocosm, and this rational order produces a bond between men.

5. Rescher, p. 143.

6. This is the view expressed by R. W. Meyer in *Leibniz and the Seventeenth-Century Revolution,* pp. 61-62. *De principio individui* and *De arte combinatoria* appear in Gerhardt, *P. S.* 6:15-26 and 27-104.

7. The religious nature of Pythagoreanism is discussed by Martin A. Larson in *Religion of the Occident,* pp. 155-176. The relationship between the religious and scientific aspects of Pythagoreanism is discussed by Arthur Koestler in *The Sleepwalkers,* pp. 26-41.

8. Meyer, pp. 88-89. For this information regarding Leibniz' education, Meyer relies upon a nineteenth-century study by E. Speiss, *Erhard Weigel, der Lehrer von Leibniz und Pufendorf.*

9. Though F. M. Helmont seems to have been the source for Leibniz' adoption of the term "monad," Giordano Bruno's works, with which Leibniz was familiar, also used the term. For Lull's influence upon Bruno, see Frances A. Yates, *Giordano Bruno and the Hermetic Tradition,* pp. 96 and 195 et passim.

10. Leibniz, *De arte combinatoria,* in Gerhardt, *P. S.* 4:61-74.

11. The particular work referred to is G. H. R. Parkinson's translation and study, *Leibniz: Logical Papers* (Oxford, 1966). I can detect only one reference to Raymond Lull, and this is highly perfunctory and makes no mention of Lull's art. What makes the omission doubly surprising is the reputable nature of this study. Apparently, the author feels that his restricted subject matter allows him to omit these references, but one cannot help wondering how true such exclusiveness is to the Leibnizian spirit.

12. Leibniz, *Scientia generalis. Characteristica,* in Gerhardt, *P. S.* 4:199.

13. Leibniz, *Theodicy,* pp. 104-105.

14. Leibniz, *The Preface to Leibniz' Novissima Sinica,* p. 74.

15. See Louis Couturat, *La logique de Leibniz* and *Opuscules et fragments inédits de Leibniz;* Bertrand Russell, *A Critical Exposition of the Philosophy of Leibniz.* A clear and concise criticism of Russell's position on logic in Leibniz' philosophy can be found in Gottfried Martin, *Leibniz: Logic and Metaphysics,* pp. 1-3 et passim.

16. It should be noted that Buddhist logic was a development primarily of India and Tibet and was little cultivated in China. The classic study on Buddhist logic has been that of Theodore Stcherbatsky, *Buddhist Logic.*

17. According to Loemker, "A note on the Origin and Problem of Leibniz' Discourse of 1686," p. 449f, Leibniz first conceived of this plan for the Catholic demonstrations under the influence of Boineburg at Mainz in 1669 or 1670. Loemker interprets the *Discourse on Metaphysics* as part of the prolegomena to this work and maintains that Leibniz sent a summary of the *Discourse on Metaphysics* to the Jansenist Arnauld in order to evoke a favorable response and the consequent influence Arnauld's blessings would bring. Leibniz' complete outline of the plan for the Catholic demonstrations appears in *Sämtliche Schriften und Briefe,* edited by the Prussian Academy of Sciences, 6:i:494f.

18. See F. C. Happold, *Prayer and Meditation,* p. 24.

19. Meyer, pp. 146-147.
20. Leibniz, *Animadversiones in partem generalem principiorum Cartesianorum,* in Gerhardt, *P. S.* 4:390-392.
21. Meyer, p. 68.
22. See Russell, chap. 1. For some insightful comments into the relationship between Russell and Leibniz, see G. H. R. Parkinson's obituary of Russell in *Studia Leibnitiana* 2(3)(1970):161-163.
23. One of the more modern uses of Leibniz' work has been the application of binary arithmetic to computer operations on the grounds that its two numerical units greatly reduce the number of components ordinarily required by a denary or ten-unit numerical system.
24. Galileo's most complete statement on the relationship between religion and science is found in his "Letter to the Grand Duchess Christina" (1615), which is translated with notes in Stillman Drake's *Discoveries and Opinions of Galileo* (New York, 1957). A useful analysis of Galileo's religious views is Giorgio Spini's "The Rationale of Galileo's Religiousness," in Carlo L. Golino (ed.), *Galileo Reappraised.*
25. One of the most frequently cited statements in contemporary China on the importance of intellectuals' serving and learning from the masses is Mao Tse-tung's "Talks at the Yenan Forum on Literature and Art" (May 1942). See the English translation in *Selected Works of Mao Tse-tung* (Peking, 1967) 3:69-98.

*Chapter 7*

1. David E. Mungello, "On the Significance of the Question: 'Did China Have Science?' " *Philosophy East and West* 22(4)(1972):467-478; 23(3)(1973):413-422.
2. The contemporary Jesuit missionary William Johnston seeks a reconciliation of Christianity with a Japanese essence. The Japanese experience is relevant to that of China not merely because the language and much of the Japanese culture, including its well-known Zen Buddhism, have been derived from China, but also because a flourishing Christian church in Japan of 1600 experienced devastating suppression and persecution caused by xenophobic and political fears. By the end of the seventeenth century, Christianity was a mere underground movement in Japan, and the Chinese missionaries, particularly the Jesuits, sought to avoid the mistakes of their persecuted fellows in Japan. In his book of reflections on Zen and Christian mysticism, Johnston states that many of the past difficulties in the Christian experience in Japan were due to the failure of Christianity to move beyond its status as a foreign religion. See Johnston's *The Still Point* and *Christian Zen.*
The spirit identified with the name of Matteo Ricci is given a modern form by a former missionary to China, George H. Dunne, S. J., in "The Missionary in China: Past, Present and Future," *Ampleforth Journal* 78(3)(1973):9-42.
3. Johnston, p. 134.
4. *Shen-tu* (watchful while being alone) is an essential element in the *Great Learning* and was greatly stressed by Neo-Confucianism; *jen* (Humanity) was an object of great Confucian concern from the time of Confucius himself.
5. Leibniz, *New Essays,* pp. 23-25.
6. Leibniz, *New Essays,* pp. 24-25.
7. Leibniz, *New Essays,* pp. 56-58.
8. Johnston, p. 189.
9. *Discourse* MS, p. 10a.

Chin Ssu-piao　金四表

Chin Te-ch'un　金德純

Ch'in t'ien chien　欽天監

ching　靜

ching-tso　靜坐

ching-t'ien　敬天

Ch'ing K'ang Ch'ien liang ti yu t'ien-chu-chiao ch'uan chiao shih
　清康乾兩帝與天主教傳教史

Chou-i ku-ching chin-shu　周易古經今註

chu[a]

chu[b]　主

Chu Hsi　朱熹

Chu Tsai　朱才

Chu-tzu ta-ch'üan　朱子大全

Chu-tzu yü-lei　朱子語類

Ch'uan hsi lu　傳習錄

ch'üan　犬

chun-shen　辟神

chün-tzu　君子

Chung-kuo je-hsüeh yüan-lun　中國哲學原論

Chung yung　中庸

Chung yung chi-chieh hsü　中庸集解序

Erh-shih-wu-yen　二十五言

Fan Ch'ih　樊遲

fang-pien　方便

Feng Tso-min　馮作民

Feng Ying-ching　馮應京

Fo-Lao　佛老

fu[a]　伏

Fu Hsi　伏羲

fu[b]　復

Gorai Kinzō　五來欣造

Han Yü　韓愈

Hou Chi　后稷

hsi[a]　義

hsi[b]　犧

hsin　信

hsin-min　新民

10. *Discourse* MS, p. 11a.

11. Arthur Waley, *Analects of Confucius,* p. 126.

12. The translation of *Analects* 7:3 is my own; that of 7:6 is from Waley, pp. 123–124. Rather than follow Waley's use of "detraction," I chose a term with more positive connotations.

13. Confucius himself did not practice farming, nor did he propose that *chün-tzu* (gentlemen) do so. See the *Analects* 13:4. During Confucius' time there was a competing school known as the *Nung-chia* (School of Agriculture) which held that each person should produce his own food. As time went on, however, the Confucian school absorbed elements from this and several other schools. For a reference to Wu Yü-pi (K'ang-chai) (1391–1469) see the section on Wu K'ang-chai (Yü-pi) in Huang Tsung-hsi (1610–1695), *Ming-ju hsüeh-an* (Writings of Ming Confucianists), chap. 1, pp. 3–7. Also compare references to Wu Yü-pi in William Theodore de Bary (ed.), *Self and Society in Ming Thought,* p. 7 passim.

14. A pertinent project now underway is described in a paper by Charles Wei-hsun Fu entitled "Confucianism, Marxism-Leninism and Mao: A Critical Study" in the *Journal of Chinese Philosophy* 1(3–4)(1974):119–151. While not attributing deviation from the Marxist path to Mao Tse-tung, Fu sees Mao's thought as a dialectical synthesis of Marxism-Leninism and the ethical humanism of Confucius. Fu further shows himself to be in the Chinese moral tradition in his creative treatment of Mao as the true apostolic successor to Marx and Lenin, based on Mao's attempt to initiate a proletarian transformation of human nature on fundamentally moral grounds. Another paper with a number of fresh insights on related matters is Henry Rosemont, Jr.'s "Confucian Perspectives on Contemporary China," *Canadian Forum* (September 1974), pp. 13–19.

15. One dimension of Confucian spiritual and moral cultivation that is continued in contemporary China is the concern over the unity of knowledge and action or theory and practice. One of the foremost Confucian spokesmen on this dimension was Wang Yang-ming (1472–1529). See Wang Yang-ming, *Ch'uan hsi lu,* pp. 3–4. The modern Chinese concern over this dimension is expressed by Mao Tse-tung in the essay "On Practice," *The Selected Works of Mao Tse-tung* (Peking, 1967), vol. 1, pp. 295–309.

16. Recent attempts at reconciling Christianity with traditional Chinese religious categories have failed for somewhat different reasons than in Leibniz' time. For example, recent attempts at such reconciliation in Hong Kong have failed because many Hong Kong Chinese no longer subscribe to traditional Chinese religion and culture. A discussion of this failure and a proposal for a new approach that comes to terms with modernization in Asia is presented by Peter K. H. Lee in the article "Indigenous Theology—Overcropped Land or Undeveloped Field?" in *Ching Feng—Quarterly Notes on Christianity and Chinese Religion and Culture* 17(1)(1974)5–17.

17. There is no reason to think that such beliefs must be grounded in Christianity, though Christianity is one source from which to build to an accord. A number of Christians have been attempting to develop new approaches to contemporary China, and it may be useful to refer to some of them here.

A contemporary assessment written in the spirit of Matteo Ricci contains what could be useful guidelines for a program by Christians in China. Note that the author does not see a return of Christian missions in the traditional sense to China. See George H. Dunne, S. J., "The Missionary in China: Past, Present and Future," *Ampleforth Journal* 78(3)(1973):9–42. Also the Christian Study Centre on Chinese

Religion and Culture in Hong Kong is making honest attempts to confront the realities of the present demoralized state of Christianity in mainland China. See their quarterly publication, *Ching Feng—Quarterly Notes on Christianity and Chinese Religion and Culture*. It is published in both Chinese and English editions at Tao Fong Shan, Shatin, New Territories, Hong Kong.

A secular or humanitarian program born of a deep Christian commitment is found in the "People-to-People" program of the Division of Overseas Ministries, Christian Church (Disciples of Christ) of Indianapolis, Indiana. Inspired by Dr. Joseph Smith, who spent considerable time in the Far East the program stresses unofficial contacts between Chinese and Americans. Friendship, not conversion, is the explicit aim.

# *Glossary of Chinese Terms*

Alternative names and characters are included in parentheses. The abbreviation "T." designates the *tzu,* which are included here only because of the lesser availability of the Chinese names of Jesuits in comparison with the Chinese themselves. The Chinese names for Jesuits in the China mission may be found in Aloys Pfister's *Notices biographiques . . .* and, in more organized and readily available form, in Joseph Dehergne's *Répertoire des Jésuites de Chine de 1552 à1800.*

An To P'ing-shih　安多平施
Chang Ch'eng Shih-chai　張誠實齋
Chang Hsing-yüeh　張星曜
Chang Tsai　張載
ch'eng　誠
Ch'eng Hao (Ming-tao)　程顥(明道)
Ch'eng I (I-ch'uan)　程頤(伊川)
chi　極
Chi-ho yüan-pen　幾何原本
ch'i　氣
ch'ien　乾
chin　巾
chin-min　親民
Chin Sheng　金聲
Chin-ssu lu　近思錄

Hsien-t'ien tzu-hsü　先天次序
Hsing-li ta-ch'üan shu　性理大全書
Hsiung San-pa (T. Yu-kang)　熊三拔（有綱）
Hsü Erh-sheng　徐日昇
Hsü Kuang-ch'i　徐光啟
Hu Kuang　胡廣
Hu Wei　胡渭
Huang-chi ching-shih　皇極經世
Huang Ti　黃帝
Huang Tsung-hsi　黃宗羲
i　易
I ching　易經
I-hsüeh hsiang shu-lun　易學象數論
I-hsüeh t'ao-lun chi　易學討論集
I-hsüeh ch'i-meng hsü　易學啓蒙序
i-san　一三
I-t'u ming-pien　易圖明辨
jen[a]　人，亻
jen[b]　仁
K'ai-chiao san-ta chu-shih　開教三大柱石
K'ang Hsi　康熙
Kao Hsiang　高享
ko-i　格義
kou　姤
kuan　觀
kuei　鬼
kuei-shan　鬼神
k'un　坤
k'ung　空
k'ung-li　空理
Lao Tzu　老子
lei　類
Lei Hsiao-szu　雷考思
Lai-pu-ni-tz'u(tzu)　萊布尼茨（茲）
Lai-pu-ni-tzu de chou-i hsüeh　萊布尼茲的周易學
li　理
li[a]　里
li[b]　裏

li<sup>c</sup> 立

li<sup>d</sup> 禮

Li An-tang　利安當

Li chi　禮記

Li Ch'eng-kang　李證剛

Li Chih　李贄

Li Chih-tsao　李之藻

Li Ching-te　黎靖德

Li Kung　李塨

Li Ma-t'ou (T. Hsi-t'ai)　利瑪竇（西泰）

Lieh Tzu　列子

ling-hun　靈魂

Liu Pai-min　劉白閔

liu-tsung　六宗

Liu Ying Sheng-wen　劉應聲聞

Lu Jo-han　陸若漢

Lü Tzu-ch'ien　呂祖謙

Lun yü　論語

Lung Hua-min (T. Ching-hua)　龍華民（精華）

Ma Jo-se　馬若瑟

Meng Tzu　孟子

mien　宀

Min Ming-wo (T. Te-hsien)　閔明我（德先）

Ming-Ju hsüeh-an　明儒學案

ming-li　名理

Nan Huai-jen (T. Tun-pai)　南懷仁（敦伯）

Pa Yung-lo　巴庸樂

pi　比

pien　偏

po　剝

Po Chin (T. Ming-yüan)　白晉（明遠）

Pu Chih-yüan　卜致遠

pu Ju i Fo　補儒易佛

san-chiao i-ho　三教一合

Shang shu　尚書

shang-ti　上帝

Shao Yung　邵雍

shen　神

Shen Ch'üeh　沈㴝
shen-ling　神靈
shen-tu　愼獨
shih　十
Shih chi　史記
Shih ching　詩經
shih-li　事理
Ssu-ma Ch'ien　司馬遷
Ssu-pu pei-yao　四部備要
Ssu-shu chi-chu　四書集註
Ssu-shu ta-ch'üan　四書大全
Sung-Yüan hsüeh-an　宋元學案
ta　大
ta-ch'üan　大全
Ta hsüeh　大學
t'ai　太
t'ai-chi　太極
T'ai-chi t'u-shuo　太極圖說
t'ai-hsü　太虛
t'ai-i　太一
t'ai-i fen erh kuei t'ien-ti　太一分而規天地
t'ai-i han san　太一函三
T'ang Chün-i　唐君毅
T'ang Jo-wang (T. Tao-wei)　湯若望（道味）
tao　道
Tao Hsüeh　道學
te　德
Teng Yü-han (T. Han-p'o)　鄧玉函（涵璞）
ti　帝
t'ien　天
t'ien chih tao　天之道
t'ien chu　天主
T'ien-chu-chiao tung-ch'uan wen-hsien su-pien
　天主教東傳文獻續編
T'ien-chu shih-i　天主實義
T'ien-hsüeh pen-i　天學本義
T'ien-hsüeh shih-i　天學實義
T'ien Ju yin　天儒印

t'ien-li　天理
t'ien-tao　天道
tsai　宰
tung　動
T'ung Chien　通鑑
Wan Tsu-t'ung　萬斯同
wang　望
wang[a]　王
Wang Yang-ming (Shou-jen)　王陽明（守仁）
Wang Yi-yuan (T. T'ai-wen)　王豐肅（一元）（泰穩）
Wei K'uang-kuo (T. Chi-t'ai)　衛匡國（濟泰）
wen-jen　文人
wen-li　文理
wu　無
wu-chi erh t'ai-chi　無極而太極
Wu ching ta-ch'üan　五經大全
wu hsing　五行
wu-li　物理
Wu Yü-pi (K'ang-chai)　吳與弼（康齋）
Yang T'ing-yün　楊廷筠
yin　禋
yu-hun　幽魂
yü　玉，王

# Bibliography

Abraham, William E. "Complete Concepts and Leibniz's Distinction between Necessary and Contingent Propositions." *Studia Leibnitiana* 1(4)(1969): 263-279.

Alexander, H. G., ed. and trans. *Leibniz-Clarke Correspondence*. Manchester, 1956. Reprinted 1970.

Archivum Romanum Societatis Jesu. Rome.

Aristotle. *Metaphysics*. Translated by Richard Hope. Ann Arbor, 1960.

Attwater, Rachel. *Adam Schall: A Jesuit at the Court of China, 1592-1666*. Adapted from the French edition of Joseph Duhr, S. J. Milwaukee, 1963.

Augustine, Saint. *Confessions*. Translated by R. S. Pine-Coffin. Baltimore, 1961.

Baddeley, John F. *Russia, Mongolia, China*. Vol. 2. London, 1921.

Barber, W. H. *Leibniz in France, from Arnauld to Voltaire: A Study in French Reactions to Leibnizianism, 1670-1760*. Oxford, 1955.

Bernard, Henri, S. J. "Chu Hsi's Philosophy and Its Interpretation by Leibniz." *T'ien Hsia Monthly* 5(1)(1937):9-19.

———. *Matteo Ricci's Scientific Contribution to China*. Translated by Edward Chalmers Werner. Peiping, 1935. Reprinted Westport, Connecticut, 1973.

Bodemann, Eduard. *Der Briefwechsel des Gottfried Wilhelm Leibniz in Königlichen öffentlichen Bibliothek zu Hannover*. Hanover, 1889.

———. *Die Leibniz-Handschriften der Königlichen öffentlichen Bibliothek zu Hannover*. Hanover, 1895.

Bouvet, Joachim, S. J. *Portrait historique de l'Empereur de la Chine*. Paris, 1697.

Carr, Herbert-Wildon. *Leibniz*. London, 1929. Reprinted New York, 1960.

*Catholic Encyclopedia*. Vol. 2. New York, 1907.

Chan, Wing-tsit. "Chu Hsi's Completion of Neo-Confucianism." *Etudes Song-Sung Studies*. Series 2, no. 1. In memoriam Etienne Balazs. Edited by Françoise Aubin. Paris, 1973.

———. "The Evolution of the Neo-Confucian Concept *li* as Principle." *Tsing Hua Journal of Chinese Studies*, n.s., 4(2)(1964):123-148.

———, trans. *Reflections on Things at Hand, Complied by Chu Hsi and Lü Tsu-ch'ien*. New York, 1967.

———. *A Source Book in Chinese Philosophy*. Princeton, 1963.

Chu Hsi. *Chu-tzu ta-ch'üan*. Edited by Chu Tsai. Ssu-pu pei yao edition. Reprinted Taipei, 1966.
_____. *Chu-tzu yü-lei*. Edited by Li Ching-te. Circa 1270. Reprinted Taipei, 1962.
_____. *Ssu-shu chi-chu*. Reprinted Taipei, 1969.
Copelston, Frederick, S. J. *A History of Philosophy*. Vol. 4. New York, 1963.
Cornelius, Paul. *Languages in Seventeenth- and Early Eighteenth-Century Imaginary Voyages*. Geneva, 1965.
Couturat, Louis. *La logique de Leibniz*. Paris, 1901.
Creel, Herrlee Glessner. "Was Confucius Agnostic?" *T'oung Pao* 29(1–3)(1932):55–99.
Cronin, Vincent. *The Wise Man from the West*. New York, 1957.
Daniel-Rops, Henri. *The Church in the Eighteenth Century*. Translated by John Warrington. New York, 1966.
De Bary, William Theodore, ed. *Self and Society in Ming Thought*. New York, 1970.
Dehergne, Joseph, S. J. *Répertoire des Jésuites de Chine de 1552 à 1800*. Rome, 1973.
Demiéville, Paul. "The First Philosophic Contacts between Europe and China." *Diogenes* (Montreal) 58(1967):75–103.
Dewey, John. *Leibniz's New Essays on Human Understanding*. 1888. Reprinted in *John Dewey: The Early Works*. Vol. 1. Carbondale, Illinois, 1969.
Drzewieniecki, Walter M. "The Knowledge of China in XVII Century Poland as Reflected in the Correspondence between Leibniz and Kochanski." *Polish Review* 12(3)(1967):53–66.
Duhr, Joseph, S. J. *Un Jésuite en Chine, Adam Schall*. Paris , 1936.
Dunne, George H., S. J. *Generation of Giants: The Story of the Jesuits in China in the Last Decades of the Ming Dynasty*. Notre Dame, Indiana, 1966.
_____. "The Missionary in China: Past, Present and Future." *Ampleforth Journal* 78(3)(1973):9–42.
Eichorn, Werner. *Chinese Civilization*. Translated by Janet Seligman. New York, 1969.
_____, trans. *Die Westinschrift des Chang Tsai*. (*Abhandlungen für die Kunde des Morgenlandes* 22[7]). Leipzig, 1937.
Eliot, T. S. *The Four Quartets*. London, 1959.
*Encyclopedia Cattolica*. Vol. 3. Vatican, 1949.
Feng, Tso-min. *Ch'ing K'ang Ch'ien liang-ti yü t'ien-chu-chiao ch'uan chiao shih*. Taipei, 1966.
Fischer, Kuno. *Gottfried Wilhelm Leibniz: Leben, Werke und Lehre*. Heidelberg, 1920.
Franke, Otto. "Leibniz und China." *Zeitschrift der Deutschen Morgenländischen Gesellschaft* 7(1928):155–178.
_____. "Li Tschi und Matteo Ricci," *Abhandlungen der Preussischen Akademie der Wissenschaften* (1938)5, Berlin, 1939.
Franke, Wolfgang. *China and the West*. Translated by R. A. Wilson. Oxford, 1967.
Frankfurt, Harry G., ed. *Leibniz: A Collection of Critical Essays*. New York, 1972.
Fu, Charles Wei-hsun. "Confucianism, Marxism-Leninism and Mao: A Critical Study." *Journal of Chinese Philosophy* 1(3–4)(1974):119–151.
Fülop-Miller, Rene. *The Jesuits: A History of the Society of Jesus* (original title: The Power and Secret of the Jesuits). Translated by F. S. Flint and D. F. Tait. 1930. Reprinted New York, 1963.

Fung, Yu-lan. *A History of Chinese Philosophy.* Translated by Derk Bodde. 2 vols. Princeton, 1953.

Gale, George. "The Physical Theory of Leibniz." *Studia Leibnitiana* 2(2)(1970): 114–127.

Galileo, Galilei. *Discoveries and Opinions of Galileo.* Translated by Stillman Drake. New York, 1957.

Geymonet, Ludovico. *Galileo Galilei.* Translated by Stillman Drake. New York, 1965.

Gorai, Kinzō. *Jukyō no Doitsu seiji shisō ni oyoboseru eikyō.* Tokyo, 1929.

Grimm, Tilemann. "China und das Chinabild von Leibniz." *Studia Leibnitiana,* Special Edition, 1(1969):38–61.

Guhrauer, Gottschalk E. *Gottfried Wilhelm Freiherr von Leibniz: Eine Biographie.* 2 vols. Breslau, 1846. Reprinted Hildesheim, 1966.

Happold, F. C. *Prayer and Meditation.* Bungay, Suffolk, England, 1971.

Hazard, Paul. *The European Mind, 1680–1715.* Translated by J. Lewis May. Cleveland, 1963.

Heeren, J. J. "Father Joachim Bouvet's Picture of Emperor K'ang Hsi." *Asia Major* 7(1932):556–572.

Hsi Tse-tsung, et al. "Heliocentric Theory in China." *Scientia Sinica* 16(3)(1973): 364–376.

Hu, Kuang, ed. *Hsing-li ta-ch'üan shu.* 70 vols. 1415.

Hu, Wei. *I-t'u ming-pien.* 10 vols. 1706. Reprinted Shanghai, 1935.

Huang, Siu-chi. "Chang Tsai's Concept of *ch'i.*" *Philosophy East and West* 18(4) (1968):247–260.

————. "The Moral Point of View of Chang Tsai." *Philosophy East and West* 21(2)(1971):141–156.

Huang, Tsung-hsi, ed. *Ming-ju hsüeh-an.* 62 vols. 1888. Reprinted Taipei, 1965.

————, ed. *Sung-Yüan hsüeh-an.* 100 vols. Supplemented by Ch'üan Tsu-wang. 1846. Reprinted Taipei, 1966.

Hughes, E. R., trans. *The Great Learning and Mean in Action.* New York, 1943.

Hummel, Arthur, ed. *Eminent Chinese of the Ch'ing Period (1644–1912).* Washington, 1943. Reprinted Taipei, 1970.

Ignatius of Loyola. *The Spiritual Exercises.* Translated by Anthony Mottola. New York, 1964.

Johnston, William, S. J. *Christian Zen.* New York, 1971.

————. *The Still Point: Reflections on Zen and Christian Mysticism.* New York, 1971.

Jordan, G. J. *The Reunion of the Churches: A Study of G. W. Leibnitz and His Great Attempt.* London, 1927.

Kao, Hsiang, ed. *Chou-i ku-ching chin-chu.* Shanghai, 1947. Reprinted 1949.

Koestler, Arthur. *The Sleepwalkers.* New York, 1963. Reprinted 1971.

Lach, Donald F. "Leibniz and China." *Journal of the History of Ideas* 6(4) (1945):436–455.

————. "The Chinese Studies of Andreas Müller." *Journal of the American Oriental Society* 60(4)(1940):564–575.

————, trans. *The Preface to Leibniz' Novissima Sinica.* Honolulu, 1957.

Larson, Martin A. *The Religion of the Occident: The Origin and Development of the Essene-Christian Faith.* Paterson, New Jersey, 1961.

Latourette, Kenneth Scott. *A History of Christian Missions in China.* London, 1929. Reprinted Taipei, 1970.

BIBLIOGRAPHY

Le Comte, Louis, S. J. *Nouveaux Memoires sur l'État present de la Chine.* 2 vols. Paris, 1697.

Lee, Peter K. H. "Indigenous Theology—Overcropped Land or Undeveloped Field?" *Ching Feng—Quarterly Notes on Christianity and Chinese Religion and Culture* 17(1)(1974):5–17.

Legge, James, trans. *The Chinese Classics.* 4 vols. 2nd ed. revised. Oxford, 1893. Reprinted Hong Kong, 1966.

———, trans. *The I Ching.* 1899. Reprinted New York, 1963.

———, trans. *Li Ki.* The Sacred Books of the East series, vols. 27 and 28. Edited by Max Muller. Oxford, 1885. Reprinted New York, 1967.

Le Gobien, Charles, S. J. *Histoire de l'Edit de l'Empereur de la Chine en faveur de la Religion Chrestienne.* Paris, 1698.

Leibniz, G. W. *Discourse on metaphysics and correspondence with Arnauld.* Translated by George R. Montgomery. La Salle, Illinois, 1902. Revised by Albert R. Chandler, 1924; reprinted 1968.

———. *Discourse on the Natural Theology of the Chinese.* Translated, with an introduction, notes, and commentary by Daniel J. Cook and Henry Rosemont, Jr., Society for Asian and Comparative Philosophy monograph 4. Honolulu, 1977.

———. "Discours sur la theologie naturelle des Chinois" (Lettre sur la philosophie chinoise a M. de Remond). Hanover, Niedersächsische Landesbibliothek, MS 37, 1810, no. 1.

———. *Gottfried Wilhelm Leibniz's General Investigations Concerning the Analysis of Concepts and Truth.* A translation and evaluation by Walter H. O'Briant. Athens, Georgia, 1968.

———. Hanover, Niedersächsische Landesbibliothek, Leibniz-Briefwechsel (designated by Leibnizbriefe number).

———. Hanover, Niedersächsische Landesbibliothek, Leibniz-Handschriften (designated by MS number).

———. *Leibnitii opera omnia.* Edited by Ludovici Dutens. 6 vols. Geneva, 1768.

———. *Leibnizens mathematische Schriften.* Edited by Carl Immanuel Gerhardt. 7 vols. Berlin and Halle, 1849–1863.

———. *Leibniz-Faksimiles.* Hanover, Niedersächsische Landesbibliothek. Hildesheim, 1971.

———. *Leibniz: Philosophical Papers and Letters.* Translated and edited by Leroy E. Loemker. 2 vols. Chicago, 1956.

———. *Leibniz: Selections.* Translated and edited by Philip P. Wiener. New York, 1951.

———. *Logical Papers.* Translated and edited by G. H. R. Parkinson. Oxford, 1966.

———. *Monadology and Other Philosophical Essays.* Translated by Paul and Anne Schrecker. New York, 1965.

———. *New Essays Concerning Human Understanding, by Gottfried Wilhelm Leibniz.* Translated by Alfred G. Langley. New York, 1896.

———. *Novissima Sinica.* Hanover?, 1697; 2nd ed. 1699.

———. *Opuscules et fragments inédits de Leibniz.* Edited by Louis Couturat. Paris, 1903.

———. *Die philosophischen Schriften von G. W. Leibniz.* Edited by Carl Immanuel Gerhardt. 7 vols. Berlin, 1875–1890.

———. "Preliminary Transcription of the Leibniz-Bouvet Correspondence." Edited by Alan Berkowitz, Chris Benoit, and Thatcher Deane. Photocopy.

Burlington, Vermont: Center for Area Studies, University of Vermont, 1975.
_____. *Sämtliche Schriften und Briefe.* Edited by the Prussian Academy of Sciences. 6 vol. in progress. Darmstadt and Leipzig, 1923-.
_____. *Theodicy.* Edited by Diogenes Allen. Translated by E. M. Huggard. Abridged. Indianapolis, 1966.
_____. *Vivi illustris Godefridi Guil. Leibnitii epistolae ad diversos* . . . . Edited by Christian Kortholt. 4 vols. Leipzig, 1735.
_____. *Zwei Briefe über das binäre Zahlensystem und die chinesische Philosophie.* Translated by Renate Loosen and Franz Vonessen. Stuttgart, 1968.
Li, An-tang, [Antoine de Sainte-Marie, O. F. M.]. *T'ien Ju yin.* In *T'ien-chu-chiao tung-ch'uan wen-hsien su-pien.* 3 vols. Taipei, 1966.
Li, Ma-t'ou [Matteo Ricci, S. J.]. *Chi-ho yüan-pen.* 6 vols. Peking, 1605.
_____. *Erh-shih-wu yen.* Peking, 1604.
_____. *T'ien-chu shih-i.* Nanking, circa 1595. Reprinted Taipei, 1967.
Liu, Pai-min, trans. "Lai-pu-ni-tzu de Chou-i hsüeh." In *I-hsüeh t'ao-lun chi.* Edited by Li Cheng-kang. Shanghai, 1941.
Liu, Shu-hsien. "The Confucian Approach to the Problem of Transcendence and Immanence." *Philosophy East and West* 22(1)(1972):45-52.
_____. "The Religious Import of Confucian Philosophy: Its Traditional Outlook and Contemporary Significance." *Philosophy East and West* 21(2)(1971): 157-175.
Loemker, Leroy E. "A Note on the Origin and Problem of Leibniz's Discourse of 1686." *Journal of the History of Ideas* 8(1947): 449-466.
_____. *Struggle for Synthesis: The Seventeenth Century Background of Leibniz's Synthesis of Order and Freedom.* Cambridge, Massachusetts. 1972.
Longobardi, Nichola, S. J. *Traité sur quelques points de la réligion des chinois.* Paris, 1703.
Mackie, John W. *Life of Godfrey William von Leibnitz.* Adapted from Guhrauer. Boston, 1845.
Malebranche, Nicholas. *Entretien d'un philosophe chrétien et d'un philosophe chinois sur l'existence et la nature de Dieu.* Paris, 1708.
Martin, Gottfried. *Leibniz: Logic and Metaphysics.* Translated by K. J. Northcott and P. G. Lucas. New York, 1967.
Mason, H. T., ed. and trans. *Leibniz-Arnauld Correspondence.* Manchester, 1967.
Maverick, Lewis S. *China: A Model for Europe.* San Antonio, 1946.
Merkel, Franz Rudolf. *G. W. von Leibniz und die China-Mission.* Leipzig, 1920.
_____. *Leibniz und China.* Berlin, 1952.
Merton, Thomas. *Mystics and Zen Masters.* New York, 1961.
Merz, John Theodore. *Leibniz.* New York, 1948.
Meyer, R. W. *Leibnitz and the Seventeenth Century Revolution.* Translated by J. P. Stern. Chicago, 1952.
Moore, Charles A., ed. *The Chinese Mind.* Honolulu, 1967.
More, Louis Trenchard. *Isaac Newton.* New York, 1934.
Müller, Kurt. *Leibniz-Bibliographie.* Frankfurt am Main, 1967.
Mungello, David E. "Leibniz's Interpretation of Neo-Confucianism." *Philosophy East and West* 21(1)(1971):3-22.
_____. "On the Significance of the Question: 'Did China Have Science?' " *Philosophy East and West* 22(4)(1972):467-478; 23(3)(1973):417-422.
_____. "The Reconciliation of Neo-Confucianism with Christianity in the Writings of Joseph de Prémare, S. J." *Philosophy East and West* 26(4)(1976):389-410.

184                                                                  BIBLIOGRAPHY

Navarette, Domingo Fernandez. *Tratados históricos, políticos, ethicos, y religiosos de la Monarchia de China*. Madrid, 1676-1679.
Needham, Joseph. "Chinese Astronomy and the Jesuit Mission: An Encounter of Cultures." China Society Occasional Papers, no. 10. Edited by Cyril Birch. London, 1958.
_____. *Science and Civilisation in China*. 7 vols. in progress. Cambridge, England, 1954-.
*New Catholic Encyclopedia*. Vol. 2. Washington, 1967.
O'Briant, Walter H. "Leibniz's Project of a Universal Language." *Southern Humanities Review* 1(1967):182-191.
Parkinson, G. H. R. "Bertrand Russell, 1872-1970." *Studia Leibnitiana* 2(3) (1970):161-170.
Peursen, C. A. van. *Leibniz*. Translated by Hubert Hoskins. New York, 1970.
Pfister, Aloys [Louis], S. J. "Notices biographiques et bibliographiques sur les Jésuites de l'ancienne mission de Chine, 1552-1773." Bound and photocopied manuscript, Jesuit House Library, Rome, 1868-1875.
_____. *Notices biographiques et bibliographiques sur les Jésuites de l'ancienne mission de Chine, 1552-1773*. Variétés sinologiques, nos. 59-60. 2 vols. Shanghai, 1932-1934.
Plato. *The Timaeus*. Translated by Francis M. Cornford. Indianapolis, 1959.
Prémare, Joseph Henry-Marie de, S. J. "Selecta quaedam vestigia praecipuorum Christianae Relligionis dogmatum, ex antiquis Sinarum libris eruta." Canton, 1724.
_____. *Vestiges des principaux dogmes chrétiens tirés des anciens livres chinois*. Translated by A. Bonnetty and Paul Perny. Paris, 1878.
Regis, Jean-Baptiste, S. J. *I-king, antiquissimus Sinarum liber*. 2 vols. Stuttgart, 1834, 1839.
Reichwein, Adolf. *China and Europe: Intellectual and Artistic Contacts in the Eighteenth Century*. Translated by J. C. Powell. New York, 1925. Reprinted Taipei, 1967.
Rescher, Nicholas. *The Philosophy of Leibniz*. Englewood Cliffs, New Jersey, 1967.
Ricci, Matteo, S. J. *China in the Sixteenth Century: The Journals of Matthew Ricci, 1583-1610*. Edited by Nicholas Trigault, S. J. Translated by Louis J. Gallagher, S. J. New York, 1953.
_____. *De Christiana Expeditione apud Sinas*. Edited by Nicholas Trigault, S. J. Augsburg, 1615.
_____. "Entretiens d'un Lettre chinois et d'un Docteur européen sur la vraie idée de Dieu." In *Lettres edifiantes et curieuses écrites de Missions étrangères*. Vol. 14, pp. 66-248. Edition of Lyon, 1819.
Rommel, Christoph von. *Leibniz und Landgraf Ernst von Hessen-Rheinfels*. Frankfurt am Main, 1847.
Rosemont, Henry, Jr. "Confucian Perspectives on Contemporary China." *Canadian Forum* (September 1974), pp. 13-19.
Rouse, Ruth, and Neill, Stephen Charles, eds. *A History of the Ecumenical Movement, 1517-1948*. 2nd ed. London, 1967.
Rowbotham, Arnold H. "China and the Age of Enlightenment in Europe." *Chinese Social and Political Science Review* 19(2)(1935): 176-201.
_____. *Missionary and Mandarin in China: The Jesuits at the Court of China*. Berkeley, 1942.
Roy, Olivier. *Leibniz et la Chine*. Paris, 1972.

Russell, Bertrand. *A Critical Exposition of the Philosophy of Leibniz.* 2nd ed. revised. London, 1937.

Sainte-Marie, Antoine de [Antonio Caballero a Santa Maria]. *Traité sur quelques points importants de la mission de la Chine.* Paris, 1701.

Santillana, Giorgio. *The Crime of Galileo.* Chicago, 1955.

Shao, Yung. *Huang-chi ching-shih.* 7 vols. Reprinted 1935.

Sivin, Nathan. "Copernicus in China." *Studia Copernicana* 6(1973):63–122.

————. "Why the Scientific Revolution Did Not Take Place in China." Transcription of a talk given to the Metropolitan New York Section, History of Science Society, 22 April 1975.

Speiss, E. *Erhard Weigel, der Lehrer von Leibniz und Pufendorf.* Leipzig, 1881.

Spini, Giorgio. "The Rationale of Galileo's Religiousness." In *Galileo Reappraised.* Edited by Carlo L. Golino. Berkeley, 1966.

Stcherbatsky, Theodore. *Buddhist Logic.* 2 vols. Reprinted Atlantic Highlands, New Jersey, 1958.

Suzuki, D. T. *Mysticism: Christian and Buddhist.* New York, 1957. Reprinted 1971.

T'ang, Chün-i. "Ch'ang Tsai's Theory of Mind and Its Metaphysical Basis." *Philosophy East and West* 6(2)(1956):113–136.

————. *Chung-kuo je-hsüeh yüan lun.* 2 vols. Hong Kong, 1966–1968.

Tu, Wei-ming. "*Li* as a Process of Humanization." *Philosophy East and West* 22(2)(1972):187–201.

————. "The Neo-Confucian Concept of Man." *Philosophy East and West* 21(1)(1971):79–87.

Waley, Arthur. "Leibniz and Fu Hsi." *London University School of Oriental Studies Bulletin* 2(1921):165–167. [Review of Waley by Paul Pelliot, *T'oung Pao* 21(1922):90–91.]

————, trans. *Analects of Confucius.* London, 1938.

Ward, A. W. *Leibniz as a Politician.* Manchester, 1911.

Wang Yang-ming, *Ch'uan hsi lu.* Reprinted Taipei, 1971.

Wiener, Philip P. "G. W. F. Leibniz: On Philosophical Synthesis." *Philosophy East and West* 12(3)(1962):195–202.

Wilhelm, Hellmut. *Change: Eight Lectures on the I Ching.* Translated by Cary F. Baynes. New York, 1960.

————. "Leibniz and the *I Ching.*" *Collectanea Commissionis Synodalis in Sinis* 16(1948):205–219.

Wong, George H. C. "The Anti-Christian Movement in China: Late Ming and Early Ch'ing." *Tsing Hua Journal of Chinese Studies,* n.s., 3(1)(1962):187–222.

————. "China's Opposition to Western Science During the Late Ming and Early Ch'ing." *Isis* 54(1)(1963):29–49. [Response by Nathan Sivin, *Isis* 56(2)(1965):201–205.]

Wyngaert, Anastasius Van den, O. F. M. ed. *Sinica Franciscana, Relationes et Epistolas Fratrum Minorum.* Rome, 1929–1936.

Yates, Frances A. *Giordano Bruno and the Hermetic Tradition.* 1964. Reprinted New York, 1969.

Zacher, Hans J. *Die Hauptschriften zur Dyadik von G. W. Leibniz.* Frankfurt am Main, 1973.

Zempliner, Artur. "Gedanken über die erste deutsche Übersetzung von Leibniz' Abhandlung über die chinesische Philosophie." *Studia Leibnitiana* 2(3)(1970):223–231.

————. "Leibniz und die chinesische Philosophie." *Studia Leibnitiana Supplementa* 5:15–30.

# Index

Abstinence, sexual, 104–105, 114
Academies of learning, 128
Acceptance, 141; joyous, 142–143
Accommodation: attitudes on Chinese rites, 19; attitude, 20; of Christianity with Confucianism by Ricci, 20–21; view toward Chinese rites, 21–22; view in missionary methods, 31; theory of Ricci, 70
Adam (first man), 55
Agnosticism, 107; of Confucius, 106
Alexander VII (pope), 11
Alexander VIII (pope), 11
Altdorf, University of, 2
America, 145–146
Amitabha, Western Paradise of, 28; Buddhism, 152–153
Amphiboly, 10
*Amphitrite*, 43
*Analects (Lun yü)*, Jesuit translation of, 6, 24; cited by Leibniz, 72; cited by Sainte-Marie, 88–89; Confucius' view of spirits, 106–109; spiritual cultivation in, 143–144, 165
Ancestors, 78, 104; rites, 11, 19; ceremonies, 12; Chinese cult of, 115; worship of, 115–116; tablets, 118
Ancient Chinese: philosophy of, 101;

versus modern Chinese, 21–22, 73, 74–75, 142; culture of, 147
Ancients, versus moderns, 81
Angels, 100, 101
*Animadversiones in partem generalem principiorum Cartesianorum,* 127
Anti-Confucius Campaign of 1973–1974, 145
Antiquity, Leibniz' awareness of Chinese, 33, 71, 74, 75
*Apologie des dominicains,* 13
Arabs, mathematicians, 52
Aristotelianism, qualities, 54; influence on Leibniz' youth, 121
Aristotle, 2, 10, 54, 76, 101
Arithmetic: in tutoring the K'ang-hsi emperor, 57; versus geometry, 57, 148; of Pythagorean numbers, 122
Arithmetical progression, in the *Changes* diagrams, 46, 147–148
Arnauld, Antoine, 3, 10, 13–14, 151, 169
*Ars combinatoria.* See *De arte combinatoria*
Assimilation: of Jesuits into Chinese culture, 22; of Christianity, 137
Astronomy, 18, 33, 36; Arabic, 34; Chinese, 34

# *About the Author*

David E. Mungello is assistant professor of history and religion at Briarcliff College, Briarcliff Manor, New York.

He received his A.B. degree from George Washington University and his M.A. and Ph.D. degrees from the University of California at Berkeley.

Journals in which his writing has appeared include *Philosophy East and West* and *Journal of Asian Studies*.